The Business Transformation Field Guide

What they are saying about this book …

"This book is a valuable and comprehensive collection of lessons learned for BPMS enabled transformational projects. It helps avoid costly pitfalls and should be included in any project tool box." Marc Scharsig, Enterprise Process Management Executive, BPM Global Services LLC.

"The authors of the Business Transformation Field Guide have distilled decades of hands on experience into an easy to read and comprehensive guide to successfully running large, complex enterprise projects. The advice is refreshingly practical and contains insights that you don't often find in books about business change. This is a book that all business transformation professionals should not only read but read and read again as there is such a wealth of knowledge that new ideas and tips can be picked up on each reading. It's like having your own personal business transformation mentor available on demand." Diana Davis, Senior Editor, PEX Network

"I feel the Business Transformation Field Guide is a tremendous resource and absolute must have for every professional that is tasked with executing, participating, or directing business operational change" William LaFollette, Operational Excellence Leader, Accumen, Inc.

"The Field Guide is an all-encompassing look at how to run a modern business transformation project from starting strategy to completed project and beyond. Although it leans toward Business Process Management (BPM) projects, this practical guide, by senior business consultants who have "been in the trenches", is a major how-to guide for running any significant project. Business transformation projects are more important than ever and doing them right can be difficult. This guide illuminates why Project Managers are so valuable and covers a vast array of topics from how to build a Center of Excellence (CoE) to how to deal with temporary outside resources (contractors) and even what to include on weekly status reports. Great work by a great team!" George Barlow, CBPMP, OCEB, CSO, Trisotech

"This 'Field Guide' provides practical advice for all phases of a process-led transformation. It shares valuable lessons learned that every process improvement initiative can benefit from. The book is a great read for process management practitioners." Dr. Mathias Kirchmer, Managing Director and Co-CEO, BPM-D

"There are a lot of 'how to' books written on this subject. Typically I review them with a skeptical eye, which was the case here. After reading the Business Transformation Field Guide, my first thought, 'where was this book when I started?' This Guide would have been instrumental in avoiding many pitfalls that leaders face. As a seasoned leader, we can't remember or know everything. The guide helps to ensure you are thinking holistically and reinforcing critical areas that are key to successful transformation. I would recommend this book to transformation leaders regardless of their years of experience." Eric Thompson, VP Operational Excellence Wyndham Worldwide

"A broad yet acceptable explanation of a wide range of issues and pragmatic considerations for business practitioners. Takes the reader through the journey of business transformation by providing clear and pragmatic nuggets of experience and expertise that the authors call "hints." All in all, a really practical field guide structured around a comprehensive business transformation methodology. Denis Gagne, CEO & CTO, Trisotech

The Business Transformation Field Guide

Daniel Morris

Keith Leust

Rod Moyer

Meghan-Kiffer Press
Tampa, Florida, USA, www.mkpress.com
Visit our Web site to see all our specialty books focused on
Innovation at the Intersection of Business and Technology
www.mkpress.com

ISBN 0-929652-58-4 ISBN 13: 978-0-929652-58-0

Published by Meghan-Kiffer Press
310 East Fern Street — Suite G
Tampa, FL 33604 USA

Meghan-Kiffer books are available at special quantity discounts for corporate education and training use. For more information write Special Sales, Meghan-Kiffer Press, 310 East Fern Street, Tampa, Florida 33604 or (813) 251-5531 or email info@mkpress.com

Meghan-Kiffer Press

Tampa, Florida, USA

Innovation at the Intersection of Business and Technology

Printed in the United States of America.   SAN 249-7980

MK Printing 10 9 8 7 6 5 4 3 2 1

Dedication

Sometimes, if we are lucky, we are touched in profound ways by special people. Parents, brothers, sisters, spouses and children are high among the list of those who guide us and shape us. Then sometimes, there are those we meet on our journey through life who have an equally great impact on us and help shape who we become. All too often these people are taken from us much too soon.

This Field Guide is dedicated to those who have been lost to us. We will always remember them and how they helped to shape us into the people we have become.

Acknowledgements

We would like to thank Mr. Neelesh Harmalker of PWC for the time and energy he put into helping us. As the first editor, Neelesh gave the book its "cold" review. That means that he was the one who had to determine if the hints made sense and if they were in the right places. That is always a sobering time for authors – especially if the first editor is honest and really tries to help make the book better.

We would also like to thank Wendy Morris and Anneliese Lust for their time and contributions in editing the book and helping us to make it read well and comply with the rules of written English.

This Field Guide is a quick reference manual that contains short "hints" intended to help managers and staff members understand business operation change and how it can be executed.

These hints leverage a variety of professional disciplines including:

- Business Process Management
- Business Architecture
- Enterprise Architecture
- Process Architecture
- Project Management for business transformation and improvement
- Project Execution for business transformation and improvement
- Lean and Six Sigma
- Togaf® (The Open Group Architecture Framework) and the Zachman Framework
- Change Management.

The hints are organized by, and apply, to the phases of a Business Process Management Suite (BPMS)-enabled BPM project. While this creates some overlap, since hints can apply to more than one place in a project, we have tried to keep the overlap to a minimum.

The hints are not meant to be read as a regular text or business book – front cover to back cover. Rather, the book is meant to be read in sections that apply to a specific area of activity in a business operational program or project. It is also recommended that all team members working in a given part of the project read the hints that apply to them beforehand. This will help the team to reach a mutual understanding about the way the project might or should be executed.

Who is this book for?

This book is written for professionals who wish to accelerate their learning by leveraging the lessons of others who have already faced the business and organizational challenges that are inherent in all organizations. The hints are not to be treated as "written in stone" and followed blindly. They are lessons that are a result of decades of successes and failures. They are the essential hints that, when followed, will make you, your project, and your organization more successful.

The book should serve to create open and blunt discussions around the transformation process. It is also important to note that this book is written from a business perspective. While IT topics and hints are included, these serve mainly to help further the discussion between project sponsors, business managers, business improvement teams, and other collaborators to ensure that all responsible parties are on the same page.

Lastly, we believe that anyone who is involved in business change can benefit significantly from this Guide. It covers all aspects of a change project from the approval of a project's request to the eventual delivery and move to a state of continuous refinement so optimization can be maintained.

Why read this book?

No one knows everything about anything. Our main goal is to share what we have learned and help those who read this book avoid mistakes and the infamous "land mines" that have resulted in many projects failing in the past. We are business process management (BPM) evangelists and we know the potential of these methods, techniques, and technology. We also know that BPM is under-utilized and not living up to its potential. We want to help you excel as a practitioner in transformation. By leveraging the information in this book, any company's BPM projects can be improved and the benefits the company will realize can be both proven and expanded.

Approach Assumptions

1. For purposes of the more technical steps in this Field Guide, it is assumed that a company's business transformation and operational improvement efforts will be supported by a Business Process Management Suite (BPMS). A BPMS is an integrated set of tools that allows the project teams to generate computer applications. In lieu of a BPMS, some entities may employ a collection of at least some BPM tools that carry out portions of the capabilities supported by the integrated suites. These tool suites have process modeling tools, rules definition engines, and computer application generators.

    The Field Guide does, however, contain a wealth of hints that address topics independent of a BPMS and therefore will be of value to those who have no access to a BPMS.

2. The more advanced of these tool suites have moved to an intelligent Business Process Management model and offer workflow simulation, performance analytics, and an ability to generate Social Media Apps. Some of these tools are easy to use and some are difficult. Some are more business staff oriented (for information entry) and some are very technical. In organizations that use the more technical BPMS tools, you may find separate Business Process Analysis tools used as modelers and simulation engines.

3. The discussions often mention iBPM (intelligent BPM) concepts and capabilities. This includes the use of simulation modeling and analysis tools and the inclusion of advanced analytics to support performance management and business intelligence reporting.

Terminology

BPM terminology definitions vary by company and often by group within a company. There are no commonly accepted definitions. BPM terms may have multiple definitions, making their meaning interpretive based on context as well as the mindset of the user.

This leads to misunderstandings as well as the potential challenges that accompany communication style differences between business areas and IT. It is therefore recommended that the BPM team work with IT and other stakeholders to create a company dictionary that all must use. An example is *"project management"* compared to *"project execution."* To many, these terms are synonymous. To the authors, they are very different. Project management is the ability to manage a project, including managing people, tracking progress, and controlling budgets. This has little to do with the actual execution of tasks that need to be performed. Project management activities can be used in any type of project. This is not true of project execution. Project execution is related to a specific type of project and the tasks that need to be performed to create a solution. Execution is thus related to a specific project and is not generally applicable to many other projects.

A second example is the word, *"process."* To some it is an end-to-end aggregation of all the work needed to deliver a specific product. To others it is any type of job, or a group of activities done by a person. These activities may or may not be automated or supported by applications. To still others it is anything they do. In one case, a person defined the process as taking a document out of a pile, scanning it, and then putting it in another pile. Who is right? All of these are right – within the context of the specific operating environment of each individual. However, within the context of a project there must be a uniform understanding of what is meant by the term process so that these various understandings do not lead to confusion or errors.

These examples are extremely important. Can all terms be defined? Of course not. Many will look at the definition of terminology as an unnecessary exercise; however, experienced project managers will have a different opinion. We suggest that the team start by identifying at least 20 key terms that they use frequently and move everyone on the team to these definitions. Additional terms can be added as the need to be clear arises.

Contents

Foreword

When I was asked to write a foreword to "The Business Transformation Field Guide", I thought "uh-oh," another one of those dry methodology books with lock step approaches. **Turns out I was wrong**. First of all, this book contains a remarkable set of guidelines, pearls of wisdom, and practical steps for successful transformation efforts. It is especially good for transformation projects with a process focused approach aimed at desired business outcomes run by changing goals and KPIs. Not only that, there are multiple starting points to transformational efforts identified here; this book can help no matter where you start your transformation efforts.

I was particularly struck by the depth of experience the collective authors have on various process based projects and efforts. There's extensive expertise displayed here particularly on business strategies, competencies, architectures, process methodologies, and project methodologies. The level of practicality displayed in the guidelines was refreshing and I found myself going back to my experience on transformational projects and nodding my head in agreement. I really liked Wendan's Laws section as an overall guide to project success.

I like the fact that this book has a context rich process focus. Since almost all the projects I've worked on have at least one major process component, I found it extremely practical for supporting process projects. The book doesn't stop there because it also considers several contexts for these process efforts including "To Be" architectures and "As Is" architectures. At the same time other contexts are considered for a holistic approach for transformational process projects.

Unlike other methodology books, the approaches here leverage the best of rapid development along with the guardrails of rich and complete methods. This book strikes a real balance between the speed of development and completeness of context and outcomes. Transformations will be essential to progress in digital and process evolution and this book helps those efforts.

Jim Sinur

CEO of Flueresque and former Gartner VP

> *Editor's note: For information about Jim's upcoming books and blog, see Jim's bio at the end of this book.*

Preface: About the ADDI methodology

The authors are the creators of the ADDI iBPM/iBPMS methodology. ADDI stands for Architect, Design, Deploy, Improve. This is the only formal iBPM execution and orchestration methodology and the only methodology that supports the combination of Waterfall and Agile approaches, while incorporating Lean, Six Sigma, Zachman's Framework, Togaf®, Business Architecture, Process Architecture, Enterprise Architecture, and Change Management.

ADDI is built to handle business transformation and improvement projects of all sizes. The methodology presents a comprehensive list of over 1,500 tasks in seven phases that should be considered when planning and executing a project. Depending on the size, scope, complexity, and impact of the project on the areas of the business in scope, the project manager can remove any tasks that are not needed to eliminate any non-value add work and then create the project plan. The ADDI product suite also contains a comprehensive "How To" book, aligned to the task list, a project estimation tool, and both accelerators and templates. Links embedded in the task lists allow the project manager to make certain that standards and other information are considered by the project team at the places in the project where they apply.

This makes ADDI unique. It is also the only formal methodology to leverage a multi-view perspective of success and both the IT "Stub and Driver" concept and the IT model office evaluation concept. Together the concepts, techniques, and approaches in ADDI represent business transformation experiences, IT experiences, and project rescue experiences of the authors.

When fully applied, ADDI significantly mitigates risk and greatly reduces the possibility of delivering a solution that fails to provide the required capabilities, quality, and performance improvement defined in the project charter.

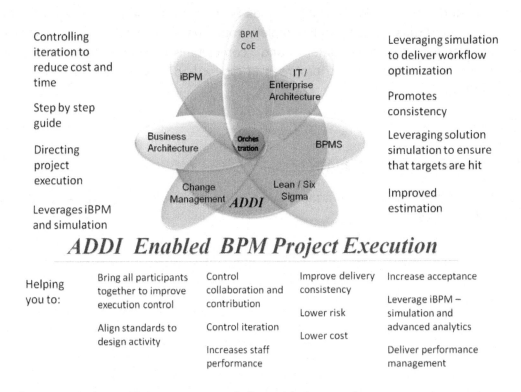

ADDI Enabled BPM Project Execution

Helping you to:	Bring all participants together to improve execution control	Control collaboration and contribution	Improve delivery consistency	Increase acceptance
	Align standards to design activity	Control iteration	Lower risk	Leverage iBPM – simulation and advanced analytics
		Increases staff performance	Lower cost	Deliver performance management

Success is never a given. But, you can push the odds in your favor.

The hints provided in this book are based on tried and proven lessons that the authors have learned in the field – working on and managing transformation projects in virtually all industries.

These hints have been proven in over 15 years of projects by the authors. They are thus not theory. They have all been used and all been proven. They will help you unlock the doors that keep shutting on most projects.

Whether you are currently carrying out business transformation projects or just now building your team to reach that level, this book provides a wealth of practical information to improve your outcomes while reducing risk. Decades of experience have been distilled into over 800 hints that address activities, concepts, techniques, and recommendations that have been proven through hands-on fieldwork. Many of these hints will help you tackle complex issues while others share small details that can make a big difference in how smoothly a project goes and how effective the outcome is.

The hints are organized into an easy to use format that tracks a comprehensive transformation life cycle from project set-up through post-project continuous refinement activities. Accordingly, the book is not really meant to be read cover-to-cover, rather it is intended to share information that is relevant to the project phase that you are addressing at any given time and that can be applied immediately. Readers can get into the information they need to do a set of tasks, and then get out.

Introduction

This Field Guide was created by senior practitioners for practitioners and is based on the belief that no one person knows everything or has encountered every situation. It is not another book on theory, nor is it advice from people who review what others write and then synthesize a point of view. Dan, Rod and Keith have lived in the business transformation trenches since it first started to evolve in the early 1990's. They have led dozens of projects – from large transformations to smaller improvement efforts and everything in between. They have also helped pioneer many of the concepts used by big consulting firms. Based on their combined experience and knowledge, many regard them as true thought leaders within the transformation industry.

Further, the advice that is offered in this book has been battle-tested through numerous scenarios, across various projects, and utilizing a wide range of project teams and team member skills. It also has been tested in the tough environment of consulting - where client expectations shift constantly and few accept excuses. The hints are down to earth and when adjusted to the reality of the situation by practitioners, they have been proven to work.

This Guide will cover most of anything you will run into, but there will still be situations that are new. If for no other reason, it will be because technology keeps changing the rules we work under. Stay flexible and evolve with it and look for future updates as we all adjust and learn more.

Important

Many companies go directly from a high-level conceptual new business design, or even with no new business design, to the identification of use or business cases and their redesign/development in Agile sprints. This is popular in IT and espoused by many BPMS vendors. While this approach is useful for small, narrowly focused projects, it is not what we recommend for larger transformation projects.

These larger projects require a formal business redesign, then a technical solution design based on the business design, and finally the application of an approach like Agile. The hints in this book can be used in both situations. However, the team should recognize the need to go beyond Agile for larger, high visibility or mission critical projects.

Even though the BPMS technology has a lot of largely untapped capabilities and thus an ability to help in ways that many companies have yet to really discover, BPM is NOT a technical play. It is a business play and it MUST be approached from a business perspective. The real business perspective can easily be lost in a company's rush to deliver something. Such an approach should be relegated to history. Failure to build solutions within the context of a business perspective can also damage the credibility of IT in companies.

It is less expensive and disruptive to take the time to do it right and deliver a great solution. The "deliver something quickly and then improve it" interpretation of BPM and Agile is doing great damage to the way companies look at both BPM and IT within their organizations. However, this can be changed by rethinking how both can be used.

BPMS-enabled BPM, coupled with a proper use of an industry recognized project management tool, can make a big difference in a company's ability to compete and survive. To do that requires an evolution of the way we look at change and the role of both BPM and Agile within the company. The fact is that while Agile alone may be fine for smaller projects that are narrow in focus, it is only part of what is needed for larger projects. For these larger, more complex projects, Agile should be used in conjunction with a proven business operation redesign method and then applied to the results of the business redesign and the solution models that the redesign creates. Together, when used in this way, the combination is formidable.

We have divided the process transformation/improvement project into a business and a technical side. The project starts with the creation of a foundation in the "As Is" design to determine how the business operation is actually working and a "To Be" or future state design. This "To Be" design is not looked at as a possible solution. It is the solution.

As such it will need to be heavily reviewed and have evolved through business manager and staff reviews and reviews by collaborative partners. It will evolve in both content (the activities that are performed) and execution (workflow, rules, data use, etc.). This evolution is where simulation modeling comes in and where we recommend both simulation-based solution efficiency proof and, using proven techniques, a testing of the solution for the delivery of project targets – before the parts of the solution that are outside the BPMS-generated applications are built. This saves time and money and ensures delivery of the project goals.

The hints in this book are focused more on the business redesign side of the project. This is because this is where most projects have problems. The overlap or handoff to the technician is also addressed. But we are not presuming to tell any company how to use their version of Agile, PMI and other project management tools. So, beyond the handoff at the technical design, we move to addressing how the business team members should continue to be involved as the solution is created.

As a result of our combined experiences and the techniques we have introduced to companies, there may be hints that will not seem to apply for a given BPM group at the moment. When these are encountered, it is recommended that you consider if these concepts, techniques, and approaches should be introduced.

We believe that BPMS-enabled BPM is the breakthrough that has the ability to totally change the way business is approached. However, to have that impact, BPM must move from projects with a narrow focus to true business transformation. This does not mean that continuous improvement approaches should be abandoned – they are needed. It does mean that BPM-supported (not driven by) BPMS needs to evolve and become more focused on making the company more competitive and on increasing revenue.

The hints in this book will help every BPM practitioner evolve their personal capabilities and skills – reducing project risk and increasing the benefit and value of the solutions that are created.

Levels of detail (How models fit together)

There is no single reference model that defines the levels in a BPM business process model. The names and the number of levels vary. For this reason, the levels and names in the model below may be different in your company. However, the model below is provided to show the way we look at the different levels in a BPM decomposition.

Because we believe that the high level business operating model is the foundation needed to provide context for change and show how change supports strategy, our model starts with strategy and then Business Architecture to show the way the different operating units fit together

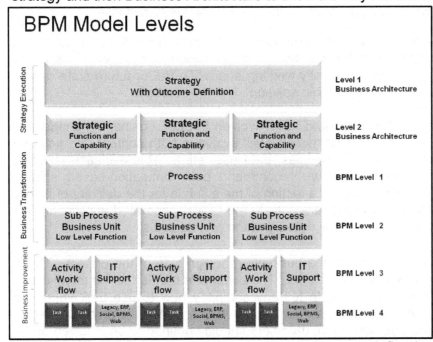

to support the strategic goals of the company. At this level, models show business function and business capability. Once the business functions in the strategic outcome model are defined, the functions that are needed to deliver them are defined and built. The capabilities will now be aligned to process in order to tie process to business strategy. The BPM sub-process level is where major components of a deliverable are aggregated and tied to the business units that create the components. Within the business unit, the activities are defined as logical sequential groups of tasks and their related application support. Application use, data use, problems and opportunities are noted at this level. The final level is where tasks are performed. These tasks contain the steps and the support needed to actually perform the work.

Together, this model represents the emerging way to look at business change.

How to use this Field Guide

Start anywhere... Go anywhere...

We have designed this Field Guide so that you can start anywhere and follow the threads of hints. We have also structured the contents to follow a simple seven-step methodology which we call Architect, Design, Deploy, Improve, or simply *A.D.D.I.* (see **About the ADDI methodology** at the end of this book.) This is a proven approach to setting up, designing, executing, and implementing a business transformation or improvement project of any size and complexity.

Imagine if you could ask the most experienced project/business/BPM/BPMS experts that have ever worked in the field what critical pieces of advice they could give you. Then pick up this book and begin reading. We have assembled over 800 hints of all types, be it how to manage a project, how best to design the future state, when and how to optimize business operations, and best practices in implementing your solutions. We have even captured hints around how to improve and expand the skills and capabilities of the BPM and BPMS Center of Excellence (CoE).

In addition, the Guide is *not* meant to be read from cover to cover – front to back. Rather, it is meant to be used as a *reference* as you start to perform different tasks in a business operation improvement or business transformation project. Due to the intent and design, the Guide is a type of BPM expert mentor. It is meant to help you succeed and avoid the project and transformation land mines the authors have stepped on and had to adjust to. This is a set of helpful guidance which we wished we had years ago when we were struggling to make this all work and be consistently successful.

The Field Guide is organized to follow a project's life cycle. It begins with hints on the initiation and setup of the project (change management and PMO or another project management methodology), moves through current state definition and baseline simulation to create a new business design, and then proves that it delivers the goals of the project – before money is spent to build the IT part of the solution. Next, it builds the IT support side and moves to a user-based test in a model office environment. The ADDI project execution approach controls iterations, limits risk of acceptance issues, and ensures that all benefits, goals, improvement standards, and value objectives are delivered.

The hints are meant to help you understand the options you have in each type of activity that you become involved in. Our focus is on the business side of transformation. This is where failure lives. If the design is not on target, the creation of any support is a moot issue – it will be wrong and the project will fail.

The real problems can often include that the wrong capabilities are built as a solution, that the way applications interface may not deliver what the business really needs, or that the solution may simply not support the business in the right way. These are design issues, not technical issues, but many design issues are caused by technicians trying to tell a business how to operate and how to perform activities and at a lower level of detail, tasks. Business Architects need to define strategic outcomes and translate the outcome definitions into high-level business functions and then into business capabilities. Further, Process Architects need to translate these capabilities into operational work and align it to processes and sub-processes. They can then align the sub-processes to organization and, within the organization, to operational (low-level) functionality. These low-level functions are then the drivers for activity and flow requirements, which are executed in tasks and at a still lower level of definition, steps. This execution level design is the realm of the business analyst.

On the IT side, the needed technology infrastructure, the communications network capability design and the application portfolio architecture are the responsibility of the Enterprise Architect. Specialty IT architects for data, user interface, and other areas will support the Enterprise Architect. All of these people work with their business counterparts in defining solutions, identifying constraints, and redesigning optimal ways to deliver better business operations that contain more flexibility, are more cost effective, and provide an improved quality and customer interaction experience.

In conclusion, we hope that the Guide is helpful and we welcome any suggestions on how it can be improved. Please send them to us at: daniel.morris@wendan-consulting.com.

Wendan's Laws

These "laws" should be considered for any project, BPM or otherwise.

	Laws that will help you succeed
1.	Do no harm to the business operation – always leave a business operation more effective and efficient than it was when you first got there.
2.	Take no risk unless it is planned and controlled – and approved by anyone who may be affected.
3.	Never implement anything without first being able to back it out and reinstate the current business operation without any noticable affect on the business.
4.	Never assume that you have been told the whole story on any problem – probe and verify.
5.	Do not assume that any information you have been given is either correct or up to date. Check update dates and the update process and make up your own mind. Any data or model that is over six months old is NOT current.
6.	Old models and data are worse than no models or data – you don't know what is right and you can easily be misled and make poor decisions from out-of-date models.
7.	Always respect the people you are interviewing – they may have caused error and waste, but there were reasons you may not be aware of or constraints that limited what could be done.
8.	Never find fault with what a person has done or try to find who is to blame – both are irrelevant, just fix the problem.
9.	Be patient when trying to teach business people BPMS modeling or application requirements definition – the people are totally outside their element and you must make them comfortable and not afraid to fail in trying to use new tools.
10.	Be friendly and try to put the people you interview at ease.
11.	Obvious is often only obvious to an outsider – people tend to get too close to the operation and they don't question things.
12.	Question everything and keep at it until you get an answer – then document it.
13.	Ask the tough questions and do not accept answers that say or tell you nothing – do not accept nuance and drive for clarity. Do not let anyone go off on tangents and fail to give you the answer to the question you are asking. You are leading the interview – so lead it!
14.	There is a big difference between optimal and OK! Please don't settle for OK for expediency or to save time.
15.	Do not deliver an OK solution and count on iteration to eventually get you to a good solution – the business managers will not be happy and there is a high probability that no one will keep evolving the solution once it is delivered. This drives a company to mediocrity.
16.	If applications are not directly defined by a new business design, they will likely not be used as anticipated or as designed from requirements.
17.	There is no room for ego on a business transformation team
18.	The people who do the work are actually the people who know the work. Talk with them and listen carefully.
19.	Use a formal methodology that is capable of aligning to the different discipline tasks and techniques of the various collaborative partners and controlling activity among all the collaborative groups.
20.	Always define success at the beginning of a project and get agreement on how success will be measured and evaluated.

BPM Project Performance

Hints

0.0 Thinking about BPM

Before getting into the first step of setting up the project, the authors felt that there were some general hints that would help to set the tone for thinking about BPM in your organization. These hints reflect our overall perspective of how BPM should be viewed and leveraged and, as such, provide some insight into how and why we think the hints in the remainder of this Field Guide can help obtain and maintain high value.

Any manual process is prone to inconsistent processing and variances in results. This is often referred to as human error. While people do make the decisions that cause the variations, the real issue is often that the processes are poorly defined, the decision rules are seldom known or managed, and the people are under tremendous pressure to "get the job done." While the wisdom of creating this environment can be debated, this is the way it is and we need to find ways to deal with these situations within the framework of corporate operations and the company culture.

In addition, in many places, business transformation has been relegated to the IT department. Experience shows that depending on company culture this may cause an issue. If the business areas look at BPM-based operational transformation as a technical function, it simply becomes another IT approach that the business managers place in the IT box and leave alone. When this happens, business transformation is in trouble.

Business transformation and business improvement are both business activities that are supported by IT applications. IT approaches are meant to create application systems and when applied broadly often fail to deliver expected results – some reports place failure at up to 60% (over time, over budget, reduced functionality, failure to deliver expected benefit). In this book, we follow a business-oriented approach that has been built into the ADDI iBPM transformation project orchestration methodology. This blends IT Agile, ITIL, Change Management, Business

Architecture, Enterprise Architecture and other specialty methodologies around a central core orchestration and execution methodology that call the others as needed. This approach supports the BPM collaboration and iteration concepts and adds in iBPM simulation, mobility, and analytics. Thus, it provides a project execution focus in the organization of the hints.

An unrealized promise of BPMS-supported BPM is solution development speed. This is obtainable, but it also requires a new approach to leveraging BPMS and emerging technology. Even with BPMS tools, few companies have been able to keep up with automation needs even though IT is one of the biggest budget line items in company budgets. To exacerbate this problem is the fact that technology is evolving faster than most companies can keep up with. But mobility device vendors leverage this emerging technology and significant segments of the population rush to obtain the latest versions of their products. While this is good for them, it is bad for most companies – it creates capability expectations in the public that few companies can meet, let alone keep up with the evolution.

A big part of the reason is that many companies simply try to build solutions the way they have always built them – just using a couple of new tools. BPMS-supported BPM is, however, different than traditional approaches and requires different practices to optimize their use.

These are only some of the issues that companies must face in their move to operational modernization. But they are real and failure to leverage all the new concepts and technology in any business transformation will seriously limit the ability of the company to compete. It is, therefore, incumbent on the business transformation project leaders and team members to push the capabilities of any solution as far as they possibly can and be as creative as they are allowed to be.

Have you ever thought, "Why are we still doing manual paperwork processes outside core enterprise systems?" Many companies still take the manual route with key processes even if the systems they use are capable of automating it. Outdated technology solutions, which do not incorporate and automate key business functions, can leave you dangerously out of touch. A lack of available business information can become a significant problem, no matter how many spreadsheets and workarounds have been developed. The BPM team should be a strategic partner who helps the business address key gaps between manual and automation by developing new solutions that are trusted to deliver in actual practice, not just in theory.

BPM was originally developed as a focus on end-to-end processes. This intent has evolved in the last decade to encompass any type of change that follows BPM principles. The concept of business transformation is evolving and becoming a term for an approach that includes activity from BPM, BPMS-supported BPM, Business Architecture, Enterprise Architecture, Data Architecture, Change Management, and other disciplines.

BPM-based projects are becoming larger, more complex, and mission critical. This is creating the need for a new way to approach these projects – a new type of methodology. We believe that a hybrid methodology needs to be developed and customized for each company's real operating environment. Creating or obtaining this methodology is critical to legitimizing any project approach, and the project direction and control that it carries with it.

Business transformation is a business activity first and foremost. It is supported by IT changes, but it is not an IT project.

Project size and impact fall across a continuum. There are small projects that are very local and have a nominal impact to the business. These are often referred to as "fingers and toes" projects since they are small, relatively low risk, and provide only limited business benefits. As a result, they do not receive much attention from leadership and can often be dismissed as not significant. The risks to these efforts are that they are not seen as significant and their value is often never recognized. Worse, the team members are not recognized as having contributed much to the business and their effort is not well appreciated. If project managers, BPM or other internal professionals find themselves on too many of these projects, their value and contribution to the business will be questioned as these projects are not making a significant impact to key business objectives. On the other end of the continuum are large company-wide transformation projects. These can be multi-year, vast in scope, and consume tremendous amounts of resources. These are clearly aligned with and are expected to make a significant contribution to key business objectives. Careers are advanced with their success or crushed with their failure. Unfortunately, the vast majority of transformation projects do not meet their original objectives (see hints on transformational project success).

Most projects change over their duration. Managers, sponsors, and project participants learn more and understand the issues at a deeper level. An analogy is from construction – rehabilitation in particular. You see a stain on a wall and press on it. It is a little soft and you decide to cut it out and patch it. When you open the wall, it is full of mold and insects. So the wall you first thought was sound and then thought needed a small patch now needs to be removed, the leak needs to be found and fixed, and the insect damage needs to be repaired – after the insects are killed. Most projects are like this – even though many hate to admit it and many try to hold teams to the original estimates. This is the reason for assumptions in the project request and charter. The fact is that there are unforeseen problems that will arise. When they do, a decision needs to be made to either deal with them or ignore them. Experienced project managers build in contingency time and budget, as well as put assumptions about estimate review at milestones with project change orders for approved project expansion.

When determining the importance, value and priority of a project ensure that you are aligning each project to strategic business objectives. These should include the following:

- Growth and scalability of the business
- Creation of differentiation and strategic capabilities
- Delivery of customer experience

These are universal objects and should always be considered as vital elements when assessing the relative value of a project investment.

Before any project is started there needs to be a clear and agreed to method to determine the return that the business expects to be delivered for the investment. Successful projects are those that are clearly aligned and demonstrate how they contribute to and drive strategic business objectives in clear measureable ways. Too often projects are launched with unclear definitions of expected returns.

Building teams and working with people

We firmly believe that BPM is about business and business is about people. BPM in organizations is often also supported by technology, however, that may not always be the case. Business, in our view, ends up being all about people even when there are a lot of bells and whistles. It will be people who gather the information, find creative solutions, and ultimately do the work, so working with people and building high functioning teams is critical. People make or break any operation.

In addition, we believe in a collaborative approach that engages people from all affected business areas, multiple IT areas, and possibly customers. These collaborative groups offer different views and perspectives that are often not otherwise considered. Collaborative teams require different management and different project planning approaches. It represents more of a consensus approach and an ability to find common ground. However, we believe that you will find the outcomes of projects to be more readily accepted.

Always be non-threatening and if at all possible, avoid confrontation. This is a hard lesson for most of us to learn. However, you will get a lot further by proving a statement or position is wrong through a roundabout questioning process than by confronting someone you know is wrong or is purposely not being honest. Start asking questions that have nothing to do with the point and build your foundation information until you can say 'so in other words, because of X, Y and Z, A will be the outcome.' Here the outcome is what you knew it would be and the error/falsehood is exposed. Lastly, pick any battle carefully, but avoid battles if you can. This does not mean to give in or to do something you know is wrong. Just be careful and do not confront people directly in meetings unless what they are saying or doing will hurt the project. If a confrontation seems inevitable, have the discussion privately.

Poor performers on your team should never be tolerated, and if excuses begin to appear, the situation should be addressed immediately. If there are team members who appear to be at risk for not delivering the work that they are assigned, they might jeopardize the work of the entire team. When a poor performer is identified, immediate action must be taken. When a potential problem is identified there must first be a non-confrontational effort to determine what might be causing the problem. People may have difficulty carrying out their responsibilities for a variety of reasons which can include:

- Assignments that exceed knowledge and/or skill levels
- Personal problems
- Interference from managers and supervisors
- Imbalance of daily job responsibilities and team responsibilities
- Resistance to the project/project concepts
- Poor work habits
- Etc.

The underlying reasons will need to be addressed in ways consistent with those reasons. Where possible, corrective steps should be taken and the situation monitored to see if performance becomes acceptable. Unfortunately, there may be circumstances where there is no acceptable corrective action or where performance does not improve. It is important in these circumstances to remove the problem person from the team as soon as possible to mitigate any risk to the project and to the team as a whole.

Do not be publically judgmental. Do not put a business manager or staff member down and do not ridicule an IT programmer for poor application systems. Things are the way they are for a reason. You do not know the long list of circumstances that led to the current process or operation. Your job is to fix it, not to make people feel bad.

Poor behavior can occur on the part of the most seasoned or the most inexperienced team members. Every project needs to be managed professionally and poor behavior towards any person or the work being conducted is not to be tolerated. When poor behavior is identified, immediate action must be taken. If it is not, the team will begin to form groups or camps that can become hostile toward one another and virtually kill the project. Although uncomfortable for many managers, action must be taken. This includes one-on-one coaching by the project manager, communication with the individual's manager, engaging human resources, and, when necessary, removal of disruptive people from the project team. Do not expect others on the team to intervene on behalf of the project manager. It is the project manager's job to ensure professionalism of every member of the team at all times.

In any team there will be participants who are vocal and even outspoken as well those who are quiet or even silent. Every team member is there for a reason and one of the challenges for the project manager is to elicit the thoughts, concerns, and ideas of each and every participant. Sometimes input can be gained from less vocal team members by simply going around the room and asking each person for their input. There may be situations, however, when getting a person to share their thinking will work best in a one-on-one conversation or by asking for written input directly to you as project manager. If you have participants who you can see squirming in the context of a larger group, you should take steps to gain the input without putting the person on the spot.

Projects are both work and learning environments. Small investments in the learning portion can pay big dividends over the life of one or more projects. Coaching, mentoring, and taking time to explain some details or complexities can both uncover and build competencies that were completely unknown originally. The authors have each discovered very talented people of all ages who ended up contributing far more than ever envisioned when they were assigned to the team. Investing in team members also builds strong relationships and trust.

No matter what the nature of a project is, the project manager must create, encourage, and maintain a culture and environment that supports responsible and professional work habits, encourages and promotes constant critical thinking, and engenders mutual respect and trust. In this culture and environment, however, there will be variability in how well team members demonstrate each of the attributes. Some people are just better at critical thinking than others, some people are better at preparing documentation or asking the right questions, etc. These problem identification/solving skill differences may lead to adjustments in assignments to maximize individual skill sets. Mutual respect and trust, however, cannot be allowed to be variable and if problems are seen regarding these attributes, they must be addressed immediately. Failure to maintain respect and trust can seriously impair a project that otherwise appears to be on track.

1.0 Preparing for the project - foundation

One of the biggest reasons for project failure is a lack of proper preparation. Today with BPM, collaboration is emphasized more than at any time in the past, which adds significant complexity to the project. In addition, most companies now recognize that simply telling an IT systems analyst "what you want a system to do" is not really adequate and seldom delivers the results the business needs.

In addition, a serious mistake that is often made is the belief by many that certified project management people will make a big difference in BPM projects. This is simply not true. While it is true that project managers need to be experienced and need to understand how to manage a project, these capabilities alone do not really help with project execution. For a successful BPM project, a good understanding of the activities and steps is needed to allow for the project to be executed and orchestrated. The larger the scope and the more complex the initiative, the higher the need for advanced understanding and competencies. It is a big mistake to think that these projects are performed the way projects have been performed in the past.

One of the key differences lies in change management and the alignment of all project participants who will be affected by the project outcome (business operation, production, sales, finance, legal, etc.), as well as the alignment of IT support capabilities and limitations. Coordinating this alignment is neither simple nor easy. Each manager will have their own agenda and their own needs. Obtaining agreement on the outcome of a project that will cause changes in more than a single business function in a single department is not for the faint of heart.

Setting the foundation for the BPM- and BPMS-supported BPM project is critical, but difficult, because it requires new considerations that increase the level of difficulty in this activity.

1.1 Project execution

Project execution is different from project management. Project management is the process of managing people and the progress of the project. Project execution refers to the tasks that need to be performed, the order they will need to be performed in, the inputs to the tasks, and the products of the tasks. The execution plan must identify and define the work that needs to be done by each participating group/role. Project execution deals with what should be done and how it should be done. It has little to do with the actual assignment of people, the tracking of work, and the tracking of progress. For any project that is relatively complex or fairly important, you need both project management and project execution capabilities.

This distinction is needed because it is not enough for a BPM- or BPMS-supported BPM project to be managed by a project manager with a PMI or other project management certification. Obtaining that certification should indicate that the project manager knows how to run a project. However, there are thousands of different types of projects – each with its own unique approach and type of tasks. This is where execution specialization comes in – someone must know what you need to do to perform the project and deliver the goals and objectives. This execution specialization in BPM projects covers both business transformation operational redesign and IT applications redesign and construction.

BPM and BPMS are two halves to the same equation. One without the other often results in disappointing outcomes. For a project to truly deliver value, the BPM and BPMS professionals need to work together in determining the best requirements that address the business needs, identify how best to envision the future solution, and together bring to bear the best of their respective tool sets to create and implement solutions that bring real and lasting value to the business. BPM alone defines better processes, while BPMS alone creates and enables automation. Individually, each will under-deliver on the real business need. Together, BPM and BPMS leverage the capabilities around efficient and effective process design, tied to the infusion of appropriate technology and automation to create around dynamic business logic and differentiated process solutions.

Creating a foundation of consensus, sound estimates, adequate budget, realistic expectations and collaboration is required for success. When this is not done or not given enough attention, the project will fail. Execution-focused project activity definition is vital to the success of the project.

Formal project definition as part of setting up a project is critical. The project definition should state the problems or issues that need to be eliminated (or solved); the impacts of each problem or issue on current state processes, the dollar savings associated with each correction, the value that the change will bring to the company's ability to execute strategy of some kind, and the impact this will have on the customer, revenue generation, and/or market share expansion. This information is the foundation for the execution of the analyses and design activities in the project. If the project request does not contain this information along with timing, constraints, staff support availability, etc., the project manager will need to develop it all before the project officially starts.

All projects are important! If not, they should not be done. Even small projects deliver value. Care should be taken to properly manage and perform even obvious improvements. This includes a formal plan with defined roles and managed assignments. If it is worth doing, it is worth doing right.

Sponsorship needs to be at the highest level of the organization to ensure that barriers, issues and resource requirements are taken seriously. If a team attempts a significant effort and does not have the backing of a senior executive, the project runs the risk of being relegated to one of the many "improvement or transformation" efforts that struggle to get attention, are short on resources and struggle to move forward. This usually leads to the project being re-scoped or terminated because sufficient progress is not demonstrated.

A good project manager will be vigilant in overseeing and managing changes to the project scope. Such changes can be driven by legislative changes, technology changes, union changes, and more. They may represent significant changes to the project and may require solution rework. As scope is changed, the entire project needs to be re-reviewed to ensure that timelines, milestones, resources, costs, and benefits still meet the needs and expectations of the sponsor and the organization. While this can be an onerous exercise, if not done, the project will struggle since the plan of record, along with resource needs, support, etc., may not be aligned with the revised scope.

A project issue log needs to be available to all team members so that everyone can see the barriers that can cause potential project risk. It is vital that this be available not only to the project team but also to leadership, so they are aware of the issues and can recognize that the project team is actively working and resolving open items. This open and honest environment builds trust and when you need a sponsor to intervene or support your project, they know that their influence is being leveraged appropriately.

Communicate clearly and often to the employees and their managers who will be affected by the changes that will be put in place by your project. Ideally, those same employees should be brought "into the tent" early so that they understand why the project has been launched, what the changes will be, and how it will affect them. In fact, the more you demonstrate your solutions and include them in the user acceptance testing (UAT), the better their adoption will be once the project is fully implemented.

Set expectations for each individual as well as for the team as a whole. Do this early on and reinforce from time to time throughout the project. This will reinforce what individuals are accountable for and ensure that there is no confusion on who is accountable for what.

There is a difference between continuous process improvement and business transformation.

Improvement and Transformation

Only business transformation can lead to operating optimization.

Improvement: small focused projects that make what you do faster, cheaper, better

The risk with improvement - it is usually narrowly focused and the impact on the overall process is seldom considered
- Over time many small individually beneficial changes can weaken the overall integrity of the process and its efficiency.
- Uncontrolled improvement thus can have a negative impact on optimization.

Transformation: the fundamental rethinking of what should be done

Because of complexity, transformation must by holistic, must be closely managed, and requires comprehensive methods and standards to succeed.
- Although IT is part of a transformation, these are business, not IT projects.
- Transformations are long, expensive, high visibility, high impact projects.
- Risk can be high if the transformation is not led by experienced Sr. Level Managers.

Expectations must be carefully managed to make certain they are realistic given the time, budget, staff, and external support assigned to the project. This is critical because the team will be held responsible for what they agree to do – setting expectations. Do not be bullied into agreeing to the impossible.

Placing Subject Matter Experts (SMEs) from relevant business areas on the project team is a good start in building a team, but history has shown that they are only a good start in understanding the business or in promoting acceptance of the project. It is suggested that in BPM projects, the approach of engaging users be followed throughout the project. This approach involves taking a little time now and then from a wide range of users. This shares the load and ensures that no one is overburdened by their involvement.

Expectations can only be managed if they are formally defined. The project manager and project team will be held accountable for what participants expect – even when the expectations were wrong or unreasonable. That is why it is important to be honest and to negotiate expectations that can be delivered. However, this is a tricky thing to do. If you try to set expectations too low, people will lose faith in you and the team. If you set them too high because someone is pressuring you to do so, you will fail. So realistic expectations are critical to the ability to succeed.

The role of a project sponsor may seem simple, but playing the role is difficult. A project sponsor needs to:

- Stay the course and not allow anyone, including leadership, the business partners, and the project team, to challenge the decisions about the projects that have already been agreed to and accepted (unless, of course, an underlying assumption needs to be revisited). Too often people will agree and then later choose to "opt out" or choose a different course of action, frequently without supportable facts.
- Provide air cover for the project so that the team can focus on getting the work done, while the sponsor focuses on ensuring continued support of the project, defusing potential internal political issues and mitigating unnecessary pressures on the project.
- Ensure that leadership exhibits patience in achieving results.

The project sponsor does this by:

- Demonstrating endurance and willingness to allow the work streams to yield value over a multi-year horizon,
- Holding the business accountable for seeing through decision commitments,
- Determination in not allowing key actors to change their mind after agreement and thus to impede success,
- Willingness to lead and make decisions that are based on the interests of the entire organization even when they may be perceived to have negative local implications.

Each role on a project is vital; the project sponsor is amongst the most important.

Formal project team status review meetings should be held every day. These should be 15-minute meetings focused on sharing status, problems, constraints, technical issues that have been encountered and what needs to be done to eliminate them. The main purpose of these daily sessions is to share problems and to find help in resolving them. The secondary purpose of these status meetings is to help the project teams better prepare for the workday.

Project success must be judged from 4 perspectives:

- Technical success (meets all requirements)
- Business success (the solution is acceptable to the business user)
- Interface success (all components and interfaces function properly)
- Customer success (all customer interactions are given high marks).

Only when success is achieved from all four of these perspectives will a solution be considered successful. A.D.D.I. views these perspectives in the order presented.

Today businesses rely on temporary external resources more and more. This allows the flexibility of acquiring specialized skills quickly and reduces the cost and management burden of a large permanent full-time staff. While this provides leaders with increased flexibility, it does present a unique set of conflicting goals. Your business will seek the best temporary resources for the shortest duration and the lowest cost. On the other hand, the vendor seeks to place as many resources, for the longest time possible, at the highest cost. These different sets of goals can come into conflict if not managed effectively, and it is the program/project manager's role to ensure that there is a balance between the need for resources and the vendor's desire to maximize their income. Depending on where resource needs are located, the project manager may have to work with senior leadership and/or operational managers to achieve and maintain this balance. If you rely on your vendor, the cost may create an unsustainable drain on your organization. When leveraging temporary resources, it is important to:

- Set clear expectations of the skills and capabilities the temporary staff must bring to the table,
- Negotiate the fees before work starts. Recognize that the longer a temporary resource is to be employed, the lower the per hour cost should be,
- Establish clear roles and expectations for the temporary resources. Ambiguity can contribute to under-performance and missed expectations, *or* it can result in over-performance by applying more resources and/or higher level resources than the project requires. Either situation can result in higher costs and unnecessary conflicts,
- Always have a set end date. Even if the date is later extended, you must have a date that the resources will exit. The lack of a clear termination date creates an open-ended invitation for the resources to remain and seek other roles, expand their scope, and create fees.

In addition to milestones, projects need to have clear checkpoints throughout their execution. Check points are formal reviews of the project to date and are used to:
Assess the overall progress of the project to plan and to discuss any known or potential new issues/risks

- Confirm continued sponsorship support of the effort. This is especially important for lengthy projects where sponsors may become fatigued or the named executive might change (due to a change in their role);
- Communicate to leadership, the team and the organization the progress to date, and reinforce the value that the project will bring to the business;
- Engage the entire team and keep everyone in the loop as to progress, macro issues, sponsorship, alignment to key business objectives;
- Align against the business objectives and confirm that the goals of the project continue to be in sync with the strategic objectives of the organization.

1.2 Select the standards, KPIs, policies, and procedures

To avoid chaos in a project and the collection of useless information, it is necessary for all BPM- and BPMS-supported BPM projects to adhere to set company standards for data collection, problem identification, performance monitoring, business modeling (BPMN is a good start, but it is only a part of the modeling picture), supporting the business methodology that will be used, etc. It is also critical that the project team understand the constraints that will apply and the ways that may be used to creatively address capability limitations.

In addition, many companies have standard improvement Key Performance Indicators (KPIs), policies, legal requirements and financial monitoring rules that must be followed. To avoid misunderstanding and the omission of a critical consideration, the project manager and team must find all project guides and weave them into the fabric of the project – making their consideration mandatory at all applicable parts of the project.

Failure to formally identify, define, and align these guiding requirements in any BPM- or BPMS-supported BPM project will increase risk, increase cost, and almost ensure rework due to a lack of solution acceptance.

Over the last several decades, the question of relevance has continued to grow in importance. If a project, its leaders and its staff cannot demonstrate a clear connection to delivering on business objectives and providing a compelling value proposition, their relevance will be measured and found lacking. To be successful in project execution and ultimately in one's own career, it is important to ensure that the question of relevancy is asked often and the answer found to be compelling enough to continue with the project. Without this, projects will be shut down, careers will stagnate, and ultimately the business will be at risk.

The BPM group within the organization or project needs to create a formal list of standards for each of the major actions that it is involved in. These standards include:
- Definition of the information to be collected at each point in the project;
- Definition of how collaboration will function – disciplines needed to be represented, roles and role tasks, disagreement mediation;
- Participant performance measurement;
- Modeling and solution design – Lean, Togaf®, Zachman Framework, and others;
- Process performance measurement and management that will be built into the solution – Six Sigma, and others;
- Simulation information to be collected;
- Solution testing, IT testing turnover.

At the start of any current state modeling, it is important to schedule time with legal and finance to identify and define all compliance requirements and compliance reporting needs. The team will also need to know how the compliance reports are constructed to help identify the best sources of data and the way evaluation formulas function.

Identify the company standards and "Best Practices" from other projects which should be considered in all areas of the project and create hot links to them. This includes compliance monitoring, Agile, change management, PMI, Legacy interfaces, data architecture, and other standards.

When company standards are collected and reviewed, it is possible that some may be incomplete or out of date. If this occurs, the "owners" of the standards should be asked to bring them up to date. If that fails, the project governance team should reach agreement on how the standards will be defined and applied within the project. This agreement must be put in writing to avoid confusion or conflict during the project.

As documents containing standards are collected, they should all be placed in a repository accessible to anyone associated with the project. A "Read Only" format should be used to avoid inadvertent changes. The repository should be a separate folder containing only standards.

Define how each standard will impact activities and how it will be used across the entire project. This definition should be formally accepted by the BPM CoE and should also be accepted and understood by all project participants. While this hint is part of the "selection of project standards," it is to be a foundation within every phase of the project.

Meetings are a necessary evil in business. To make a business meeting effective and useful, a few simple principles should be followed to maximize the time spent together. This includes:
- Have a clear set of meeting objectives and agenda (i.e., why the meeting taking place);
- Have a time-bound agenda. Outline the topics that will be covered and an estimate of how long each will take. This ensures that you get through the material in the time allotted. This does not, however, mean forcing a decision if it becomes clear that more information and/or more discussion is needed to bring a topic to conclusion;
- Ensure that people are prepared to participate and contribute. If a decision is to be made, all the facts need to be made available. Failure to have all the facts in the room will result in additional meetings being scheduled, resulting in delays and wasted time;
- If there are follow-up items identified, be sure that each is assigned to someone in the room, that a date is agreed to for the task to be completed, and that there is agreement on how the results of the action will be communicated to others;
- Document the meeting results. It is important to capture who attended, the decisions that were made, and that follow-up items are assigned. By documenting this, you have a record of the meeting that can be referred to in the future.

It is estimated that between 35% to 50% of manager's time is spent in meetings. Project teams fall victim to meetings as well. The key is to follow these simple principles and productivity will increase dramatically. In the end, a meeting should never be scheduled unless there are clear objectives, the right people can actually attend (not just get invited), and that the agenda is defined and followed.

There must be a clear understanding and commitment from top levels down that the project is a key job assignment and that appropriate adjustments to other responsibilities may need to be made. This has to be kept in mind when identifying participants.

Project status reporting, made simple. Everyone is interested in the status and more importantly, the progress of a project. Keeping stakeholders, business partners, and the overall project team informed is a key element of continued support and engagement. At a minimum, a project needs to publish a weekly status report and should contain the following:

- The status report should have an executive summary of 2-3 sentences describing at a very high level the purpose of the project and how it aligns to business objectives. This ensures that anyone reading the status report has a starting point as to what problems/ business objectives are being addressed and puts the status information in context.
- The next most vital set of project facts is indicating the key players on the project. This ensures that the sponsor, team leader, and project manager are seen as accountable for the project and that they are the "go to" contact points for any information on the project.
- Overall status should be on the top and present an easily understood message of the project. Follow the RAG Status for the project (Green = project on track, Amber (yellow) = project has some issues that are being worked on, and finally Red = project is not on track and is at risk). This simple color coding establishes the context for the overall project.
- Key activities for the period being reported on – this shows both activity and progress to goal and serves to communicate that work is moving forward;
- Activities planned for the next period – demonstrates that the team has clear focus on "what comes next" and that you are continuing to push forward;
- Risks/issues and mitigation plans capture and acknowledge barriers to progress and outline the plans to mitigate or eliminate them. It is vital that the project clearly acknowledge that there are barriers and that plans are in place to address them;
- Key action items/milestones elevate high importance activities/decisions as well as identify milestones which are a measure of both progress and completion of specific work streams/phases;
- All of this information can be captured on a one-sided page which is created by the project manager and approved by the project sponsor. Once published, this represents a formal status of the project.

1.3 Project orchestration - identify probable participants

As collaboration increases in popularity, it must be woven into the way a project will be executed and the way it will be managed. The common issues are based on conflicting timing among the different groups who will be involved and the fact that the different groups bring with them different perspectives, different beliefs on how the project should be performed, the disciplines that should be used, and how the work will be estimated and prioritized. These differences open the project to a wide range of backgrounds and experiences – which is good. However, it also opens the project to continuous disagreement, active non-engagement, and general chaos.

Controlling and managing collaboration can be challenging and it requires a strong project manager, supported by an equally strong project sponsor. This is one of the reasons that standards are so important, that formal participation commitment is critical, and that the project should follow a formal business-focused BPM methodology.

Business transformation and smaller, more narrowly focused projects today are collaborative efforts. Participants come from multiple business areas and often multiple geographies. They also bring their way of doing things and often a belief that no way but their way is possibly right. The project manager will need to orchestrate or control and direct the participation of these differing perspectives, skills, approaches, and disciplines to ensure that the right people are doing the right work for their skills, at the right times and places in the project. This is not an easy task.

The project manager's role can be looked at as one part "Mother Theresa" and one part "Attila the Hun." In fostering debate, creativity, consensus, etc., "Mother Theresa" is appropriate. In adhering to standards, policies, requirements and the like, "Attila" may be necessary at times.

Participants should include persons from all those areas of the company that are connected to the process being addressed by the project.

Participants should span a spectrum from executive level to people actually performing various tasks. Participants should be specific individuals in reality, but may initially be identified by position or location on the spectrum before specific individuals are identified, especially at the level where work is performed.

The team should also include a full continuum from executive to line staff with all management levels being represented.

One of the responsibilities of the project manager is to build and maintain an atmosphere of mutual respect. There is no denying that organizations have hierarchical structures, but the efforts by the team to identify issues, factors, and solution elements must recognize that each participant is there because of their unique ability to make a contribution and, therefore, is equally important.

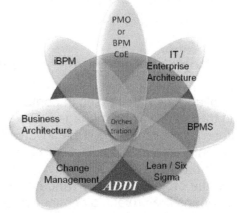

BPM Project Orchestration

The entire project is dependent on building and maintaining consensus on a constant stream of issues. Because of this, some thought should be given to whether potential participants are known to be team players and conversely, seen as bullies. While some participants may be unavoidable due to their role, other participants may have roles that allow for some choices.

If a participant, who is viewed as a potential bully, must be part of the team, the risk thus presented should be discussed with the project sponsor before real activity even begins and avenues to mitigate potential problems worked out. The project manager should remain vigilant for any emerging problems, particularly when the team includes subordinates of the person in question.

A potential participant should not be eliminated simply because they work in a remote location. It is not unusual for a key or perhaps the only person who can bring in necessary perspectives, skills, knowledge, etc., to be somewhere other than corporate headquarters. If remote simply means an hour or two away to be part of the group, remote participants should be required to come in. While teleconferencing is an easy way to address remote participants, some thought should be given to bringing remote participants in at least for important sessions. There is no team-building substitute for being face to face from time to time.

Do NOT eliminate a potential participant simply because of a language barrier. DO have someone around to translate when needed, even when it's just a hard to understand accent.

Do NOT allow a manager or supervisor to eliminate a potential team member because "They just can't be spared." The team needs the best of the best and most likely every member cannot be spared, but they will have to be. If need be, discuss any such situations with the project sponsor to find a way to include needed members and to do so in way that does not force them to work nights and weekends to perform two jobs.

For many participants, the team activities will only be a part-time responsibility. This leads to two important scheduling considerations:
- In addition to formal team work sessions, most participants will have to have prep time prior to the work sessions and some will have homework in the form of gathering information, things to document, metrics to capture, etc. It is important for the total time commitment to be honestly addressed and that the participants (and their supervisors) are not sold on just the several hours a week when the formal sessions are conducted.
- Since the team members are not doing their regular job, it is likely that team activities will require a different way of thinking and a different understanding of context than they have for their day-to-day responsibilities. It will take a little while for participants to get into "team" mode for each work session, especially if they have left behind nagging day-

to-day issues that distract them. Therefore, attention should be given to the scheduling of work sessions. Half, full and multi-day sessions will be more productive than the same number of hours scheduled one at a time and spread across the entire week. This reasoning is often used in setting up executive retreats and should be applied to team efforts.

As an important part of the project, there should be a clear understanding and clear support from the sponsor and other key executives. An issue that needs to be addressed in this support is the necessity at each level to create a work environment that recognizes that subordinates on the team will be responsible for project tasks as well as their routine work. As a result, adjustments must be made to expectations regarding routine work. In most cases, this will require some redistribution of workload within the operating unit since there will be limited opportunity to catch up on work that cannot be done while project tasks are executed. Part of the adjustment approach should be to focus on the most critical skills each team member contributes to routine work and redistribute responsibilities that can be readily carried out by other staff in the operating unit.

Project governance policies should be developed to address how substitutes for participants and ad hoc participants will be addressed. In general, substitutes should be discouraged and ad hoc participants should be limited to situations where there is a clear need for expertise, information or a perspective that is not available from any other team member. Frequent use of a substitute should be seen as a red flag that commitment and buy-in are lacking.

In any collaboration, the project leader will need to select the best approaches, techniques, tasks, disciplines, etc., for the project. This will vary by project and possibly by the project phase for larger projects. The project manager will need to follow company standards but he or she will need to make decisions on when to use such things as Lean and Six Sigma, Waterfall and Agile, etc.

Avoid approach wars -- getting into a debate between the relative merits of Six Sigma vs. Lean vs. BPM, etc. In the end, each of these methodologies is intended to enable and improve business operations. The nuances are best left at the door and, as a team, focus on creative problem solving, not whose methodology is right or the best.

When determining the importance, value and priority of a project, ensure that you are aligning each project to strategic business objectives. These should include the following:
- Growth and scalability of the business
- Creation of differentiation and strategic capabilities
- Delivery of a customer experience

These are universal objects and should always be considered as vital elements when assessing the relative value of a project investment.

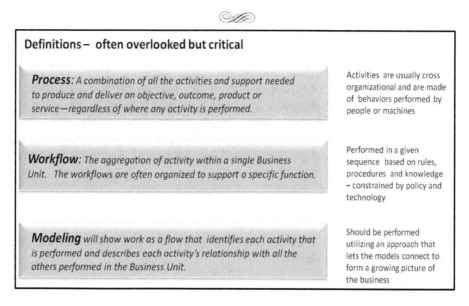

Definitions – often overlooked but critical

Process: *A combination of all the activities and support needed to produce and deliver an objective, outcome, product or service—regardless of where any activity is performed.*

Activities are usually cross organizational and are made of behaviors performed by people or machines

Workflow: *The aggregation of activity within a single Business Unit. The workflows are often organized to support a specific function.*

Performed in a given sequence based on rules, procedures and knowledge – constrained by policy and technology

Modeling *will show work as a flow that identifies each activity that is performed and describes each activity's relationship with all the others performed in the Business Unit.*

Should be performed utilizing an approach that lets the models connect to form a growing picture of the business

1.4 Align managers - project vision, goals, outcome definition, and participation

Differences of opinion are often hidden behind perceived understanding. People may think they understand something or agree with something only to later find out that they really disagree based on other's interpretations. We all filter what we hear through our understanding of vocabulary, our experience, and what we want to hear or believe.

Language alone is imprecise and easily misunderstood. Just look in any dictionary and see how many different definitions common words have. Most words have different meanings based on context and situations. The result is that it is both easy and common for people to read the same project request or description and come away with very different ideas on what the project is all about or what will be delivered. For this reason, bringing together the group of people who will participate in the project (business area managers and staff, the project team, collaborative partners, IT, and at times customers) and those who will be affected by it is important. A workshop should happen as soon as the BPM project team members are chosen and the business area/collaborative partners select their project team participants. Once together, it will be critical to lead them through a discussion to reach a common interpretation of the project, what it will deliver, and how they will be impacted. This is a key foundation activity in any project of any real size or complexity. This is a first step toward project success and collaborative team building.

A good starting point in defining BPM and BPMS terms is the Association of Business Process Management Professionals (ABPMP™) Common Body of Knowledge Glossary. Another good source of definitions is the Business Process Incubator's website at www.businessprocessincubator.com.

A good way to approach this alignment is in a workshop setting. Dialogue should be encouraged and solicited — you are seeking active involvement, not people acting on orders they are given. Executive commitment and sponsorship should be clearly visible and part of the workshop.

Always build a set of project assumptions with the project team, IT, and all business participants. These assumptions are important. They pull all participants together if they are defined collaboratively. If any assumptions are subsequently proven to be inaccurate, it may be necessary to revise project estimations or even to add some new constraints. The assumptions help to frame the scope and content of the solution. They define what the team assumes when it is defining the project, the desired outcome, and what types of technology and techniques can be used.

Keep in mind that you are selling change and that is generally a hard sell, so there has to be enthusiasm and excitement generated.

Provide team members with the opportunity to catch up on work so that when in a workshop session, they can focus on the agenda and topics at hand. This way they are not worried about falling behind on deliverables while sitting in a workshop.

You might want to consider holding the workshop off-site and/or providing lunch/snacks to establish that this is not just another meeting interrupting work that needs to be done.

People can play different roles in the same project and they can keep changing roles as they work on different tasks. But it is difficult for a person to play more than one role on any single task.

Often the existing BPMS application will be used as the dominant solution to BPM recommendations. This is kind of like using a hammer to solve every problem. There are times that the existing BPMS is not the best solution and alternative technologies should be considered. Be aware of the trap of only using tools that are at your disposal, better solutions may be available and they should be considered. In addition, when the business is constantly forced to accept BPMS solutions that obviously do not fit well, they quickly realize that the solution is not optimum and will negatively impact the credibility of the BPMS team.

BPMS is a tool used to simulate, automate, and monitor the business processes of an organization. It helps organizations to determine future strategies. It increases profitability by optimizing business processes through its various components, such as a process designer, process engine, rules engine, and process analytics. A process designer assigns logic to the process after analyzing it and the process engine allocates automated activities to applications and manual operations to employees. The rules engine ensures that the process adheres to the business rules and process analytics provides feedback on process performance.

1.5 Alignment of the project to the delivery of corporate strategy

Business transformation and improvement projects offer an opportunity not only to deliver the stated objectives/requirements/targets, but also to help the business area deliver the changes needed to support corporate strategy.

Many projects miss this opportunity to add value to the benefit the business sponsor states in the project request. This is because few projects consider both the stated cost reduction or quality improvement **and** the value that can be delivered by adding to the creation of changes needed to deliver corporate strategic goals.

Each department in a company will have some part to play in the delivery of corporate goals – and thus in the operational changes needed to support the goal or goals. These changes are often not put into a formal form or defined at the business unit level. It may be necessary to work with participating and impacted business managers to define how the strategic goals affect their operations and then factor considerations for these changes into the project's solution design.

This approach to aligning project solution design and delivery to strategic goals can create a whole new way to look at the results of a project.

While this is the setup stage of the project and is well in advance of the formal fact finding that must be carried out in subsequent stages, you will be given valuable information in the form of both objections and suggestions as you discuss alignment with strategic goals. This information should be carefully captured. What is revealed during these conversations not only forms the starting point of future fact finding, but it helps shape the fact finding agenda and approach.

As the chain of logic is traced from corporate strategic goals through KPIs, CSFs and company performance standards and expectations, it is not only possible, but probable, that both "disconnects" and even conflicts will be identified. For example, a corporate strategic goal to be "Recognized as an industry leader in customer service" may in fact be thwarted by a KPI within the Call Center that sets the expected number of calls per hour at a level that makes spending time with customers impossible. If disconnects and conflicts are identified, they need to be discussed with the project sponsor and solutions found that at a minimum balance the strategy and operational realities. It is preferable that such conflicts are resolved in favor of the strategic goal and the KPIs and CSFs adjusted.

In addition to KPIs, CSFs and other higher level performance measures that need to be aligned with the strategic goals, reviews of documentation and input from managers and operational staff may identify localized performance standards within functional areas and operating units. These may be formal and employed in performance reviews, bonus/reward calculations, employee recognition, etc. These localized standards and expectations must also be checked for alignment with strategic goals. If they are in conflict or simply do not fully align, they should become part of the overall project plan so they can transition to expectations that *do* properly align with the corporate strategy.

For most projects it will be important to gather information from Human Resources and keep them involved in making sure the human capital/talent components of the solution are aligned with the activities as well as with the strategic goals. While not all will be applicable in every company for every project, the following are some of the issues that might impact the overall success:

- Are there labor agreements that have provisions that may become constraints if changes cannot be negotiated?
- Are there general hiring terms or common employment contracts that may need to be altered, or might some of these be constraints as well?
- Are there work environment requirements such as OSHA that need to be considered?
- Do minimum hiring requirements need to be changed to make new skills available?
- Are there provisions for training and/or education that may need to be modified?

Unintended consequences that we do not plan for often lurk under the rocks. This is especially true when managing a project that is designed to make significant changes to your organization. Understanding the behavior and underlying human responses is key to recognizing that an unintended consequence is at play so that you can break out of a potentially destructive cycle. In many organizations, we are encountering and reinforcing elements of a cycle which inherently does not learn how to change fundamental behaviors, in fact we are building and reinforcing existing practices - - practices which reinforce the underlying problems.

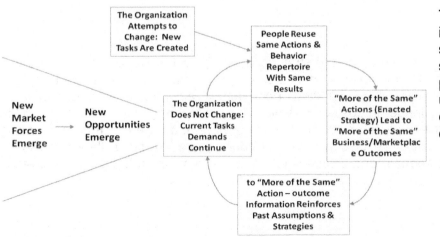

This elevates the importance of integrating solid change management skills and controls into the project team so that these unintended consequences can be identified, tactics designed, and action taken to remove them as barriers to the project.

1.6 Modify the approach to deliver success

BPM- and BPMS-supported BPM projects are often approached informally following whatever style and methodology (if any is followed) that the project manager is comfortable with. This can cause disputes when others in the collaborative project staff have different approaches that they follow. This becomes most obvious with IT run BPM projects and the popular IT application development methodology called Agile.

We have found that most methodologies are good for what they were created to guide, but fail as they are used in ways they were not designed to address. Agile is an example. It is good for application development from a set of requirements that are arranged into groups that define the support needed to do a specific job or task. This allows the team to divide the development work into small modules called Sprints. These Sprint-created modules are combined at some time into the IT application part of a business solution. However, this approach typically does not have the framework for dividing large solutions and guiding the construction of the solution from multiple modules. The impact of this and other weaknesses can be reduced by adding components of other methodologies to the group of project tasks for execution – the actual creation of the solution. These additional methods include Waterfall business project methodologies, Change Management methodologies, production capability/construction methodologies, Process Architecture methodologies, Business Architecture methodologies, Enterprise Architecture methodologies, and specialty methodologies as needed.

Creating this composite approach increases the project setup time for the first project it is used for, but following that project, the setup customization requires only focused modification to adjust to the needs of the project.

To promote consistency in project execution and project management, it will be necessary to define a standard way to approach business transformation and business improvement projects. Having a standardized approach aligns the business project methologoy with the project management methods and IT application development methodology. The result is a common set of activities that should be applied to all BPM-related projects.

Project management knowledge is necessary for success, but it is only a part of the project picture. The other part deals with execution and understanding what tasks need to be performed, when, why, and how. Both skill sets need to be present to succeed.

Agile IT methods are often different from company to company. The concepts are often close to the same, but the way they are implemented is often different. It is important for any company to formalize their approach to Agile and to include the information needed to drive Agile Sprint scopes/definitions in the BPMS standards

Be honest regarding what it will take to deliver a project. Realistic time, staff, and cost estimates are important. Have all of your supporting information available and make your case. Many projects fail because the estimates are unrealistic at the start of the project. In many companies, given cost and time pressures, creating realistic estimates are very difficult. However, changing estimates or accepting unrealistic estimates will only lead to one place – disaster.

In executing projects, actual hours spent by team members needs to be captured, and not an arbitrary figure such as a flat 8-hour day or flat 5-day work week. Failure to capture the actual effort will result in perpetually underestimating the real resources that must be available for future initiatives.

Do not continue a project if the business area managers will not engage with the BPM team at a level deemed to be necessary for success. This must be spelled out in the project assumptions and failure to engage with the BPM team is a cause for a project to be put on "hold status" that does not penalize the project team or project schedule. The business area managers will be the ultimate decision makers on project success or failure and they must be engaged at appropriate times and at appropriate levels. At the earliest indication of reluctance to engage, the project sponsor must be consulted to determine a strategy to address the risks to the project.

When the scope changes in the middle of a project, it is vital to re-estimate the impact on the timeline and project costs. A formal "go/no go" decision should be made if a project is re-estimated. If the change in scope is significant, it is vital to re-forecast the project ROI and impact on delivering business capabilities to ensure the continued relevance and value of the project. In addition, if your project is inter-dependent with other projects, it is important to meet with your business sponsor to reset expectations and obtain agreement as to the impact the changes will have on the original project.

1.7 Define Critical Success Factors (CSFs)

If you cannot measure improvement, it does not exist. If you cannot define how you will measure success and the way (formulas) it will be measured, you cannot succeed in delivering credible improvement. Further, all definitions of success must be created by those who will be affected by the project and not simply by the sponsor.

The foundation for any performance evaluation is the formally measurable target - Critical Success Factors (CSFs), improvement targets/goals (such as compliance management), and customer interaction ratings. Soft goals can also be defined, but they will be evaluated based on opinion and are thus not a real measure of success. This difference should be clearly defined in the expectation setting workshops at the start of the project. In any identification of performance measurement CSFs, etc., the way the performance improvement or the project targets will be measured is critical and must be formally defined and agreed to.

Also, these definitions must state the purpose of the CSF (or target/goal, etc.) and the benefit of measuring it. Everyone who will be measured by each CSF must also approve it.

Since different data sources will have varying degrees of data accuracy, the sources and content of the data that will be used in measuring each CSF (target or goal) should be validated by both business and IT data management (the data architects and database analysts), and the quality of the source data evaluated.

It is important to ensure that performance can be measured in any new business operation design. The way it is measured will need to be agreed upon, but different techniques can be applied to different parts of the design. For example, Six Sigma may be used in some places while Activity Based Costing may be more appropriate in other places, and volume/throughput/error rate may be the best way to look at improvement in the workflow. Pick the technique that works best in each case – there is no one right answer that should be applied for all measurement requirements.

Critical Success Factors (CSFs) must be things that are *observable* and *measureable*, not opinions.

Project success measurement by opinion is the fastest way to failure that we know of. Critical Success Factors (CSFs) must be supported by tangible actions and results that can be measured. You must be able to observe the work being measured and audit the measurements for quality and accuracy.

Poorly defined CSFs and/or poorly designed CSF measurements will produce inaccurate metrics. This must be avoided. There is a saying in IT – "garbage in, gospel out." This means that regardless of how bad the source data is and even if everyone acknowledges the poor quality of the data, once it is committed to paper, it is all that management has and it becomes the accepted truth.

In any new business operation design, performance must be measured. The way it is measured will need to be agreed upon. but different techniques can be applied to different parts of the design. For example, Six Sigma may be used in some places while Activity Based Costing may be more appropriate in other places in the workflow. Pick the technique that works best for each measurement – there is no one right answer that should be applied for all measurement requirements.

Decision Management is implicit in all project teams, but often not acknowledged or formalized. The purpose of clear decision management is to ensure that the project constantly moves forward and is not held captive to indecision or worse, retractions of previously made decisions or commitments. Factors impacting decision management include:

- Delaying - forcing/requiring additional (non-value added) analysis to be conducted which delays making a decision;
- Denial – after the fact claiming little or no knowledge of the agreements, or suggesting that the decision was in fact never agreed to;
- Appealing – initial agreement followed by back door negotiations with senior leadership resulting in special exceptions and/or undoing of the decision;
- Back Tracking – decisions that have been agreed to are suddenly recanted based on "new" information.

To address these barriers, consider clearly defining the following decision management process elements:

 Decisions that can directly or indirectly affect the direction of a work stream, an analysis, the outcome of a test are identified as KEY DECISIONS and are captured at a PMO and at a work stream level. Clearly define if there are any exceptions or conditions which would invalidate the decision. Finally the risks of non-compliance need to be discussed and understood.

 Clearly confirm the INDIVIDUALS who have agreed to the decisions and confirm that they have the authority to make commitments on the behalf of a Business Unit/process/technology etc.

 If a decision is not abided by, need clear protocols defined by the decision body outlining how compliance will be monitored and reinforced. Clear consequences of non-compliance need to be established and agreed to.

 The decisions are captured and documented including what the decisions was and in what context the decision was made, when was it made, who agreed to it and how people will be held accountable for compliance.

A decision management process is valuable to ensuring that decisions are made and adhered to.

Issue/risk management can be the undoing of any well-run project. To ensure that they do not undermine the project:

- Implement <u>mechanisms to identify and resolve issues</u> based on criticality;
- <u>Ensure appropriate decision makers</u> are engaged in the process;
- Establish a <u>clear escalation process</u> based on the type of issue;
- Facilitate <u>timely resolution.</u>

Issue escalation processes should be defined and established early in the project. The first step is to determine the type of issue that you are facing and then the severity of the issue (this is an assessment of risk the issue introduces to the project, e.g., project delay, cost increase, impact to functionality, etc.). Next, determine who the issue should be escalated to, so that it can be quickly addressed and resolved. See the following table for an illustration:

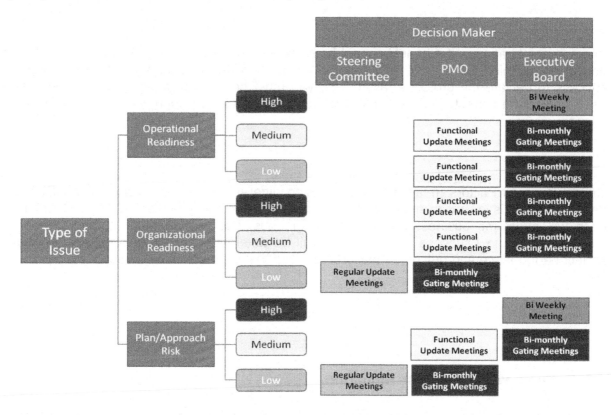

Type of Issue	Severity	Steering Committee	PMO	Executive Board
Operational Readiness	High			Bi Weekly Meeting
	Medium		Functional Update Meetings	Bi-monthly Gating Meetings
	Low		Functional Update Meetings	Bi-monthly Gating Meetings
Organizational Readiness	High		Functional Update Meetings	Bi-monthly Gating Meetings
	Medium		Functional Update Meetings	Bi-monthly Gating Meetings
	Low	Regular Update Meetings	Bi-monthly Gating Meetings	
Plan/Approach Risk	High			Bi Weekly Meeting
	Medium		Functional Update Meetings	Bi-monthly Gating Meetings
	Low	Regular Update Meetings	Bi-monthly Gating Meetings	

Establishing an escalation process will ensure that issues can be quickly addressed and any risk to the project better managed.

If a project finds itself behind schedule, over cost and/or facing significant issues/risks, it may be in need of a formal rescue plan. This is a formal recognition that the entire project is at risk of not achieving its planned targets. As a result, valuable resources have been spent and are at risk of being lost. A project rescue is a deliverable and full reassessment of the project to determine its "go forward" viability. Some projects are so far behind and over budget that it may be in the best interest of the organization to significantly scale back the effort, or even cancel the project entirely. This requires a complete understanding of the project status, an evaluation of what has been accomplished to date, and full transparency and involvement with stakeholders. Unfortunately in most organizations, projects that find themselves in this state are also risking the reputations and potentially even the careers of several individuals. The project manager who will be perceived to have mismanaged the project, the sponsor who provided their support and reputation to back a failing project, and even key business leaders such as operations or IT who have a large stake in the project's success and are now at risk of losing their deliverables. Politics and relationships will be strained and people can begin to act in unexpected ways as they either try to distance themselves from a perceived 'train wreck' or those who will look beyond politics and personal agendas and focus on the needs to the organization and the business objectives. When a project does find itself failing and in need of a rescue, it is vital that the project team be honest and completely transparent as to the issues and causes, and to recommend a course going forward.

There is an old adage, "If a benefit cannot be measured, it doesn't exist!" Do not try to justify a project on anything that cannot be measured. There will be those who use a lack of proof of success to declare the project a failure. So you must be able to measure everything that is used to justify a project. The way it is measured must also be approved by HR or Legal or finance.

Critical Success Factors mean different things to different people and companies. Formally define what this is in your company and create a collaborative way to identify them. Define how each will affect the business, what parts of the business will be involved, how it will be calculated, and how success in delivering it will be determined. Failing to do this will move project performance and outcome measurement into the world of opinion – not a good place to be.

1.8 Define Key Performance Indicators

Key Performance Indicators (KPIs) are used to measure different types of operational, quality, production, operational improvement, or financial performance. Because of this diversity in use, the project team must create clear definitions of what each KPI will be used for, why the target is realistic and how the KPI will be measured. The more concise this definition, the better.

Each KPI represents something that someone or something will be measured against. The starting position for this measurement is either the current performance level or the creation of standard targets. This definition can be based on company history, industry best practices, or studies on how the operation can be improved. The key is that every standard must be completely understood by both those being measured and by those who will use the performance information. As with all measurement, it is important that the formula for the measurement be defined prior to the new solution design and the places where the data will be captured are identified. Once identified, the team can build the measurement into the workflow design and drive reporting and evaluation as a parallel process performed by IT and business area management.

This understanding and the formal identification of purpose, standards, measurement (data sources and measurement formula) are the foundation for a formal agreement between those who will be using the data to evaluate performance and those who will be affected by the measurement. This agreement is important in using the evaluation to improve the operation. Without this agreement, any evaluation will be subject to "interpretation" and opinion, and will thus be open to debate and argument.

Performance management is defined by a set of factors in a collaborative process with business leaders and IT leaders. Once defined, management should agree on how each should be measured and the sources of information that will be used. The approach to the evaluation of the performance data should also be agreed upon so it will be accepted. Then for each activity that will be measured, performance monitoring should be embedded as part of any new business operation improvement or transformation design and built into the workflow and application support of the new solution.

KPIs must be quantifiable and agreement must be reached on what specific thresholds are to be used. Where possible, a baseline should be used (or created) to define the "as is" level.

Do not let people build in the use of KPI measurements in a new operation design to take punitive action. If that is done, the KPI will be worthless – there will be conflict in its use and the measurement will always be challenged. Instead, focus on using the KPI measurement to help show areas that need improvement so work can be focused to reduce error, improve productivity, etc.

The information used to measure performance must be from reliable sources. If the data is suspect, the KPI and the results of any measurement will have no value. Sometimes people move forward knowing the data sources are suspect – "it is better than nothing." However, bad data is worse than no data at all because it is misleading and decisions based on bad data can do more harm than good.

Care must be taken in understanding the relationship between a business operations manager's formal annual evaluation and bonus determination, and the KPIs. If the relationship is not considered by the design team, some managers will manipulate the data being used to drive evaluation and render the entire review process irrelevant.

All projects will encounter barriers, especially during the implementation phase. In addition, the larger the change, the more complex the solution, and the greater the potential barriers will become. To anticipate this, there are several key issues/obstacles that can be anticipated and planned for. Ultimately, all issues need to be resolved to ensure the success of implementation. This table provides some insights on how best to anticipate and tactics to resolve each.

Potential Areas of Challenge	Details	Tactics to Resolve
Senior Level Sponsorship	• Ad hoc support and commitment • No clear mechanism to track and communicate decisions • Inconsistent follow through	• Implement Steering committees with accountability per work stream • Define issues escalation / resolution and decision management process • Ensure project success and accountability tied to individual goals
Resourcing	• Bandwidth constraints • Inability to attract top talent	• Senior level communication about importance of the project – initiative is a top corporate priority • Ensure project success and accountability tied to individual goals • Rigorous gating process – clear process to access funds • Leverage existing talent management process to surface internal talent
Organizational Readiness / BU Engagement	• Varying cultural appetite for change • Varying individual appetite for risk • Lack of motivation	• Senior level communication about importance of the project – initiative is a top corporate priority • Ensure project success and accountability tied to individual goals • Award success; providing recognition will help raise visibility of program and support buy-in • Define clear repercussions / consequences of non-compliance • Leverage "known leaders" – people with reputation to drive change
Competing Organizational Priorities	• Focus on achieving Revenue and margin targets • Other large scale efforts, response to external market dynamics	• Interim processes for managing competing priorities • Utilize central funding (no impact to P&L's) • Alignment with Strategy and Budgeting Process • Ensure project success and accountability tied to individual goals

Anticipating barriers is the first step to removing them.

1.9 Define project success

Success means many different things based on your perspective. That is the problem. Unless it means the same thing to everyone involved and affected by a project, you cannot succeed.

Too many projects are loosely defined and success is left to interpretation and perception. Few projects are measured after delivery against stated goals to see if the delivered solution meets expectations, and most that are reviewed produce reports that are open to debate.

The place to begin any project's journey to a successful outcome is with a clear definition of what will constitute success – in the opinions of all who will evaluate the project's outcome. This definition should be written and negotiated into the project's request. If it is not, the project itself should begin with this definition.

Once agreement has been reached on what characteristics must be met for the project to be a success, the next step is to determine how success will be measured. This involves the identification and definition of performance targets, their alignment with the formal definition of success for the project, the creation of the formulas that will be used in the measurement and the evaluation criteria, and the sources of the data that will be used in the measurement. When this is all agreed to and formalized (put in writing), the project can succeed.

This definition of success with its approach of performance measurement and evaluation is the foundation for the team in producing the solution. Everyone will know exactly what must be delivered in order to succeed – no ambiguity and nuance. Project managers can now review the progress of the work against both project goals and the way the project will be evaluated.

Success will be determined by opinion or it will be determined by formal measurement. If it is left to a "feeling," the success of a project will be open to constant debate and disagreement on what has been achieved.

The project manager needs to build a composite definition of success from both the project sponsor and those who will be affected by the change. This definition should have formal targets and formal outcome measurement. It should also describe exactly how success will be determined and how it will be measured – including where the data is coming from and the current baseline. Without this comparison against baseline, even if all targets are hit, there is no way to tell what real improvement has been made.

Due to the importance of this definition, the project sponsor and all affected managers must formally discuss the definition and agree on it.

"I don't know exactly what I am looking for, but I'll know it when I see it." If you encounter this definition of success from the project sponsor, participating business managers, or affected managers, **STOP** the project until the outcome goals can be defined and performance measurement can be clearly stated. This way of thinking is really not optional. You cannot build a solution that the business user cannot define. This is not a joke. This kind of definition has been expressed by well-meaning business managers who simply have not engaged and believe the creation of the solution is up to IT or someone else. However, it is guaranteed that if they are uncomfortable with the solution, they will be the first in line to declare the project a failure.

It is entirely ok to say "no" to significant changes or requests to your project. Too often a sponsor or business leader will challenge the team to complete the project much sooner than defined in the project plan, to accomplish milestones with less than the planned resources, or even expand the scope without consideration to the impact to the overall project. When this occurs, it is vital that the project manager be very clear and accurate regarding the impact of these types of requests to the project. It is vital to determine the true impact of these requests, the risks that they present, and to communicate them to leadership. While leadership is reluctant to recognize the reality that ten pounds of fertilizer cannot fit into a five pound bag, it is the role of the project manager to tell the honest truth rather than making a vain attempt to stuff the bag with more than it can hold, resulting in a mess that will need extra time and often extra budget to clean up. In the end, leadership will appreciate your courage to stand up and tell the truth.

Project success must be formally declared. This declaration will be based on the delivery of the expectations defined earlier and approved by management. The measurement of this delivery will have been defined and the project will be measured against formal targets. This removes the success of the project from internal politics and from a "feeling" on the part of the business or IT managers.

If success is not formally defined with collaborative agreement with the business sponsor on how it will be measured, evaluation of the project's outcome will be based on subjective perception. This is extremely dangerous because you will have a hard time pleasing the business user as his/her view of success may evolve, and be very different at the end of a project than it was defined when the project was first launched.

Too often people will seek to avoid accountability on the project team. Always be clear on who is accountable for what activity/ actions/decisions/results. Having a "single throat to choke" or a "single back to pat" makes it clear to everyone what they are responsible for.

When defining project success metrics, make sure that they clearly align to the overall business objectives of the enterprise. Doing a project because everyone agrees it is important or because it is the right thing to do is NOT a reason to invest in a project. All projects must be clearly linked to and enable the delivery of the business strategy ... at all times.

1.10 Customize the project plan-define tasks, roles, estimates, and deliverables

The approach to requesting projects tends to evolve in BPM teams from ad hoc into a formal process, with formal data requirements and formal benefits estimation. For the small to moderate size projects, an ad hoc approach can work. However, as larger mission-critical projects are requested, the BPM CoE will need to formalize the process of making requests and create rules that will control what projects are accepted and provide the foundation for making these decisions. These requests should include a formal description of the problem, the probable impact, the scope, the performance issues it is creating, the constraining factors, an assessment of damage to the operation, and a description of what must change.

The project plan will now need to be formalized. This can be accomplished through a melding of:
- Activities from formal project management
- Activities from your BPM project execution methodology
- Activities from your BPMS and IT application development methodologies
- Change management activities
- IT activities related to the creation of solution requirements and technical specs (to guide IT application generation from a BPMS and the custom programming of new applications/changes to legacy applications/the creation of interfaces between programs)
- Performance management techniques from Six Sigma, Activity Based Costing, etc.

The plan should now be streamlined to eliminate any tasks that are not needed for the project from the methodology that will be followed and the plans that it will produce. Standards from BPM, BPMS, change management, enterprise management, HR, legal compliance and more should be aligned to the project's methodology and plan. Phase gates and review points should also be added to help organize work and formalize review/evaluation points.

The resulting method and plan will incorporate multiple approaches, multiple disciplines, and a variety of techniques based on these approaches. This will be the foundation for a collaborative aggregation of work from the several different groups which each have a role in the project – including BPM, BPMS, Lean, Six Sigma, change management, enterprise management, data architecture and more. Once this is in place, the project manager will be in much better position to provide realistic estimates and define the capabilities, skills, and competency levels needed in the project staff.

It is critical that the transformation or improvement project be formally controlled through a business-oriented project management methodology which directs execution and controls collaboration through formal participation orchestration.

A challenge for many projects, especially those with significant goals and deliverables, is how to phase or stage them. Should a project demonstrate interim successes along the way, or is it best to deliver a big bang? In general, it is important to recognize that most people have short attention spans. This is reinforced with the drive to deliver quarterly (short-term) results. As a result, a rule of thumb is to create project plans that have not only internal milestones and key decision points, but phases or steps where results/value can be demonstrated and even delivered to the business. Involve the business in each phase or step, so that they are materially part of the work and are as excited about progress as the project team.

We have found that applying IT project development approaches to the majority of a business improvement or transformation does not often deliver the best solution. Part of the reason is that while IT approaches/methods have evolved to help improve application development, they generally do not address business analysis or design very well. Each company may interpret these approaches and methods a little differently and apply them based on the reality of their company/their IT operations and capabilities. For this reason, some companies may have adequately expanded their IT methodologies to encompass business issues, while others may not have. It is important to obtain or create a business execution methodology which will be combined with any project management approach and then linked to the company's IT application development methodology.

A BPM business execution methodology is the standard for identifying the tasks that are needed. However, this business-focused BPM methodology will not stand alone. Other discipline methodologies will need to be melded – using different groupings of their tasks for different projects. In this way, the project methodology/approach will create a unique plan from common parts for each project. This promotes consistency in the way projects are approached. With the BPM methodology as the core, these additional methodologies include:

- Formal project management
- Business Architecture
- Enterprise Architecture
- Process Architecture
- Change Management
- Data Management
- Construction – facility or manufacturing production line

The composite methodology that is built defines the approach that will be taken and the tasks that will be executed – along with their order and dependencies. This task definition will be augmented with roles, timing estimates, phase gates, deliverables and more to create the formal project plan. This should be reviewed in a collaborative workshop with the project team and the people from the different competency areas who will serve as interfaces to those areas.

In creating this composite methodology and project plan, simple is better. Complexity can be added as needed. Unnecessary work is simply a waste.

Since refining the methodology and defining the project plan occur at the very beginning of the project, the modifications and customizations must be considered to be interim in nature. Executives, members of governance and project management must all be aware that as fact finding commences, further refinement will be necessary. This refinement should never be viewed as a series of change requests, rather as an evolving plan that continues to incorporate new information. Maintaining this perspective can be tricky, since many participants may be sensitive about issues such as scope creep, cost overruns, or having something cut out based upon past experiences. This is why refinements should be incorporated into the formal project plan. It may also be desirable to embed notes in the project plan to provide insights into why changes are made.

Named resources - Often when a project is scoped and the need for resources is identified, we create a staffing model to identify the skills and capabilities needed for successful project execution. When the project is approved and the green light given to move forward, we are often surprised to discover that key resources are also deployed on other projects. Too late we learn that Sally or John are staffed on three other projects and their time is committed 150% + and we wonder why things are not getting done! Be sure that you not only identify the type, but also the name of the resource that will be staffed on your project.

Acceleration of a time line. A project cannot be delivered in half the time by doubling the resources or investment, especially once the project is already underway. This expectation looks reasonable on paper, however in reality there are other factors that come into play. A project has significant interdependencies, the team understands the work that needs to be done and by doubling the number of people, there is not only a tremendous learning curve but this new and expanded team needs to begin to work together. In addition, there is a tendency to cut corners in the interest of "saving time." Realize that each item is on the work plan and it is there for a reason. The removal of tasks will reduce work, but it may also significantly undermine the quality of the analysis, the overall solution, and ultimately the implementation.

1.11 Prepare for collaboration - define participant groups and needed skills

One of the major advances in the BPM approach to operational improvement is the specific approach that all needed people should be involved in building the solution, thus introducing collaboration. With BPMS BPM modelers, this collaboration is supported for teams split among multiple locations. This allows different groups to work on the models or other parts of the solution around the clock, thus leveraging teams or sub teams in different geographies.

The key is that everyone who needs to be, or should be, involved can be involved at any level that they or their manager will commit to. This opens the solution design to new ideas, new perspectives, and new techniques. It also improves both the ability of a project to succeed in providing similar services to a larger part of the business – thus saving cost and improving benefit.

Collaboration-based projects are, however, much more difficult than traditional business or IT project execution. Task timing, collaborative participant commitment, approach differences, technique differences, tool differences, and methodology differences all come into play and need to be blended into a new way of performing projects. In BPM-based projects, the project manager not only has the traditional tasks (requiring traditional skills and competencies), but also the multi group orchestration management tasks to be concerned with. These tasks require new skills and competencies and a strong yet understanding touch.

However, once collaboration management has been mastered, BPM projects will provide solutions that are more accepted and provide greater value.

Collaboration is a key element for a successful project. Talk to the business managers and staff, talk to IT, talk to Legal, talk to Finance, and talk to the customers. See what is happening to drive the change, see what is expected, and see how they anticipate the operation to change. See specifically what they want from the changes and then meld these factors from all these different perspectives to form a composite view of the needs, the operational outcomes of the project, and the benefits they are looking to achieve. Next, align these expected results with the requirements stated in the project request. All too often teams stop with a review of the project request and begin moving forward with their own interpretation. We submit, that the team's interpretation is absolutely irrelevant. The opinion that counts are those from the sponsor, the business managers, and staff directly involved in the change and the expectations of those who will be affected. Those are the people who will measure success.

Initial conversations with various stakeholders will begin to define the list of people who have the knowledge to fill in specific details as well as the skills that will be needed to execute the project. These people should ultimately form the core of the project team.

If key stakeholders span multiple countries, there must be planning that addresses time zones, languages, and venue/media that will best support effective interchange and dialogue. The possibility of at least some travel for some participants should be available.

Participants must include people who actually execute the steps, tasks, and activities at the current time. Of all of the team members, they will be the only ones who actually know all of the details about how the work is executed.

Unless the project is extremely narrow in scope, the process under examination will generally span multiple functional areas and perhaps multiple types of work groups within a functional area. The team should include representatives from each.

For a variety of reasons, managers and supervisors may sometimes resist having acutal workers on the team. They may take the position that they themselves know everthing there is to know about an operation and therefore bringing lower level staff into the team is not necessary. The truth is that they do not know everything there is to know about current operations. Even if a manager or supervisor has been promoted from within after actually performing the work, today's details will be at least slightly different, and very important differences are highly likely.

In identifying the groups and types of participants, keep in mind that you will need to build a team that meets two somewhat different packages of skill sets: the skills to actually execute the *process* being redesigned and the skills necessary to execute the *project* itself. With a bit of well-designed training and education, you may be able to fill in gaps while keeping the team size reasonable.

From a slightly different perspective, the type of participants should also include attention to whether they are seen as a team player, and whether they are generally respected both up and down the ladder. Both characteristics are essential for collaboration.

1.12 Define the change management approach and build capabilities

Change management means many very different things to different groups in any company. It is important that the project sponsor and project or team leader begin the project's activity with a workshop on what change means and how it will be implemented within the specific project. For example, small projects rarely require a high degree of change management. Larger transformation projects and mission critical projects, however, do require formal change management to avoid fear and anxiety on the part of managers and staff over the potential for staff cutbacks, increased personal work, performance measurement, and more.

Of course, all of these fears are based on realistic potential changes. As a result, the project manager and team should be trained on the company's version of change management and required to use those new skills in all interactions with business area managers and staff.

In addition, it may be appropriate to implement a project website that provides project goals, progress updates, meeting schedules, training plans, data quality checks and more. This is also often used to solicit ideas from the people in the trenches.

Working with HR, the project manager should define the approach that will be used to support change management and augment the project's plans and tasks. Business area, manufacturing area, and IT area managers and staff should be encouraged to provide anonymous feedback that is monitored by HR and used to adjust the project approach to reduce risk and improve the probability of an accepted solution.

Change management is not a casual activity. Change management is the selling and implementation of change to entire operational areas in which there is a great desire to simply maintain the status quo. Specific expertise and a formal plan are necessary elements.

Change management must include constant, consistent, and accurate information that should be "pushed" to possibly affected people rather than waiting for them to access it on their own. Unfortunately, there will also be a word of mouth channel which often transmits inaccurate information and this must be offset. It may be necessary at times to directly post "rumor busting" information.

Change management must include involvement of and dialogue with many individuals on an ongoing basis, both to gain input and to gain buy-in. The overall approach must be one of doing things *with* people instead of doing things *to* people.

Change management must include specific planning for each major step from information gathering through the roll out of segments.

Change management will normally include workshops and dialogue/information sessions for affected parts of the company at key points. When there is more than one shift, these sessions *must* cover each shift and must also include any weekend staff if the environment is 24/7. If there is more than one location involved, each location must be included. If multiple shifts and/or locations are involved, sessions should be timed to be in close proximity since the word of mouth channel will go into overdrive immediately.

Language issues may need to be addressed, especially when operations are in multiple countries. This includes both the information disseminated via paper and web and change management workshops. Staff making presentations *must* be easily understood within the context of the language of their audience. In addition to the obvious differences in language, there are important cultural differences that should be considered for teams that contain people from a variety of backgrounds. There are different ways to give a presentation depending on the country that you might be working with or giving a presentation to. This is a huge factor for international organizations and projects.

If the project encompasses international operations, change management approaches should include input from indigenous staff to tailor approaches to very real cultural differences that exist. This input will help ensure that information is both clear to the audiences and sensitive to the cultural environments.

1.13 Set up the BPMS technical environment that will be used in the project

Each BPMS and BPMS modeler requires unique installation and setup to run in the company's technical environment. This need should be addressed by the implementation of the BPMS environment by the vendor and the certification of an IT BPMS administrator and solution developers. Once the BPMS environment is ready for use, the BPMS will need to be "set up" for each project. This will include the association of data elements for drag/drop capabilities in building business process models and screen/report design. It will also include the setup of a separate project or instance in the tool for the specific project's models, supporting data as well as both business and technical rules.

While this setup is an IT function led by a BPMS administrator, it should be coordinated and defined collaboratively with the project team and the BPM CoE.

If tools (such as the Trisotech simulation software solution) other than a BPMS toolset is used for modeling and analyses, these tools will need to be set up with a sufficient number of licenses to allow team members to work on their parts simultaneously.

Most efforts will be focused on how a project should proceed, tasks leading to ultimate execution, considerations that focus on BPM, etc. Often overlooked in the midst of all this activity is the importance of *where* the team will carry out its responsibilities. This can then result in tables being set up in a spare conference room that is crowded, noisy, has cables running all over, and is hot. All projects should be planned for and resourced with the same attention and priority that would be given to establishing an important new operating unit.

In addition to decent work spaces consistent with those in other operating areas, the team will need private spaces for interviews, workshops, collaboration sessions, and similar activities. To avoid conflicts on use of these spaces, which then result in delaying some activities, more than one private space should be available. This can often be accomplished by providing priority scheduling rights to existing conference rooms and vacant offices.

Create a "war room" for your project team. This is a separate space or conference room permanently dedicated to the project. It is a place that the team can hold stand up or scrum meetings, have informal discussions, and where project-related materials are kept. Use it as a "home room" for the team to connect with the project status, see a few smiling faces and get caught up on things. Post a Gantt chart and timeline on the wall to keep the team focused on key milestones and progress.

In the war room, create and post the short term (daily) and long term (weekly) objectives with status. This helps demonstrate progress made (useful in helping with senior leadership status updates, as well as employee morale to show that things are getting accomplished) and keeps the team focused on making progress forward.

Whiteboards are an excellent tool for capturing information during interviews, workshops, brainstorming sessions, etc. Rooms used for these purposes should be equipped with them — oh, and could someone please see that there are markers and erasers actually there? In fact, the team should have its own supply to take along since they will disappear quickly.

Take a picture of each whiteboard before it is erased and post these pictures in the repository where other team artifacts are located. Rename the pictures with an appropriate topic and date so that team members can identify ones that may be relevant. (A file named with only letters and numbers such as IMG0459 is not very helpful; a file named Credit Approval 10-26-14 is helpful). The project team should consider defining specific naming conventions to ensure consistency.

Part time team members who also have operational responsibilities, but are regularly scheduled with the team, should have at least "hoteling" work spaces with the team for reasons of collaboration as well as limiting distractions arising from their operational responsibilities.

While having a designated space for the team to work is important, to the extent possible this space should not be isolated from the rest of the company. Isolation thwarts problem solving and communication and once there is a closed door or restricted area, other employees will immediately begin to fear how this "secret" group will impact them. Once such fears develop, turning the fears into cooperation will become very difficult. If at all possible, team space should be close to the most affected operational area.

For those team members who will be routinely using models and/or graphic analytics, external monitors that are 27 inches or larger will need to be provided. You simply cannot see detailed business process models on a laptop screen. For workshops and collaboration sessions, rooms should either be equipped with projection screens or large HD monitors to increase the amount of information that can be included in each view and so that information can be seen.

If work sessions must take place across remote locations, each of those locations should have projection screens or large High Definition monitors.

If part of the project is to be outsourced using external consultants, engineers, etc., these people should be co-located with the team, not placed in their own separate location.

2.0 Project setup

Many projects are literally set up to fail due to a lack of attention to creating the right environment for the project to succeed. The capability to build such an environment, however, may be impaired by factors such as a "just do it" corporate culture that does not believe in spending time to establish the foundation needed for a large project and think the project team can "wing it" or "find a way to make it work."

It is our belief, based on experience, that this setup section of a project is critical. We strongly disagree with those who believe that this activity is unnecessary and that a good project manager can make the project work without taking the time for setup activities. These activities include:

- Determining the approach that will be used and then formally defining it
- Identifying collaborative partners and defining their roles
- Identifying the parts of the different collaborative partner methods and techniques that will be used and blended into the BPM methodology used by the company
- Identifying the problems that are commonly faced in the company and modifying the approach/tasks/techniques/technical support that will be used in the project to directly address these problems
- Identifying approaches that will be integrated into the project approach – including collaboration, Lean, Six Sigma, change management, performance evaluation, simulation modeling, and the creation of advanced analytics based reporting
- Obtaining commitments from all project participants
- Identifying all of the standards that apply to the project and linking them to the BPM methodology
- Identifying any constraints that limit the scope and design of an optimal solution
- Defining project success and how it will be measured
- Identifying how solution expectations can be managed in the project and defining an expectation and status update for all team members to see
- Defining how the BPMS and legacy technology will be used and how it will be interfaced

This list is meant to be an example of the types of activities that a project setup should include. The list is not meant to be all-inclusive.

The project setup should be defined as one of the first tasks in any methodology. This should begin with a clear definition of the project, including goals, savings targets, quality targets, and market share expansion. The definition should be sent out to all participants, followed by a workshop with the project team to make certain everyone is on the same page and is approaching the project activities in the same way.

The project "setup" should include an update of lessons learned from recent BPM/BPMS projects and a modification of the company's setup standards. The setup activities will continue to evolve until the BPM/BPMS project tasks and concepts are considered to be optimal.

In each phase of the project, the team will look at the who, what, when, why, how, and where information associated with each activity

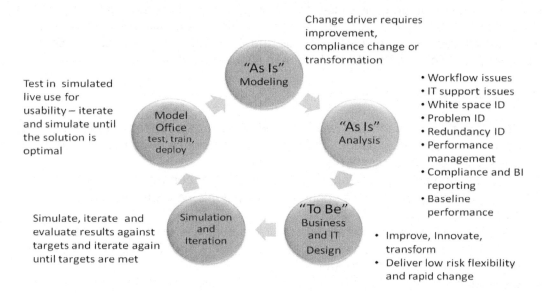

Change driver requires improvement, compliance change or transformation

- Workflow issues
- IT support issues
- White space ID
- Problem ID
- Redundancy ID
- Performance management
- Compliance and BI reporting
- Baseline performance

- Improve, Innovate, transform
- Deliver low risk flexibility and rapid change

Test in simulated live use for usability – iterate and simulate until the solution is optimal

Simulate, iterate and evaluate results against targets and iterate again until targets are met

Project setup activities will include a definition of the approach that will be taken. This can be the traditional "As Is" modeling, "To Be" design and solution construction, or it can be a variation of these phases of activity. In an iBPM (intelligent BPM) approach, these activity groups will divide further and become:

- "As Is" operational discovery and modeling
- "As Is" analysis of the operational information
- "To Be" initial design – first for the business operation, and once the technology environment has been properly documented, the business design will lead the technical design of the solution
- If simulation will be used, it will need to be included in the project setup at both the information collection stages and then again at solution development
- Testing of the business operation and IT solution will also be addressed in the setup, as will new and emerging concepts, such as the use of model office solution training and testing
- The creation or selection of standards dealing with project activities and the way analytics will be used to monitor performance and provide flexible business intelligence
- Success will also be defined at this time along with the performance management and evaluation criteria
- Collaboration should be set up and roles defined – along with specialty methods and techniques from the different groups who will be involved
- Project estimation approach will be defined and the estimates in the business case confirmed or modified
- The detailed project plan will be created

2.1 Build project foundation

A firm foundation should be constructed for all projects – regardless of size or complexity. The level of detail and the time it will take to perform this action will vary based on the size and scope of the project, but because it builds the foundation for all activity, project success measurement, and solution benefit evaluation, it should not be skipped.

This foundation includes:

- Selecting the approach that will be used – the orchestration methodology that ties all specialty methods (change management, Business Architecture, Agile, business transformation, etc.) together
- Adding supporting specialized methodologies to the company orchestration methodology
- Clearly defining the project sponsor, vision, goals, outcome definition, and identifying participants
- Identifying all existing documentation for the business area and applications that will be in the scope of the project – evaluate their quality and identify what it will take to bring these documents up to date and comprehensive
- Reviewing and accepting or modifying original project estimates in the project request
- Aligning the project estimates to the methodology and the major groups of tasks
- Selecting the standards, KPIs, policies, procedures that will be used in the project
- Ensuring alignment with corporate strategic goals or strategic change requirements (for things like a move to a digital enterprise)
- Defining project expectations and success - identifying how success will be measured
- Defining participants (collaborative partners) and project team members, roles, and commitment expectations
- Defining change management and how it will be applied to the project
- Identifying any IT infrastructure requirements – e.g., acquire a BPMS or expand communication to a new geography
- Clarifying the role of the project manager in directing collaboration and the policies for conflict resolution
- Creating the start of a common terminology dictionary – building on previous versions of a company terminology dictionary
- Setting up the BPMS tool for the project – load the data dictionary into the project instance (each project will have its own space associated with the project name) in the BPMS
- Setting up BPMS project access control and any document management and sharing site for the project

While this list of project setup activities is high level, it is fairly complete. However, each company is unique and this list may change as company requirements for project setup are considered. The key concern in any project setup is that it is the foundation for the project and will have a great effect on the ability of the project team to succeed.

In addition to project governance that is dictated by standards, it is important to determine additional governance or control mechanisms that might be required at the phase or task group level. This may include working in sensitive business areas, security access/needs, access to sensitive information, or housing sensitive information in separate "limited" access repositories.

Identify and document all changes including, but not limited to, new constraints, problems, scope changes, business design changes, IT requirements changes, budget changes, and time changes. It may be necessary to hold a work session to clarify and reach agreement around the proposed changes. Then a re-scoping exercise will need to be conducted to formally determine the impact and implications to the agreed to project, the plan, budget, and timing, etc. No project changes should be made until a complete impact assessment is done, and the implications are signed off by the project sponsors.

When making project scope changes, make sure that additional budget/time/resources are made available and added to the project. Too often projects fail when additional scope changes are made to the project and no or insufficient resources are added. The rationale is that a small change will not require re-scoping and additional resources. This may be accurate if only one small change is requested. However, over the course of a project there are many 'small' changes, which when added up make a significant impact to the overall project. Without sufficient resources, these projects are doomed to failure, or at the very least will be delivered late and create frustration with everyone including the project team, partners, sponsors, and the business.

Many projects fail because the foundation is not properly set and expectations are not properly defined across all of the key project participants and the project sponsor. Not only should this foundation be clearly and firmly established at the project launch, communication must occur in a regular and predictable manner. Sponsors should be updated at least monthly by the project manager and relevant team members.

Identify the correct security and correct access right requirements, and modify all security tables in the team BPMS or business process analysis modeling tool, the legacy applications, and other applications the team may need to use. Work with IT security to obtain access rights for the team – if background checks on the team are needed, they can be done at this time. Access must be managed and maintained. As team members roll on and off the project, the security tables need to be updated immediately.

When security and access rights are modified, care must be taken regarding information protected by the Health Insurance Portability and Accountability Act (HIPAA) and other privacy laws and regulations. This may include the need to obtain individual agreements, the posting of notices, etc.

There is a difference between project sponsors and influencers of a project. A sponsor is the business leader or executive who backs the project and puts their name on the line to ensure the project is funded and has the resources needed to deliver success. By agreeing to be the project sponsor, they are committing their reputation (and political clout) to the project and they will bear risks if the project does not get executed as planned. Typically, the project will have a direct impact on improving some aspect of the organization that the executive is accountable for. Having a clear and visible sponsor is vital. Equally important, but not so visible, are the "influencers" of a project. For example, a project team with a new engineer who is the nephew of the CFO, who does not get along well with the CIO, could potentially do what they can, without it being obvious, to undermine a project by withholding support, funding, resources, and even delaying decisions to the point that it can disrupt and put at risk project timelines. Understanding the differences between an influencer and sponsors and the dynamics they bring can significantly impact a project's ultimate success.

A change in sponsor can occur unexpectedly. This shift can be a change in politics, a promotion or transition, or even a new mandate from higher up in leadership. When this occurs, it is important that the project manager meet with the new sponsor as soon as possible to provide them an overview of the project scope, objectives, the overall status of the effort, as well as communicating any known or potential risks. During this discussion, the project manager should listen for the sponsor's level of support, hidden agendas, as well as begin the process of building a rapport with the new sponsor. These initial discussions need to confirm that the sponsor is fully supportive of the project, to incorporate any changes in scope or direction that the sponsor is looking for, and to establish a communication cadence with the new sponsor in terms of what, when, and how they want to be involved and communicated with. Finally, getting the new sponsor to meet with the entire team is the next step, so that the team can see and hear from the new sponsor first hand.

One must be constantly vigilant in keeping the project sponsor engaged and involved in the project. Their support is vital when issues beyond the control of the project team emerge. As such, it is important to have your sponsor always updated, aware of progress, and forewarned if issues may be emerging before they become serious. This goes beyond providing weekly email updates or holding monthly status meetings. As a project sponsor, they need to be engaged, and fully aware of progress and risks. As a sponsor they are responsible for providing 'air cover' and helping remove obstacles/address risks that the team is unable to. If the sponsor is not fully informed/engaged they can't to the job the project needs them to do.

Sponsors are usually high level executives who have heavy loads of day to day responsibilities. It is not uncommon for sponsors to use a trusted advisor to keep up to date. If this occurs, the trusted advisors must be kept fully informed, but the sponsor must also be kept directly engaged and regular dialogue must be maintained. At times, the trusted advisor may resist the project manager requesting time to personally update the sponsor, thinking it is their job to shield the sponsor from the mundane details of the project. This cannot be tolerated. While it is expected that the trusted advisor is providing the necessary updates at the proper frequency to the sponsor, you really don't know what is being said or how often. Having periodic face to face dialogue is essential in keeping everyone informed, aligned, and accountable.

A log of key decisions should be kept along with the rationale behind each. This way if a design is questioned at a future point, you can refer to the original decision (including what, how, why, and who was involved in the decision) and not get mired in rethinking the decision. If the decision needs to be revisited, you can re-evaluate the next steps based on the key criteria that changed, and not all the criteria.

Establishing clear roles and responsibility must be done when your project is set up and they must be communicated/reinforced throughout the project. Create a RACI (Responsible, Accountable, Consulted, and Informed) chart outlining the roles /responsibilities and decision making authority for each role type and for each individual. This reduces management and decision confusion. The RACI chart should be made available to each member of the team and housed on a team only shared document repository. If conflict or role confusion emerges, refer to the RACI rather than trying to arbitrate conflict. It provides a clear and quick mechanism to resolve issues and reinforce role definition and accountability.

When creating RACI (Responsible, Accountable, Consulted, and Informed) charts, each important activity must have an **R** (responsible person) and an **A** (accountable person), although there may be instances where **R** and **A** are assigned to the same individual. Note that these are individuals and not positions. Designation of **C** (consulted) roles should be as limited as reasonable, since each **C** occurrence can potentially delay a final decision.

Dedicated vs. part time staff is a dilemma that many project managers face. Ideally, all projects are staffed with experienced and appropriate dedicated (full time) resources. However, internal staffing limits may lead to organizations staffing a blend of both dedicated and part time resources. The challenge is with the part time resources whose time will be pulled by other projects and/or their "day" job, which will continue to demand their attention. To effectively manage part time resources, it is essential to confirm and gain clear commitment from the resources and their managers as to exactly how many hours they will devote to the project over a specific period of time as well as their commitment to complete tasks that are assigned to them within agreed to time lines. Failure to clearly outline these expectations often results in part time resources being pulled in multiple directions, resulting in a risk to your project. Risks that affect their specific deliverables and often cascade to other tasks that have interdependencies on them can quickly mount if team members are unable to complete their work on time and with the necessary level of attention.

The world of simple straight-line organizational reporting structures has all but faded. Today there is an increasing move towards matrixed organizational structures where employees have more than one boss, or at the very least, more than one person involved with setting priorities and establishing their work. Project teams make this structure even more complex. When a business Subject Matter Expert, a systems developer, and business analyst are assigned to a project, they will continue to have their "old" boss, but they now report into the project team and they are accountable to the business for delivering results. Understanding these increasingly blurred reporting relationships and lines is core to managing people and delivering on project commitments. Projects need to keep their tasks, deliverables, and overall mission front and center for the entire team, regardless of the multiple reporting relationships. Each member of the team will have tasks assigned to them that they are accountable for achieving. Focus on the work and deliverables and hold people accountable for the tasks they are assigned, regardless of other priorities they may have been assigned.

Buy a team printer and keep it available for the team in the war room. It is often difficult for folks to get access to the nearest networked printer, especially when they are not working in their traditionally assigned office location. There is also confidential information that you do not want lying around by a shared printer. It is even more difficult to get printer access for external consultants who are on your team. By having a dedicated printer, project work can move forward without an unreasonable cause for delay due to printer availability or connectivity.

Office supplies are kept locked up by the administrative staff in most companies. Gaining access to a pen, pad, or post-it notes is often a tedious and time-consuming process (if you have a box of chocolates a bit easier!). Instead of hunting for these supplies, buy a variety of supplies and keep them in your war room. It makes it a lot easier on folks when a person needs something as simple as a stapler, a marker, or some tape.

Always take detailed notes in interviews. Formalize your notes within a day or two from the interview and send them to the person or people you interviewed to confirm that you understood them properly. Accept all changes from the person interviewed, ask follow-up questions, and update your notes. Send a copy of the changed notes back to the person or people you interviewed. This will help avoid misunderstandings that could cause issues to arise. In addition to ensuring that your notes are accurate, it builds a trusted relationship with the person you were interviewing.

If a company does not have a BPM Center of Excellence, the BPM and BPMS development teams will likely be separated organizationally. While this can cause issues if not properly controlled, it allows management to focus knowledge/capability/skills into the groups they fit into best. However, although separated for skill concentration, the business redesign and the BPMS/IT application development together represent a complete change process.

For companies with a BPM CoE, both the business redesign and the BPMS teams are often combined organizationally. This recognizes that transformation projects require a seamless integration of the roles these two groups plan and the skills each brings to the project.

In both organization models, work needs to follow a common methodology. Both the business redesign and automation sides of the solution development project will still need to perform the same functions regardless of the organization structure. Although the activities of the business and technical will be very different, they will still be part of the same solution development process.

This methodology will start with the business redesign and then once the business design is optimized, flow over to include a technical application generation or development methodology. These methodologies need to be supported by standards that differ for the business and the technical sides of solution design/development.

Without this combined methodology with supporting standards and policies, the project will likely fall back on IT approaches. While this will likely work OK for small improvements, we have found that larger, mission-critical projects require much more direction and control. In addition, we believe that managers must look at the project team as a single group – regardless of the organization structures involved. We have also found that this combination of methodology and project team melding greatly improves the chance of project success.

Control and consistency need to be enabled by methodology supported and standards-driven coordination and governance.

A log of key decisions should be kept along with the rationale behind each. This way if a design is questioned at a future point, you can refer to the original decision (including what, how, why, and who was involved in the decision) and not become mired in rethinking the decision. If the decision needs to be revisited, you can re-evaluate the next steps based on the key criteria that changed rather than having to rethink the entire decision.

2.2 Move to a common vocabulary

Language is imprecise. In any company, terms are defined based on the activities and the people in each business unit. Sometimes they are defined by word of mouth and other times by internal dictionaries. Sometimes they are defined intuitively and other times they are incorrectly defined by someone who is guessing. Regardless of the source of the definition, definitions will vary within any group or company. For proof, just look in any dictionary. Most terms have multiple meanings. In addition, these meanings are flavored by the group using them. This is the reason that communication is inherently difficult and causes many misunderstandings. In any project, the team members bring their versions of term definitions – as do collaborative partners and business area managers and staff.

We recommend that a project term dictionary be created to avoid serious misunderstandings. This can build from project to project, adding terms and identifying synonyms. Over time, this company dictionary can have a great impact on improving internal communications and reducing risk.

Often it is useful to define key terms at the beginning of project documents to ensure that the common understanding is reinforced. This is especially important for longer projects as staff members may join and exit the project on a regular basis. Having a project "terms dictionary" is a great tool to keep the team in sync on language and to get new team members up to speed quickly.

Terminology definitions should not be taken for granted. People in the same groups often use terms very differently. Also, any given word will have multiple meanings that we interpret by context. This has been a problem that has caused a lot of project failures. Also, avoid nuance.

Check for any existing company term definitions with the COO, the Chief Medical Officer in healthcare, the CIO, the head of a BPM Center of Excellence, or the head of Change Management for the company. Legal, Human Resources and Finance should also be asked to contribute terms they will likely use in the project and define them.

The defined terms should be consistent with Business Process Model and Notation (BPMN) 2.0 where applicable to avoid translation issues as activities begin to be modeled. Consideration should also be given to encouraging syntax as used in BPMN, such as verb first, noun second.

A dictionary of common company terms and common business and technology terms is critical when dealing with a collaborative group that is located in different geographies with members who speak different languages. The group will probably move to English, Spanish, or another language of choice as the "host" language for the project. Because this may be a second language for many team members, clarity requires that definitions be concise, unambiguous, and without nuance. Ongoing terminology discussions, and updates to the terms dictionary, should be encouraged to make certain communication is not based on assumed understanding.

Many terms that you think are in common use are actually used differently by different people and groups. For example, the term "customer" is almost universally and improperly stated in the singular, whereas processes inevitably have multiple customers. Therefore, the term should not be used as a catchall but rather as a category that requires additional detail to ensure the correct customers are clear and unambiguous in each case. Customers of any process will have multiple personas. These personas are defined by role and by demographics. For example, in just the sales support component of a pharmacy benefit manager (PBM), the roles include internal staff, brokers, health plans, benefit consultants, self-insured employers, and RFP-based customers. Each may require different information in different forms and each must be considered in the design of solutions. On the demographic dimension, age, gender, ethnicity, locale, e-commerce familiarity, educational level, and other factors can all impact how customers need to be supported. Information gathering for all projects should include input from each type of customer that needs to be supported.

No terms should have more than one definition – e.g., definition A, definition B, definition C, as you will find in some dictionaries. A term should mean one thing and one thing only.

If a company dictionary of commonly used terms exists, have all team members review it and adopt its definitions. If a dictionary of company terms does not exist, the team will need to start one and enter definitions that the team will use for even common terms. Experience has proven that terms are often defined and used differently in different business units, by people doing different jobs, and by people with different skill sets.

Where specifically defined terms exist for certain disciplines such as Lean, Six Sigma, Agile, etc., it is important to determine if there are any differences between the discipline usage and company usage. To the extent reasonable, the discipline usage should prevail to avoid confusion, particularly where external resources are used to carry out any part of a project.

Communication is often blamed for project failure and the delivery of a solution that does not meet the needs of the group. This is easy to manage but is seldom given much consideration. The dictionary should be a living project asset. It should start with the terms that people can think of, reusing any definitions that may exist. The team should then add any new terms that may be confusing or undefined through the life of the project. This should become a BPM CoE or IT asset and reused for every succeeding project. The dictionary should be put online and shared across the organization as needed.

Six Sigma Black Belts were introduced into the world of business by engineer Bill Smith while working at Motorola in 1986 and focused on improving the quality of the output of a process by identifying and removing the causes of defects (errors) and minimizing variability in manufacturing processes. As a result, Six Sigma Black Belt professionals have a natural bias towards reducing variation and improving quality. A challenge is effectively integrating Six Sigma Black Belts and their philosophies into a BPM project. This can be done by ensuring that the project "problem/value statement" is clearly defined in business language. This ensures that the focus of all team members, regardless of which framework they ascribe to, is around the business problem, not the solution methodology.

2.3 Validate and adjust the selected project methodology tasks

The center of any BPM project execution should be the BPM business operation evolution orchestration and execution methodology. All others in the company can tie into this central methodology. It is not an IT application development methodology or approach. It is a business transformation methodology that is based on BPM concepts, principles, and techniques. This methodology can be licensed or it can be built internally. The orchestration methodology should be detailed and comprehensive, and deal with the entire development cycle of a business transformation project.

This core methodology provides the framework for all sizes of BPM projects and should result in project approach consistency since the project plans for different projects are customized versions of the core method – all based on common phases, approaches, and tasks.

Nevertheless, this BPM core methodology is not all that is needed – especially in a collaborative environment. This is where orchestration becomes important. The core method should be augmented by links to other specialty methodologies for things like change management and IT (Agile). In this way, Waterfall approach methods can be mixed with free form Agile type methodologies and each used to its greatest advantage. This also allows groups using different disciplines (such as Six Sigma) to have exits in the core orchestration method, which allow the team members to leverage other approaches and techniques at the right times in projects.

This blending represents a unique customization for each project, but because a common core methodology and approach is used, the projects maintain both flexibility and control. This reduces risk and helps bridge the gaps between different groups and different project needs.

It is important to formally revisit the project plan that has been laid out to determine if there have been methodology changes that have been removed or any added contemplated tasks based on discussions to date. Any changes should be formally documented as part of change management control and made in the overall plan, and carried through to estimations of team member time commitments as well as costs.

This is a good practice to revisit tasks that were removed from the original project plan. As the project progresses, it is possible that some tasks initially considered unnecessary need to be added back in. It is important to recheck to see if tasks that were replaced by corporate approaches are actually fully addressed by internal policies, procedures, and resources.

Double check to verify that the planned and estimated time commitments of team members is consistent with the specific tasks they will be executing and that the complexity of these tasks has been gauged as accurately as possible.

Try to be as realistic as possible about projected resource needs. There may be pressure, direct or subtle, to reduce estimates to conform to expectations that upper management has. "Low balling" estimates to meet such expectations is a mistake; the project will simply go over time and over budget and these issues will have to be confronted half way through. It is far better to adjust scope, segment parts of the project, or otherwise modify the project itself than to proceed down an unrealistic path.

A BPM group should understand the current state and then envision a potential future state design for business managers who request help. These designs must include rules definition, problem definition, application use, data use, and UI design. The business workflow designs are then passed to the BPMS group, who then returns to the business area and collects any missing information. They then build a solution with input from the BPM group.

As projects are executed, it is not unusual to identify additional complexity. This may include new tasks/activities, dependencies/inter-dependencies, as well as additional resource needs because the information being gathered paints a more complete picture of what steps will need to be taken to build a solution. As a result, the plan you are building at this point should not be thought of as static. The project itself will be dynamic and the environment the solution will operate in will be dynamic as well. The project plan should be revisited regularly to ensure that it reflects the reality that is evolving.

If team members have been added since the initial team identification, special attention should be given to bringing them fully up to speed as well as to gain buy-in and commitment. This includes an overview of the project plan and significant changes that have been made, identifying the issues and risk points, the RACI chart, and even the terms dictionary.

Team motivation is critical to maintaining the focus and pace of the tasks underway and the work ahead for everyone. It is important that the sponsor shows up periodically and demonstrates their support of the project and shows that they value the contribution that everyone is making. This needs to be sincere with the sponsor having a level of familiarity of the project, the key activities/deliverables, and a full understanding of the value/benefits the team is working towards.

2.4 Set up the BPMS tool for the project

This is the technical setup and does not substitute or replace the need for the overall setup of a BMP approach within the enterprise. The following is a basic overview of this activity.

Each BPMS or Business Process Analysis tool will support collaboration and allow team members from any geography to log into the project models and work. Of course, this access is controlled by access and activity rights – for example, only people who have the correct access rights can modify models or add information. These tools generally have reasonable access and modification security, but as the nature of mobility computing and generalized access in the cloud continues to gain in use, it is recommended that BPM tool security be evaluated on a regular schedule. This is the role of the IT security team, but the BPMS administrator should be responsible for making certain that the evaulation is performed and improvements made when needed.

In addition, any of the better BPM tools will allow for multiple projects to be underway within the tool's environment at the same time. This is supported by each project having a separate secure instance or version of the tool. Access to common libraries is also set up at this time. This includes access to the rules library. Setting up the project version or instance, along with access and action priviledges, are key parts of the BPM tool setup.

Each project will also have a unique data model that gets embedded into the project's version. This supports the tool's data element drag and drop capabilities and is used to provide shortcuts in several of the team's design activities. Although the major tools will have internal databases, they are not really meant to support heavy transaction volumes and generally support internal operation capabilities, such as work list managment and task assignment.

Since BPM Suites vary substantially with regard to the ease of use of the "front end" tools such as guided information gathering and capture, modeling and simulations of models, the business side should determine if the identified BPMS provides adequate business support for these activities. Some businesses choose to employ easy-to-use and inexpensive tool sets that export to BPMN, such as Trisotech, to facilitate these activities as carried out by business team members. These tools are generally web-based and may or may not require IT involvement for the setup depending on company policies. However, for the BPMN export to be useable, they must be vetted by IT to ensure that the feeds are workable and accurate.

If there are corporate standards for Business Process Model and Notation (BPMN) use, they should be reviewed to ensure that they are accurate and up to date. Also, see if there is need for any translation assistance, cheat sheets, or other aids so that non-technical team members can easily and correctly follow the notation symbols. If there are no company standards, they will need to be created and used for the project, and be readily available to all team members.

There should also be project CoE or corporate BPM standards for usage, terminology, etc. If these do not exist, they will need to be developed. Note that any such standards will need to apply equally to all business and IT activities.

If there is already a BPMS in use, look at what has already been developed, modeled, etc. There may be elements that can be re-used for the current project, thereby giving the project a jump start. A BPM CoE should maintain an ongoing inventory of elements as they are developed as well as those modified for re-use. If there is no CoE but a BPMS is in use, those operating it, as well as managers in relevant operational areas, need to be contacted to determine what they might have that could be re-used.

If there is a BPMS in use, the specific features and capabilities that are supported will need to be catalogued to determine if the current system can support what is expected for this project. For example, there are some BPMSs that do not support simulation. If a necessary capability is absent or viewed as weak or cumbersome, a recommendation may need to be made early on to either supplement the existing BPMS or install a more suitable system.

When looking at an existing BPMS, make sure to identify all of the available features. Determine if any are not currently turned on in the system, and if so, work with IT to have them activated and tested. In addition, it is a best practice to ensure that the BPMS available is the most current version so that new functionalities are available to the team. Also find out from the vendor if there are additional capabilities that can optionally be added. Such additional capabilities might expand solution avenues.

2.5 Obtain access to tools and information

As noted in hints group 2.4, the actual setup of the access privileges will be a technical task handled by the BPMS administrator or a BPMS senior developer. These people may be part of the company's BPM Center of Excellence or they may be in the IT department. Actual entry of this information will take place by placing the appropriate information into tables in the BPMS. People who have the authority (defined within the tool suite) to enter this information should be contacted by the project manager during the early stages of project setup to prepare the tools for use by the specified members of the project team.

The setup of access capabilities by the project team should be tested as early in the project as possible and any problems addressed. The project manager should closely track BPM tool access rights because this will define the role each team member can plan and the type of tasks he or she can perform.

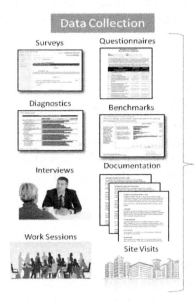

- Work is about people, process and technology

- But, activity runs on data and information

- All is controlled by rules – standards, policies, procedures, legislative requirements, schedules

- People make any change work – or kill it

- Technology enables great things when used right or acts as a serious constraint

- Redesign must consider all of these factors and it must eliminate or mitigate problems, constraints, delays, and issues with rules

- When these things are considered, effectiveness can be determined

- Finally, efficiency can be considered

Setting up access to BPMS tools is generally carried out by IT, but does include important information from the business side including:
- Identification of which team members will be using which tools
- Identification of access rights and restrictions for each team member
- Individual specification of team member ability to create, modify or delete information and at what level within the tools
- Inclusion of internal security requirements
- Inclusion of external privacy and security requirements such as HIPAA

Access to tools must be planned for carefully and thoughtfully, as well as monitored and re-checked on an ongoing basis. Few things are more frustrating than having a responsibility to carry out some task, only to discover that you are denied access to the tools required.

Access may also have to be set up for data and/or data extracts. Privacy requirements such as HIPAA may apply to these files. Be sure to have signed "nondisclosure agreements" (NDA) where necessary for people requiring access to data that could be construed as "secure data" (i.e., trade and position history; or strategic information), especially for project team members who are external consultants.

Company policies regarding "delegation" of access rights must be adhered to and if none exist, they must be created. Prohibiting delegation is not unusual.

The BPM group should define standards for a wide variety of actions and for data collection. This will ensure that a consistent approach is followed, that planning considers the same variables, that modeling is consistent (this is the foundation – BPMN is the standard for symbol use, not for how models are used or what business information they contain), etc. The standards will evolve over time, and they should fit your organization and how management wants to do business.

2.6 Train people in the BPM tool suite and other tools that will be used

Most project teams will be made up of managers and staff who have varying degrees of training and competency in the use of the company's BPM tools, in special approaches like Lean and Six Sigma, and in dealing with the more unstructured techniques of IT methods like Agile. This will be especially true in a fully collaborative project environment.

To compensate for any lack of knowledge and skills, the project manager should have added specific training time into the project set up planning. Once the team and collaborative partners have been identified, the project manager will be in a position to determine capability and skill gaps and plan to upgrade staff skills as soon as possible in the project.

This training should be delivered at this point in the project startup with time made available to test skill acquisition and competency. Currently trained staff can act as mentors throughout this training. To avoid problems, it is recommended that the best sources of training available be found and used to train the project staff. The training team should also assess the people's personal knowledge and skill levels to let new people start with the basics and others grow from their current abilities.

The project manager should work with HR in selecting training providers and obtaining skills that tie to the staff member's career growth plans.

Skill levels should be assessed and training approaches put in place for the technical BPMS activities as well as for team members who will use parts of the BPMS to carry out their required tasks. The training should be driven by the actual tools that will be used in the context of the business activities within the scope of the project. If vendors supply generic training approaches, they should be tailored to fit within the context of your project.

Do not assume that existing training materials, internal or vendor supplied, are sufficient. They should be reviewed by several team members to determine if they adequately address the characteristics and quirks of the BPMS to be used. Existing users should be asked to contribute hints that they have learned so that they can be added to the materials.

Keep in mind that the intent is to use BPM to improve business activities; therefore, the training should not be limited to or even focused on IT.

BPMS training should be structured to go down two parallel paths; technical skills and mind set. The objective is to impart sound technical abilities that support efficient and effective use of the tools while also embedding a way of thinking that constantly comes back to Who/What/When/Where/Why — the W5. The success of the project is far more dependent on the thinking than on the use of tools. The tools will quite happily display the wrong information.

BPMS training will often include identification of "go to" experts who can assist, answer questions, provide guidance, etc. Have the "go to" people maintain lists of the most frequent questions and issues and use the information to update training materials. In some cases, it may also be appropriate to pass some of the issues on to the BPMS vendor as potential improvements they might make in their UI screens, etc.

If you are new to business transformation projects, find a mentor! Reading alone will not do it. Training alone will not do it. You must be able to tie into someone with experience to avoid mistakes. We strongly recommend that anyone new to business process management obtain a copy of the Association of Business Process Management Professionals (ABPMP™) Common Body of Knowledge (CBoK) and sit for their Business Process Management Associate certification test. If you are more experienced, we recommend that you sit for the Association of Business Management Professionals Certified Business Process Professional certification test. Both tests are excellent and will clearly identify any weaknesses in a person's experience. If needed, the tests can be re-taken once you demonstrate additional training and experience.

Coaching.   Projects often need the project management team to provide business and operational coaching to the internal clients. This is to ensure that they truly understand the implications and impact that the project will have on their role and their career in the organization. We will often agree that change management work needs to be done; however, this is typically focused on helping people see their way from the current to the future in terms of how work will be organized and/or done. Generally, little is done to help people transition to completely new roles that have a direct impact on their previously stable career.

2.7 Implement change management

Change management should begin with a workshop that provides a clear definition of the project and what is expected for each participant. If the company has a formal change management process, it should be applied to the project following the specialty methodology that was linked to the core project orchestration methodology.

In reality, change management will involve multiple actions that are applied at different points in the project. At this point, the project participants should be brought to a common understanding of the project and its goals. They should also be involved in deciding how ongoing information will be distributed and what type of approach will be used in addressing those affected by the project and those in other areas of the company.

Transformation projects naturally cause fear as people wait to see if they will lose their jobs, or be transferred to another group or location. The sooner steps are taken to address these concerns, the less disruptive they will be. However, care must be taken in all communications about the project. Messages should be honest but portray the project in a favorable light. All interaction should follow formal company change management procedures, if they are available. If they are not available, the project sponsor and project manager should create a formal change management approach and evolve it as they learn more about what works and what does not in the culture of the company.

It is important to have people understand what the project is seeking to accomplish and how it will unfold. Information gathering will be significantly easier, as well as much more accurate, if people begin to buy into the overall concepts and approaches. In some cases, critical information is not recorded anywhere and is held solely in the brains of individuals, so it is much better to have people volunteer this information than to have to pry it out at a later date. It is not unusual for information gathering efforts to miss asking key questions because there is nothing on the surface that suggests that they should be posed.

One specific focus of the change management plan should be to stress the importance of people sharing anything they know that *might* have an impact on the activities that are being examined. It is much easier to discard things that prove not to be relevant than it is to discover things that may be missing.

Always include the entire team in the kickoff meeting of a project. This includes the project management team, all the SME's, the business partners, and of course your sponsor. This gets everyone together and ensures that the entire team receives the same communication, expectations, and role setting together.

A formal project kick-off meeting should include the following topics:

- Everyone introduce themselves and their role on the project
- An introduction by the sponsor of their role and why they are supporting this project
- Summary of what business problem or capability is being addressed by this project and the benefit to the organization
- Overview of the project deliverables and how they tie to the business objectives
- Summary of key milestones/decision points/go no-go gates
- Outline the communication plan and methods
- Identify how risks/vulnerabilities should be surfaced and escalated
- Discussion on how issues/risks should be raised/escalated/addressed
- Outline how discussions will take place and how they will be documented
- Review the change control process
- Set expectations on how team members should be communicating and sharing information
- Discuss training on how and where information/documentation/work product will be stored and how to gain access
- Review the cadence of the periodic status reports and who will be on the distribution
- Overview of standard meetings, including the purpose/agenda, who will lead them, who should attend, optional attendees, location, and time
- Have a little fun to get to know one another, some sort of team building exercises

The intent is to ensure that all team members are on the same page and solid working relationships are established at the start of the project.

At the end of each project phase, combine the issues, constraints, etc., from each task group and identify how each was mitigated or eliminated. The problems, constraints, etc., that were not removed will require a combined review to determine remaining impact. The project sponsor and business managers will need to help remove these problems and constraints and make a determination of their true impact.

3.0 Current state – "As-Is" – business definition and analysis

The creation of a current state or "As Is" model is often erroneously maligned as unnecessary. As veterans of a great many business transformation projects, our experience is that the "As Is" discovery process is critical to understanding the way the business operation functions and the problems managers and staff face. We also have found that few people really understand how any operation actually works. Certainly many understand business unit activity at a conceptual level and it is clear that the more experienced staff understand their jobs. There is no question about those things. But it is a different thing entirely when you try to model any business unit's workflow(s). Here, finding a single person who knows what everyone does in each task at a detailed level is hard. This is clear when you try to find all of the tasks, all of the business rules, the use of data, or how what one person does affects others. It is also a reason that a single dedicated business user for projects often is not adequate in creating an optimal solution in a transformation project.

A big part of the reason is that the business operation changes constantly at a detail level. Because few things are really documented and in many cases those things that are documented are out of date, there is seldom a reliable single source of truth that a team can find and use as a baseline.

The result is that even if you would like to start a new solution design with a blank sheet of paper or today, a blank modeling screen, you really shouldn't. The "As Is" provides the context and background that is needed for reality to creep in. A theoretical blank sheet design can be great and optimal in the pretend environment of free blue sky thought. But then operational reality and constraints and problems and people and financial reality creep back in.

We have found that the creation of the "As Is" model and the research it takes is the best way to understand the business operation, how it fits into the organization and processes, and how any solution needs to accommodate real constraints in the business, laws, unions, competition, finance, and that pesky thing called corporate culture. These things are critical and any BPM project team must understand them if it is to succeed in designing a solution that can be implemented and can be of real benefit.

This discussion and the ones related to process in the following sections of this book are related to the levels that are commonly found in both current state and future state modeling and design. These levels are shown in the diagram in this section introduction.

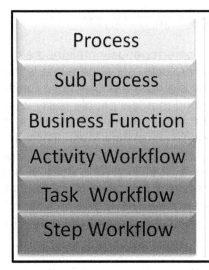

The level names in this model will vary by vendor and by company.

What is important is that everyone recognize that there are levels in defining how work is aggregated and that they agree on the number, names and content rules of the levels .

These levels have a different meaning to IT than to business – business just has one level: what they do.

Levels are critical in modeling because they allow the information to be summarized and to be shown at different levels of detail.

The process level is an aggregation of end-to-end sub-processes that combine to form a cross organization model of all activity needed to create and deliver a product or service.

Sub-processes are groups of work that support unique business functions (defined as create or produce or provide something). Each sub-process produces a component that is needed to complete the product or service that is delivered by the process.

The business functions in a sub-process are each performed or produced in a given business unit. They can be part of the work of the business unit or all of it. The key here is that the business function at this level of detail is the way processes and sub-processes are linked to business units and the business operation.

Every business unit performs work that is grouped into workflows. These workflows aggregate tasks and show their relationship to one another. Business rules, decisions, problems, legal requirements, performance, application use, and reporting are typically performed at this level.

Work is actually performed by people at the task level – it shows what they do. Many models will stop at this level. These models describe each job a person does, the screens and reports or source documents that are used, the data that is used, the data edits, and the problems that are encountered in doing the tasks. This includes compliance, timing, and other constraints.

For complex tasks, it may be necessary to break them to a lower level of detail. This is the step level. It shows the work done in a task and the relationship of each step in this work to the task's steps. Here again, documents, screens, reports, data used, decisions that are made, etc., are shown as decomposed from higher level models.

As a check, it is recommended that all problems, etc., from each level in this model hierarchy be aligned to the one above and the ones below that are in its decomposition tree.

3.1 Orchestration - control participation

Project participant orchestration is a relatively new need. It is a direct result of collaboration and the expanded role played by participating managers and staff that are indirectly affected by a BPMS-enabled BPM project. This collaborative participation complicates mid and large sized projects and adds a layer of management needed to coordinate activity among several groups who each have a primary concern for their own needs and requirements.

In this sense, orchestration is related to the need to define roles of collaborative partners and more traditional team members and to then plan for the use of people in these roles through the different phases of the project – moving people, groups, skills, competencies, and perspectives into the project and out as their participation ends and that of others begins. This movement of different participants and the blending of capabilities and skills are referred to as project orchestration.

This activity is fairly new and an important part of any BPM-based approach to business transformation. In it the project manager looks at all roles in terms of how they contribute and then controls how they are applied.

When doing data collection and analysis, always include members of the business. This ensures that the correct and representative information is captured and that the business supports the analysis that is conducted. Better to have the business "in the tent" from the beginning, rather than having them dispute the data and the team's findings later in the process.

Orchestration is the management of people and their contributions to the project. This includes defining what skills/perspectives/disciplines will be needed, the role they will play, and the tasks they will each participate in. This focuses and organizes timing and provides governance around how things will be accomplished and the decisions that support project activities.

One of the challenges in orchestration is that the dynamics of the functional organizational structure are very present but cannot be allowed to drag the team down. Hierarchy and personalities will come into play and may need to be neutralized. The tone needs to be set at the outset and the message must be that, in executing respective tasks and activities as well as contributing thoughts and ideas, everyone is equally important.

Because the hierarchy continues to exist, you may have to take steps to encourage some team members to fully commit and contribute. Normally such steps will not be needed as the project proceeds and team members will become comfortable with their roles and with fellow team members. Ask questions, solicit reactions, and draw them out. You might also have them present a key finding or a work product to build their confidence as well as building respect from other team members.

There may be participants who cannot fully leave their status in the hierarchy behind when assuming their role on the team. This most frequently shows up as disdain directed to lower level staff members in other functional areas because most of the time there is mutual respect among people in the same vertical organizational silo. If this arises, the issue must be discussed with the project sponsor immediately and an approach for remediation worked out.

Projects today promote collaboration among the different groups involved in the project. These managers and professionals represent multiple disciplines, different perspectives and ways to do things, and different business concerns. All will need to be understood, appreciated, engaged and their work on the project controlled - governed. They must use the same formats, follow the same standards, and work according to the same time table for the overall project to be successful.

At different points in the project (after major deliverables or phase gates) reconfirm the project request with the sponsor and those affected. Things that should be reviewed include confirmation of the purpose of the project, scope, targets, benefit estimates, participation commitments, and the way success will be evaluated. Note any changes in a formal project change note, and have all participants sign it – this may require a workshop to reach consensus.

3.2 Enterprise activity alignment - high level current and future state

Information will be gathered from multiple sources including documents, interviews, workshops, observations, reports, and informal discussions. As such, the information can be expected to overlap in some places and be contradictory in other places. There will be differences and disagreements between people interviewed as well as people in workshops. This will be true in both "As Is" information discovery and in "To Be" model reviews and detail activity discussions. You will need to ask and answer the question – so what is correct? What do we go with?

The way to answer these questions is to align all information from all sources into general information, and then further into information that applies to processes, sub-processes, business functions, and then to information within business units for workflows, activity, task, and possibly step – see the 3.0 section introduction.

The information that is collected should be guided by company standards, team analysis needs, and by any BPM tool information needs. This should include the Who, What, Why, When, Where (W5), and How of the business activity. It should also include volume, timing, quality, problem, constraint, known future regulatory, and other changes. While this list of information elements that are needed is important, it is even more important that the list be a company standard that is applied to all projects. This will allow different project groups to work separately and then combine information to create the ability for everyone to analyze activity and need in the same way.

W5=H
No, it's not math class. **WHO, WHAT, WHEN, WHERE, WHY = HOW**
The W5 must be determined for each step to define how things are done and how they must change.

Once aligned to these groupings, the team can look for overlapping information, contradictory information, information currency, and information holes. We suggest that the business manager for each area of W5 information be asked to make a decision on what is correct. A formal information document (in bullet form if possible) should be issued to all who participated in designing the process and to the business area manager who made the decisions on what information is correct. A disagreement mechanism should be put in place and, if needed, a workshop held to resolve disagreements. Once all disagreements are resolved, the information packet will be sent to all team members, collaborative team members, and all business managers and staff who contributed to it. Issues that are raised at this point should be resolved as quickly as possible and a project information baseline put on the project website or other sharing site.

Once this alignment is completed, it will be possible to look at data at multiple levels and work upward or downward in the data detail hierarchy to provide a complete picture of the information in an easily consumed form.

"Buy-in" on the part of the people actually carrying out each task is absolutely critical for achieving success. Buy-in can best be obtained by actively involving the line staff throughout the term of the project, not just at the beginning and at the end. Buy-in from supervisors and managers is necessary for the project to proceed and, once completed, to be declared a success, but the workers must buy-in for the solution to be adopted. That engagement starts with the "As-Is" discovery activity.

Listen to the managers and people who do the work today. The process and the procedures may be old and they may be broken, but no one knows the work better than the people who are doing it today. Even if you are planning to totally redesign the operation, you must still understand what is done, why, when, how, and by whom. You also need to understand constraints, rules, decisions, decision limits, and escalation procedures, and a lot more. Only the current managers and staff will have this understanding.

Take the time to know what information the team will need to collect in interviews – it is more than just finding out "what do you do?" and "how do you do it?" The information that will need to be identified should be:

- Business functions in the area in scope
- Responsibility of each business function
- Reason for the function and basically what it does – what value does it provide
- If the function has customer interaction, then how and why is this interaction done
- Operational problems – definition and impact (quantified)
- IT problems – applications, support – definition and impact
- Application system use
- How computer screens are used to do the task/work assigned
- Activities and their relationship to one another, including what passes into and out of the activity
- What passes into the activity, how it transforms and why
- Rules governing the information/product/service transformation in the activity
- Business rules governing each activity and performance measurements
- Decision definitions with any rules or special considerations
- Decision logic (how the decision is made and the rules that are followed)
- Decision exit probability
- Volume metrics by activity – target vs. actual – e.g., number of transactions, average/high/low volume, timing of volume, error rate over a given time period, staff number, number of transactions per staff member over a given time unit (and more, customized to your simulation modeler needs)
- Other metrics or information that the team may need to get them ready to innovate and create a new design that meets the project outcome goals.

Create a matrix that lists all of the information that is in your information collection list. We recommend that you have the information items on the horizontal axis and the people you interview on the vertical axis. Send a list of this information out to the person/people being interviewed a few days ahead of time so they understand what you will be asking about and can research the information and be prepared for the discussion with you. Fill in the cells from the notes taken in interviews – they may or may not have the information written on your questionnaire. Get back to the people who were interviewed and ask for any information that was missed. Summarize the information on the matrix for help in the analysis activity. It is also a good idea to number your notes and cross-reference the summary matrix to the notes in the different information cells.

The team should have developed its own vocabulary and its own data dictionary as part of the project setup. This is done to ensure consistency of use and consistency of understanding within the team. The people who are interviewed will use the vocabulary and the data terms that are in use in their operational areas and each of these must be explored enough so that they can then be translated into the project terminology. Do not attempt to "correct" the person you are interviewing to use your terminology—it will simply confuse things and may also be annoying.

When a BPMN modeler is in use, everyone on the project should have enough of a basic understanding of the elements and qualifiers to at least be able to follow flows on a screen or that could have been printed. However, the project should have a cheat sheet available by every screen that will be used and a printed version should be sent with every diagram. There will be team members who simply do not use BPMN frequently enough to reliably remember the difference between a "**+**" and an "**o**" inside a gateway.

If possible, use some type of Business Process Analysis (BPA) tool or a Business Process Management Suite (BPMS) automated BPM support tool suite. Even a simple business modeler is acceptable if it supports BPMN (Business Process Model and Notation which is an industry standard symbol set that standardizes the use of symbols among BPM tool vendors). BPMN symbols fall into two basic groups – a business group and a technical side group for application design and in the case of BPMS tools, application generation. The symbols for each side are different and it is generally not productive to have business people, who do the workflow design, also figure out how the applications should work and enter the technical side application definition symbols.

When possible, conduct information gathering interviews with two people – one to ask the questions and the other take notes. There should never be more than two people as it will overwhelm the one being interviewed. Once the interview is complete, the two interviewers should combine and review the interview notes, and then send them to the interviewee for their comments and edits to ensure that the information was captured accurately. This approach to information collection vastly increases the amount of information that can be obtained and level of detail that is captured and made available to the project team. This approach also reduces the number of times people have to be re-visited to clarify and/or gain additional details about what you thought you understood. One person simply cannot think, ask questions, and record results in detail simultaneously as effectively as two people can. Plan for project staffing accordingly.

Try to avoid having an interviewee's superior present when conducting an interview. Having them present may reduce candor and have a chilling effect on details as well as ideas. If the superior is present, go ahead and conduct the interview, but it may be a good idea to discuss the occurrence with the project sponsor since it may be indicative of a potential problem.

There is not anything unprofessional about being friendly during interviews. A friendly attitude often elicits more information and begins to build a little trust. Being "all business" can be seen as picking one's brain and perhaps also taking credit for one's thoughts and ideas.

Interviews should seek to get the facts, but they should also seek to identify nuances as well as information that is less visible because the interviewee assumes you would already know something or because you didn't ask. Follow up questions are very important as well as any signs that someone was going to say something else and then stopped.

Never answer your own question or fill in the blanks if a person pauses—even if you think you know the answer or what they were going to say. It is OK so start out by saying "This is how I understand that this works" as long as you then follow through to getting them to provide the details. "Uh huh" is not all the information you need when you are stating a high level understanding.

If the quality of team member notes is not where is should be, consider recording the meetings. This can be done with phone meetings much easier than with workshops or face-to-ace meetings. Also, most people resist recorded meetings and if they participate, they are very guarded in what they say. When recordings are done, it becomes a substitute for taking good notes during the interview and actually increases the amount of time that is required for the interview process. Listening to, transcribing, and then determining what is important is like doing the interview a second time. Ultimately it wastes time and is not a good practice. Instead use experienced interviewers with a solid agenda and predetermined questions.

There is often a big difference between what is being done and what should be done. BPM is designed to identify what should be performed along with what is being done. The difference is the ground for immediate improvement.

Question the business managers and users for ideas on what should be performed and ask both why it should be done and what value doing it brings to the company. If the value is small or the business manager/staff cannot justify the work, consider deleting it.

Often business focuses on improving the current operation without considering the bigger picture. The result is often doing the wrong things better or continuing to do unnecessary work faster, cheaper and much better. Alignment between what is being done and what needs to be done clearly shows the differences and provides opportunities to eliminate work. Management can now justify the differences or delete the work.

Any work that does not need to be done should be eliminated as soon as possible. This work should not be redesigned for improvement because it is not needed. It should be eliminated in the first group of changes to the business operation. Efficiency and quality changes should only be made to the remaining work.

A determination that a particular task does not need to be done and should, therefore, be eliminated must include upstream and downstream views to be certain it is not essential elsewhere. If a task seems necessary for upstream or downstream purposes, but not where it is currently carried out, relocation of the task should be considered.

Based on the alignment of the change to business capability, the original scope of the project may need to be revalidated. This may change the cost and benefit estimates of the project and may require a decision on the new value of the project.

All of the business operations managers must "buy-in" to the project and be willing to support it. If not, the issue must be brought to the project sponsor immediately for resolution. If the manager(s) remain reluctant, consider cancelling the project – a lack of commitment to project will increase the risk of success to an unacceptable level.

It is important to build current state business process models to understand how the business really operated – it will be different than most managers think it is. For instance, while most managers do not know much about the details of operations outside of their groups, sometimes even fewer managers really know how the details work in their groups. This is due to the fact that there are constant low level changes caused by people adjusting to business changes, process changes in other groups, IT applications changes (even at times to applications that other groups use), interpretation of law and compliance, and the list goes on. Business is dynamic and it is hard to keep up with the lower level changes.

In the "As Is" discovery interviews and workshops, note all problems and define them. Capture their impact and the benefit that can be expected if they are eliminated. This is a little tricky because people deal with the results or symptoms of problems. Care must be taken in aggregating these symptoms and in finding the root causes of the problems, issues, constraints, etc.

Link all business problems to activities/process elements. This is a quick way to do root cause association and to determine the potential source of the "pain point." These potential source points must be analyzed for their causes and for how they add from one to the next to build smaller issues until a critical problem is reached. Build problem matrices – problem/timing/root causes/impacts on one axis and the activity(ies) it impacts on the other axis.

Most managers do not have a good handle on all aspects of performance for their group. The creation of a current state simulation and performance models, with the needed information, can be an eye opener.

Collecting information for performance measurement may be fought and collecting it may be resisted. Even the manager will not sign off on the data, it is necessary to start someplace. To do this, do a fast, high level time and motion study. Count everything for each task and then apply it to the full workflow model. Perform the analysis that standards require and produce version 1. Then a week later, do the same thing. If time permits, do it again another couple of times. You now have a trend. It may be inaccurate to apply this model to all time periods, but over time it will be adjusted and made better – but you must start someplace.

Information collection must support project information and data collection standards. It will be collected through interviews, questionnaires, documentation review, and workshops. The information collection activity should be aligned to the business functions performed by the business unit. This focuses on the scope of work in order to deliver a specific outcome, product or service. This allows the work considered in task groups that deliver a specific outcome, product, or service.

Follow the formal work definition levels that are defined in company BPM modeling standards. There are multiple versions in the industry, so each company will need to define its own level of detail layers and naming. One that is commonly used is defined by the Association of Business Process Management Professionals (ABPMP™):

- Business strategy and strategy outcome definition and model
- Business strategy outcome high level business function
- High level business function capabilities
- Business Function Capabilities alignment to process – process definition
- Process decomposition to sub-processes
- Sub-process alignment to business area(s) – where they are supported
- Business area execution functions – workflow activity level
- Activity decomposition into tasks
- Task decomposition into steps

A simple business transformation hierarchy is:

- Strategy
- Capabilities

- Process
- Sub-Process
- Workflow – activity level
- Workflow – task level

The work in each business function-related group of tasks will have a specific starting point that forces activity into that function and a specific end point that passes activity to another business function – that may or may not be within the same business unit. If work does cross organizational boundaries, the exit and entry points should be documented.

Processes are not clean, straight-line aggregations of tasks. They branch and the work may flow into and out of the specific department/function/business unit. These interface points should be identified and the information that is passing identified/defined. The standards for this hand-off should be considered when reviewing the interface point. This interface to another process or sub-process may or may not be automated. In both cases, it must be tracked and the movement of any data, unfinished product, etc., should be time stamped and tracked.

The data passing at any interface point should be jointly controlled by both, the passing and the receiving business unit, for quality, timing, and completeness.

All interfaces, where the handoff sends something back, should be controlled by performance and quality monitoring – information must be made to be returned according to standards and quality must comply with accepted standards.

Any interface that passes new information, product component, etc., through a handoff should be controlled by standards that govern what is passed, when, its content, and the quality of the information.

Basic information that should be collected during "As Is" discovery includes (but is not limited to):

- Activities and their relationships to other activities (flow)
- What is passed to start processing work in each activity (input)
  - Internal document
  - Email
  - Data in an application
  - Mail

- Event - timing
- What is produced/changed in each activity
- What is passed from each activity
- The logic/rules for processing in each activity
- The applications that are used in each activity
- The screens used in each application for the activity
- The data that is used and how it is used or transformed
- The edits or reference to the edits that are used by each application supporting the activity
- The problems and impediments each activity must overcome and their impact
- Hold state information – why, how long (minimum/average/longest) and any related compliance regulations
- Government compliance processing and reporting requirements
- Legal or financial constraints
- Notes on the processing or on improvements

Information supporting each activity or task that should be collected includes, but is not limited to:

- Staff level and cost
- Volume passing each activity
- Processing time per unit
- Number of exceptions, standards (Key Process Indictors)
- Number of forms/information points/applications needed in each activity or workflow task

Business rules are really in the form of "if situation X, then do activity Y, or if situation Z, do activity G." The way these rules are entered (coded) into each BPM rules engine/repository is somewhat different. BPMS vendors have different coding patterns that they believe give their tool a competitive advantage. Whatever the coding format, it is important to describe the rule to the rules engine in as efficient coded representation as possible. And, this "efficient coded representation" will change by tool. This is critical in how the rule will execute by the application using the rules engine. An improperly coded rule can cause big problems. It is a good policy to check the meaning of all coded rules against the meaning of the rule and then against how it will execute.

Rules supporting each decision in a workflow must be associated with the decision and with each conditional exit from the decision.

Many activities will be governed by unwritten rules. As these rules may make up the majority of rules that run any business, it is important that these informal rules be identified and defined –

within the context of their use. This will happen in the interview process and may require a review of old documentation.

Rules discovered through interviews and old documentation must be vetted with the business unit managers. Rules that deal with compliance, standards, or legal issues should be reviewed and approved by the appropriate special group. **This is critical**. Many business systems or manual groups are using incorrect or even unlawful rules that were once OK, but have now become an issue. This is the reason that all rules dealing with finance, legal issues, or HR must be checked.

Because the team members will perform this task individually, it is important that an approach that best supports the entry of these rules into the company rules engine (usually within the BPMS, but may stand alone) be built and followed. It is also important that the entry of rules into the spreadsheet be managed and all duplicates eliminated at the time of entry into the spreadsheet.

Information needed to support current state model baseline simulation will be determined by the simulation modeler use for the project. This information should be considered as the simulation data collection standard for the team.

Define any decision or process-based workflow scenario identification and modeling as a repeating aggregation of work for a given common situation. Model the work as "whenever X, do A, B, C" following rules Y and Z. Use this approach when the response to a given situation is always the same.

3.3 Identify conceptual business change requirements

Change requirements start with the project request document. These are augmented with legal compliance and reporting requirements and with both HR and finance requirements. To these requirements will be added problem resolution related requirements, operational simplification and streamlining improvement related requirements, and customer interaction requirements.

Care must be taken in identifying and defining these requirements to make certain they are presented in an understandable manner. All of the requirements should be reviewed together to identify overlaps and conflicts, and any issues that are identified then eliminated. Finally, the requirements should be reviewed with IT to determine feasibility and estimate effort/impact.

Once in good condition, the requirements should be reviewed with affected business managers and IT in a workshop where everyone has an opportunity to speak. The resulting changes will finalize the requirements and be used to gain broad approval.

Most projects require direct data collection to clearly understand the business requirements and often the current state of the organization. It is vital that the business experts and their managers are involved throughout this process so that the information that is gathered represents a full view of the business and does not miss any critical aspects of business needs/operations. Worst case is that the project team will collect valuable data and miss something that is critical because the business SMEs were not involved to point out the gap. In addition, be sure that the business is involved with the analysis of the data so that they are completely 'in the tent' and are also accountable for the accuracy and quality of both the data collection and its analysis. This minimizes the risk that at a point in time well into the project's lifecycle that the business can come back to the team and disagree with the requirements, data, or its analysis. By keeping the business close and involved, these risks are significantly reduced since they were part of the entire process from the beginning. Failure to do this can create potential future project vulnerability from which the team might not be able to recover.

Conceptual business change requirements are identified through organized information gathering and discovery processes, not simple opinion. Core information is often obtained through one or more workshops designed to begin defining the parameters that will then be evolved and massaged into the conceptual requirements.

The conceptual business change requirements must ultimately be consistent with and support strategy; therefore, the starting point should be the current strategy document. Ideation sessions such as these typically yield a lot of concepts and each should be examined from the perspective of how the concept supports the strategy as currently articulated. Normally, not all of the concepts will survive. Those that do not should be captured within a "Parking Lot" for subsequent examination. Some "Parking Lot" concepts may eventually be used to refine strategies going forward.

The context for conceptual ideation sessions must include all identified constraints for two reasons: first, to avoid expending efforts on paths that may be blocked by the constraints and second, to determine how to reach objectives in spite of the constraints.

Part of the collaboration dialogue that takes place in arriving at a conceptual design may result in the identification of new constraints. These need to be added to the formal project documents that define limits on the project.

Understand dependencies and project backlog. Approved projects are rushed into existence and often we neglect to look at the overall volume of work and ultimately change, that is being expected of the organization. IT often is criticized for project delays, scope creep, and over runs. However, internal benchmarking tells us that a driving cause is an organization's attempt to simply do too much at once. Even if all the resources are made available, we find people stepping on one another's toes as a BPM project meant to improve processes runs into a separate project team upgrading the operating system, while still another group is trying to conduct compliance training, all targeting the same internal team of employees. This overwhelms the employees and slows project execution.

3.4 Determine the optimal approach to delivering the solution

Business transformation and business improvement projects should be formally controlled by a business-focused methodology. But here there is a problem. IT specialists insist that an Agile method is all that is needed. Lean and Six Sigma specialists insist that all that is needed is a Lean, Six Sigma method to ensure optimal solutions. Business Architects follow suit and insist that either Zachman Framework approach or *The Open Group Architecture Framework (TOGAF®)* is all that is needed. The list goes on.

Among the authors are certified Business Architects, certified Business Process Architects, and a certified Six Sigma Black Belt. We can assure you that all of the groups are wrong when it comes to business transformation. The fact is that all are needed. No one has all the right answers and the best approach. But when the best parts of each are combined and called by a central orchestration methodology, their individual strengths combine into something much more useful than any one of them alone.

Experience has proven that an IT Agile based approach alone is not sufficient to provide the context for change and the broad perspective in redesign that are needed. The same is true for change management, Lean, Six Sigma and other approaches. We recommend that a formal waterfall-based approach be built into a business change method that has been adjusted to accommodate either BPM or iBPM (intelligent BPM) concepts and techniques. This method should serve as the core methodology of a group of unique separately focused specialty approaches and methods. These other methods and techniques should be called from the core methodology at the points in the project where their capabilities can best be applied.

Corporate culture, operating environment, staff capabilities and more must also be considered in creating the standard approach that will be used in the company. Experience has also shown that any company's approach to transformation projects will also evolve as management and the business and IT teams become more familiar with the approach and find innovative ways to improve it.

However, the key is that any designated approach and the methodology that supports it must be standard in the company for BPM- and BPMS-enabled BPM projects. This is necessary to constantly improve the company version of the methodology and to limit risk and cost, while improving the probability that changes will be easier to make in the future.

Every BPM team should leverage a full BPM/BPMS lifecycle methodology. This method will orchestrate all activity and all groups who are involved in creating and in installing the solution. To support this collaboration, the method will promote integration with other specialty methodologies – such as Data Architecture. This also enables the BPM CoE to move into an iBPM future of methodology support simulation modeling, advanced use of analytics, embedding performance measurement in the design, and the activities needed to create a solid foundation for the project.

The optimal approach should represent a complete picture of what all of the parts of the solution will look like when knitted together and is normally a model that pulls together all the sub-processes that will need to be executed. The conceptual model will normally have identified business capabilities and IT capabilities that need to be supported. It is suggested that the sub-processes and capabilities be compared. Capabilities that cannot be located within the model will indicate gaps, while sub-processes that are not associated with a capability may not be needed.

To begin to design the optimal approach, a wide range of people in various roles will need to be sought out for input. While input is clearly necessary from SMEs and high-level personnel, the team at this point should include a full spectrum from those actually executing tasks through executive levels. This team should then interview additional people within all of the affected functional areas to get as wide a view as possible.

The optimal design must be business oriented. While technical components must clearly be addressed, the focus should be on what is needed to support the business activities. The design must be presented in a way that the business staff can follow the flow and comment on benefits as well as potential problems since their input will be critical to refining the design.

The pace of a project must be maintained to ensure that leadership, the team, and the business sponsors constantly appreciate the dedication of the team and that progress is constantly being made. Projects that are perceived to be slow or faltering are at high risk of being defunded, scope reduced, and/or cancelled due to the lack of real/perceived progress. Pace is maintained by setting and achieving interim goals/deliverables, and by communicating milestone progress to the business and sponsors. This will keep the project relevant and supported.

3.5 Technical analysis of the business area's IT support

The question in the creation of any new solution design is "what capabilities do I have to pick from in creating a new business design, the way IT will support it, and the way customers can interact with the part of the company being changed?"

Do you or does anyone on the team have an inventory of what capabilities and what data is available for the solution? You will know what the current applications provide if the application capabilities are identified during the "As Is" business operation and IT support discovery. You will have a general idea of some of the things that IT can support. But you will likely not know of everything. For example, what are the capabilities and limitations in creating and using social mobility apps? What can the cloud be used for? In manufacturing, what advanced robotics are on the table and can be used? What type of analytics can be supported? Does the company use Six Sigma monitoring software? Can it be reused – or are there license issues? What new hardware, communications, and software tools (like a BPMS) are available or will be available soon?

These questions and more need to be considered in a technology analysis. The team should have this information available to it along with IT or other specialists who understand what the information really means and how it can be leveraged.

The ability to leverage this information is a key part of the foundation information that supports design creativity and innovation. It is also important to maximize the tools and capabilities available in the company when creating solutions.

It is important to identify team members who have a thorough understanding of both the current business capabilities and the current technical capabilities where capabilities are defined as the ability to execute activities and tasks.

A common problem is to overlook business capabilities that actually exist but are not currently employed or used in current operations or are not being exploited to their fullest potential. These may include skills, knowledge, tools, and information on the business side. On the technical side, there are often tools, features, functions, and data elements, etc., that have never been turned on or which were active at some point but are not currently used.

Never rely exclusively on pre-existing documentation to identify capabilities, either business or technical. Documentation typically starts with gaps and begins degrading as soon as it is produced. Unfortunately, most operations that attempt to maintain procedure manuals do not have the time to keep them updated and they are thus typically not representative of what the operation is actually doing on a day-to-day basis.

As part of the identification of IT capabilities, the team must look at future plans for the next year as well as plans that may extend out 3 years. Capabilities that are anticipated to be coming on line in the near terms can be woven into the overall approach and ultimate BPM/S solution design.

The technical review must include all manufacturing and other equipment that may be part of the activities and tasks under consideration, as well as any planned upgrades and replacements that may yield additional capabilities.

3.6 Modify the current technical environment if necessary

Keeping up with technology advances is almost impossible for most companies. In truth, a lot of new technology is not really needed in many business transformation projects or improvements. However, the available technology inside the company and available in the market should be reviewed and analyzed to see if something may be beneficial in creating an optimal solution and increasing the ROI of the project.

Also, it is possible that new technology and new technology approaches (such as advanced social mobility apps, design simulation, application generation, cloud use, research data lakes, and more) are being considered by IT and may be available before the project solution will be constructed.

If new technology is needed, it should be analyzed and a formal Cost Benefit Analysis that follows company standards should be built. If it is justified, this new technology will need to be integrated into the current IT environment or manufacturing production environment and the resulting operation certified for use. At that point, it will be available to solution testing and implementation.

As soon as any new technology is approved and budget committed, the business transformation team should consider it for inclusion into the new operational solution design.

BPM is not just about cutting cost. It is also about leveraging new and emerging tools to innovate and gain an advantage for the company. The business operation redesign team should be able to look at this technology and work with the IT team members to see how they can creatively use it to improve the business, reduce waste, reduce error, improve the way it interacts with customers, and helps the company improve its ability to change quickly, with low risk.

The BPM CoE should work closely with IT strategy and the Technology Officer to understand what new technology is becoming available in the market and what capabilities it will provide to the business. The Process Architects can then leverage this knowledge both proactively and reactively to help form solutions that maximize the benefit of the change to the company.

The new technology may or may not be built into the project estimate. If possible, each project request evaluation should consider the potential of leveraging new or emerging technology so the benefit of this technology can be considered and contrasted with the benefit of using the technology that is in place in the company. This will allow management to gain a better understanding of the incremental value that technology will bring to the project.

The BPM CoE should list all new technology the company will license and provide information with IT on the new technology that is being looked at and even further, the technology that is emerging. Information on technology and applications that is being replaced or sunset should also be available to the business design teams. This information will help provide an environment for innovation and thinking in new directions based on new technical capabilities.

The business operations design may leverage technology that is new to the company. This technology may take any form – from advanced analytic support and business intelligence to social media with mobility apps and cloud computing. In the future, there is no telling what technology will be available. The key is that it may be necessary to leverage this advanced technology to deliver a capability that the business needs to be competitive or to gain market share.

It is important for a BPM practitioner to keep up to date on technology and the capabilities each new solution or trend (such as mobility computing, the next iterations of cloud, etc.) brings to the table. This knowledge, along with an understanding of current and emerging business transformation techniques, approaches, and trends can be used to set professional BPM practitioners apart from people who simply "talk the talk."

Technical changes will be controlled by the IT Enterprise Architect and carried out by IT. It is possible that some changes cannot and will not be made for a variety of reasons. These become project constraints and must be addressed by the project team to devise a solution within the boundaries these constraints create.

Changes to the technical environment must be understandable by the business team members so that they can understand and plan for new capabilities and limitations. This may require some translation between the technical and business sides. There should also be planning for training and change management to address those technical changes that will impact business staff within each applicable functional area.

The use of any technology will obviously need to be approved by IT senior management and funded. The request for this new technology should be made as early in the design process as possible. If it is approved, the new technology will need to be used, so the request must be serious and it must be backed by anticipated benefit. If the request is not approved, the design will need to remove any capabilities related to this technology. That is why the request will need to be made as early in the design as possible.

3.7 Build "As Is" business process models showing IT support

The objective of "As Is" modeling is to create a comprehensive and deep understanding of the current business operation and its IT support. "As Is" or current state business process models are the foundation for defining the following:

- How the business really works
- What rules are applied
- What decisions are made
- What data is used and how it flows and changes
- What problems are affecting the business operation
- The applications that are used
- The compliance measurement and monitoring that must be applied
- Transaction volumes
- The sources and timing that drive the start of work and the products that end a work stream

To be useful, any current business process or workflow models must be up to date. To be used, they should be accurate. It is OK if they are not complete – they will need to be reviewed and their accuracy confirmed as a starting point in project work and can be completed at that time.

We recommend that standards be created and used to determine what information is needed in these models. If iBPM concepts are followed, this data collection will need to include the data that the simulation tool needs. This simulation will be the only accurate way to determine the efficiency of the current operation. This is the baseline of the operation and allows for the accurate measurement and analysis of all performance improvement – as shown in the "To Be" business solution design.

The "As Is" models and information are created through a discovery and analysis process that leverages document review, individual interviews, workshops, observation, and informal discussions to collect information and build a picture of the operation. It is important that in the creation of these baseline models, the team confirms everything in the models and supporting information with the business managers and staff. This eliminates assumption-related mistakes and supports open communications which will be critical in the "To Be" or future state solution design.

At the start of any current state modeling, it is important to schedule time with the Legal and Finance departments to identify and define all compliance requirements and compliance reporting needs that are within the scope of the business processes being evaluated. The team will also need to know how the reports are constructed to help identify the best sources of data to ensure compliance.

Work with HR, Change Management, and IT to create a project website where people can post questions that the team can answer. The project sponsor and project manager should keep this website up to date and share status and findings, as well as post references to how the business and specific business people are involved with the project and the important role they are playing.

Data that is used in processes, as well as data gathered to support performance measurement, must be standardized and agreed upon. There are generally multiple data elements that may have the same name and yet contain information that is not the same thing, information that has been transformed, information that has not been updated uniformly, etc. In addition, measures may be created that use terms that are not the same as underlying data elements or rely on the selection of a particular data element out of multiple possible choices. As a result, the project team must agree on a data dictionary that:

- Adopts a uniform name for every data element
- Specifies exactly which data element in which system populates that data element
- Validates that the identified source provides the uniformly most accurate source of the data
- Tests these definitions in simulation to ensure that there are no unexpected results.

If the company has a formal data governance structure, they must be involved in the determination of the data elements to be used. Testing the effectiveness of data governance will ultimately happen as simulations are run.

Issues with the uniformity of data and source elements will become more complex in companies that have grown through mergers and acquisitions and therefore have multiple systems that ostensibly contain the same information. Attention must be paid to the selection of the most accurate source as well as formatting issues such as field length, treatment of leading zeros, use of special characters, sequence, etc.

Companies operating in multiple countries face additional challenges in ensuring uniform data. For example:
- Comma vs. decimal
- M-D-Y vs. D-M-Y
- Local time vs. UTC±
- Treatment of language-specific characters
- USD/£/€/¥ etc
- Address codes
- Etc.

Once you have identified and defined the level in the BPM modeling hierarchy that you will be working at, identify the activities that are performed and their relationship to one another – flow. We also recommend that the following information be considered and that once decided upon, the information needs to become a company business and IT standard:
- Title of people and brief definition of what they are responsible for – decision levels, etc.
- How many staff and does staffing vary by seasonal transaction volumes
- Maximum, minimum, and average transaction volume by month
- Quality – is it measured, how, formula and how evaluated (standards, opinion, formula)
- Waste – is it measured, how, formula and how evaluated (standards, opinion, formula)
- Problems with definitions and their impact – dollars, time, quality, etc.
- Applications used and their relationships to one another with a brief description of how each application supports the activity
- Data used and screen names
- Number of errors – rejections and a description of what is done with errors
- Constraints on the activity – time, authority limits, legal requirements
- Compliance reporting description
- Observations and staff improvement recommendations

This list will change depending on the company and the standards that it follows for business modeling. The list will also change depending on the IT environment – is a BPMS being used or a modeler? Is the tool robust or limited? The key is that as much of the data that will be needed at some point needs to be collected at one time – to save cost and business unit manager disruption.

Always confirm any data you are given with the originator (source) and identify the quality (data completeness, accuracy, on time). Make a decision as to whether the data should or should not be used. If it should be discarded, the analyst should define why and work with the project sponsor, project manager, business manager or staff member who provided the information to improve it.

When collecting information, care must be taken to clearly understand what it is you have collected. The fact is that many companies do not have current business process models, operating information, or updated procedure manuals. Cost reduction has caused even more problems with the orphan of business operation – operational documentation. However, out of date business process models are more dangerous than no model – you don't know what is right and what is wrong. If you make decisions based on these out of date models, you could be making very bad decisions, creating risks to the business. For this reason, time should be built into any project with existing business process models, to verify the models and information with the business manager before they are used. If necessary, time will need to be spent updating these models and information before work can really start.

Keep personal notes on everyone you interview – what the person likes, teams they are a fan of, what are their kids' names, and their school or college. Have them talk for a while about themselves to break the ice in the interview. Ask how everything is going. You do not want to be a counselor or social worker, but you do want people to know you care about them as people and about how you can help them succeed. Be friendly and if possible reassure everyone that you are not there to get rid of people. Also reinforce that their comments will be kept confidential and not shared outside the core project team. Business interviewers need to be able to build trust to get people to open up and share their true thoughts and beliefs. Treat everyone with respect and kindness. No one will open up to someone they think will ridicule them or break their trust with the confidentiality of the interview discussion.

After each interview, go over your notes with the person or people you interviewed and check all of the data you collected. Make any changes the person who was interviewed wants to make. Using this technique also provides an excellent opportunity to go into further detail on anything a person wants changed.

Even documentation that is presented as new and up to date must be carefully validated to determine if it actually reflects the reality of how work is done. This validation does not mean asking a manager if it is correct. One of the best practices is to have a business analyst learn tasks as an apprentice to a person trusted as an operational expert in the tasks being examined. The operational expert should be someone identified by peers. The go-to person they identify will have a lot of influence on how work actually gets done. That business analyst should then compare the actual experience against what the documentation says.

When collecting data in interviews, make sure that there are two members from the project team present. One to ask the questions and the other to take notes. There should never be more than two people as it will overwhelm the person being interviewed. Once the interview is complete, the two sets of notes should be combined and the notes reviewed, and then sent to the interviewee for their comments and edits to ensure that the information was captured accurately.

It is quite possible that the way work actually is executed as determined by observing, apprenticing, etc., is not completing the way work must be done to be compliant with laws and regulatory requirements, such as those establishing acceptable business practices in healthcare, insurance, finance and life sciences. There is often a required and government reviewed Policy & Procedure Manual that specifies how activities are to be carried out. A quick way to get an indication of whether these manuals actively guide work is to determine how often they are consulted. If they are now accessed electronically, see if IT can report the number of hits on a regular basis. Also ask line level staff to show you how they log in to check them. If the Policy & Procedure Manuals are still on paper, a quick look will tell you if they are pristine or if they have flags, sticky notes, and spilled coffee on them. If they are not being used, chances are there are violations. Fixing a finding that there are violations should be immediate, with longer term changes incorporated into the revised processes.

One of the most critical components in constructing how activities are executed are steps that are "invisible" where there is no evidence of any information being consulted or present, and the action taken comes out of the head of the person carrying out that step. "How did you know that?" is a very important question to ask to identify hidden factors that can affect how steps are handled.

The project manager and the sponsor should formally communicate to the manager of each business unit that members of their staff will need to be interviewed or involved in a workshop. Provide the timing of the workshop and the participation needed – the roles of the people who will attend the workshop or are to be interviewed. This communication should also describe what will be done in the workshop or interview, the questions that will be asked, the reasons behind the workshop or interview, and the way it will be performed. It is vital that the project team recognize that their presence can be disruptive to the business and that the team is taking this into account by talking with the business managers well in advance about the need to interact with their people.

Always send the meeting notes to all participants and require them to comment – either OK or anything that they would like changed. These notes are critical. It is important that the team properly understood what the people being interviewed are really saying. Messages and truths are hidden sometimes, but they must be heard to understand the real operation and its problems.

Starting the "As Is" or current state modeling – identify the "low level" business functions in the business unit (what it does) and the workflows that support them. You will usually find that each function is a separate workflow. This is more difficult than it sounds. Just asking what they do will get you a lot of tasks and the interviewer or workshop facilitator will need to bring everything up to a grouping of activity that produces a result or service or component of a product. At times, everyone gets the leveling wrong and mixes activities, tasks, and functions. These will sort themselves out as you start to work with them. The key is to be flexible and not try to keep something at a level where it really doesn't belong.

A business area or business unit will support one to several lower level business functions. At this level the business functions usually stand alone and are represented by separate workflows – each business function will thus decompose separately to describe it in additional detail. These business functions will each have a different purpose and a start that is initiated by some event or action, a group of activities that are performed, and then a specific deliverable(s) that is produced.

Workflows are comprised of activities that relate easily to other activities and form natural flows. Activities can be further decomposed into tasks such as register a new customer. Tasks can be broken into steps – confirm that all information has been supplied, check credit, check address, check personal information, and check demographic information. This lowest level of work decomposition (work breakdown) is often necessary to describe complex action in preparation for either business redesign or for application requirements definition.

The first step in determining the work that is in a business unit/business area's business functions is to identify the trigger action/event/timing/document/email/inquiry/order that starts the work in the workflow. Note the timing, volume, quality information, source, transformations, and supporting documents. It may be helpful to start by looking at the business function as a single entity and then look at what starts the work (input) and then what is produced (output). Once you know what starts the work and what it produces, you can start to say, "When you receive an X, what do you do?" You can also make certain that at the end of the work, the right thing is produced.

Starting at the work initiation point for the business function, identify and define each activity that is performed in the sequence that they are performed in. Note all wait times and all processing branches. Identify all volume and timing information for each activity. If metrics are not being kept, it is often helpful to initiate a monitoring activity with the business unit manager and collect basic volume, timing, and other information. The "As Is" discovery work will take time and thus will allow at least some relevant information to be collected during this activity.

When asking business managers or staff about the work and identifying activities, always ask what it does, what problems it has, and why it is needed – what value does it provide? Also try to find out if the activity can be combined with something else or if it can be deleted. The people who perform the work will have a lot of insight into what is busy work and what is actually needed. Listen to them before you make up your mind about what is needed and what can be eliminated.

Identify and define all decision points and identify what decision is being made. Determine if the decision is really needed. Many operations have unneeded decisions that were never taken out of the workflow as it changed over the years. Assuming it is needed, capture the volume into the decision and the volume out of each exit. These exit volumes will help you define path probability for simulation. The decision will be driven by specific rules that control how the decision is made. This must be captured along with a brief discussion as to the meaning of the rule, the way it is really applied, and if it delivers the accuracy that is needed in the decision. If the rules do not deliver solid results today, identify what the issues are and why the problems are occurring.

Work with the business managers and staff as you go through the "As Is" discovery and look for quick changes that can have a noticeable immediate impact if implemented. These things should be defined as "low hanging fruit" or easy changes and they should be spun off to people who can make the changes immediately. This can often help pay for the project while it is in progress. These quick changes can have a very high return when looked at cumulatively.

Identify and define all problems with the business operation at a general level first and then for each activity or decision. Note the impact of each problem on the operation and time, cost, quality. Capture any staff thoughts on how to remove these problems. Create a problem matrix with problems on the vertical axis and the business activities they impact on the horizontal. Put the impact in dollars for each activity in the cell at the intersection of the problem and the activity. This can be at any level – process to task. It just depends on what you are trying to show. The total impact of any correction can then easily be seen by totaling horizontally at the right side of the chart. This impact analysis is a great guide in justifying immediate corrective action and also in adding to the projected project benefit.

Identify all applications that are used for each activity and define how each application is used. Note who is responsible in IT for each application. Also note problems with the system's use, problems changing it, how well it supports the activity, and the quality of the application's data. Identify the screens that are used in each activity and the data that is used, modified, created in each activity. Note all constraints and problems. Work with the business staff using the application to identify how it could be improved and see if there are significant improvements that can be made quickly at low cost.

It is important that the project manager and key members of the project team have complete understanding of all the applications that their project will potentially touch or be affected by. To do this requires having access to an IT Enterprise Architect or a member of the Technology Strategy Office who can provide a detailed understanding of the application environment as well as the "go forward" application roadmap. This ensures that interdependencies on current applications and potential future changes can be incorporated as both interdependencies and risks to project execution.

Identify and define all workflow handoffs to different workflows and capture the associated timing information. Identify the probability that the work products or data will be returned on time – according to company standard or agreed timing standard. Determine the accuracy of the data that is added by the other group or the decisions that have been made. If the level of quality is unknown or in dispute, it may be necessary to perform a quick quality assessment of the information that is added or modified by the other group.

Identify all timing issues and other constraints that need to be applied to business activities, collaborative interactions, customer interactions, IT applications, or other support. Place these in notes or in data fields associated with the activities they apply to.

Identify all internal Service Level Agreements (SLAs) and validate them with the business to ensure their accuracy. Ask how non-performance to SLA's is addressed and how often it occurs. These are valuable insights into how well a process or operation is performing, and what is, or is not, being done in cases of poor performance.

Identify and define all performance monitoring and measurement that is being performed today and the sources of all data that is used. This may be manual, it may be semi automated with daily word processing or spreadsheet notes or it may be fully automated as part of an automated application. Find out what is being collected, why, and how it is evaluated. Also identify acceptance issues and problems. Put this collection into the workflow according to your company business modeling standards.

Identify all federal, state, foreign country, mandatory tracking, and reporting requirements that are built into the current workflows and identify any problems with the way this information is collected or measured. In the case of clinical reporting, such as CMS reporting for Medicare and Medicaid, determine based on reporting results if something in the work needs to change to improve the reporting score. Also, capture who in the company and the business unit needs to be involved in compliance signoff for these requirements. Identify any legacy or licensed applications that support this reporting today and identify how they are supporting the requirements – how they work and how they capture data. You will need to understand everything about compliance measuring and reporting requirements before the new design is started. When dealing with legal compliance and reporting, the only opinion that matters is that of the company's lawyers – get them involved, sooner rather than later.

Identify by activity or at a lower level, each task in an activity, the number of people performing the task, special training/skills/certifications that are needed, and the competency level by skill needed to perform each task. Identify any scheduled training and define what will result from the training.

We recommend that a formal project team wrap-up session be held at the close of the official business day, each day. The purpose of these meetings is to share significant findings from the different workshops, document reviews or interviews. This is needed to keep everyone on the team up to date with what is going on and the information that has been found.

3.8 Analyze "As Is" models for business and other problems

A great deal of information will have been collected in the "As Is" business operation modeling discovery process. If approached properly, this information will have been vetted and aligned to ensure its completeness and accuracy. The project team will now need to analyze this information to determine improvement opportunities, new rules, rule modifications, and problems that can and should be resolved in the new operation, and a variety of other considerations that will turn into requirements and constraints for the new operation design and solution definition.

Part of this analysis will be based on efficiency shown in the simulation models and part will be based on the performance results of the "As Is" operation, again as shown in the simulation models. Regulatory and financial compliance issues will also be identified, as will compliance with corporate policy and possibly compliance with union contracts.

In performing this analysis, the project team will work with the collaborative partners and IT to gain a broader perspective of how each requirement may be fulfilled and how, when applied to the business operation, it might change. This mixed team will also consider the best use of existing and anticipated new tools and techniques.

Together with the requirements from the initial project request, these issues along with opportunities to improve the business operation by doing work differently, will form the majority of the requirements for the new business operation. Some of these requirements will be met with manual operational changes, others by changes to existing applications, and still others by the construction of new applications. This analysis will form the foundation for determining the approach that will be taken in delivering each of the requirements that are defined.

Identify all problems in the activities in scope. Work with the business managers and staff to identify the problems and define them. The definition should follow BPM project standards. The definitions must also be reviewed by all project participants and formally approved by all managers as being correct.

Generally, what people will call a problem is really a symptom of root problem – the results. It should be noted that any problem can have several contributing factors or actions (symptoms). Combine the symptoms into logical groups to identify and define the problems. Track all problems back to the actions in the workflows or to decisions that cause them. This is referred to as root cause analysis.

Create a problem matrix to organize problems and understand true impact. On the vertical, list place the problem name. On the horizontal, list the low-level business functions/workflows. Define the impact in the intersections of problem name and impacted workflow or business group.

The problem matrix should also be analyzed to see if several problems have similar root causes. If they do, see if they should be cross-referenced or potentially combined. It may be possible to eliminate multiple similar problems with a single change. This is important determining the impact of a problem (or group of similar problems) and in prioritizing problem elimination.

The team should start their analysis at defined problem areas and starting at each impact, work backward through the workflows to determine where the problems are being caused and the actions that are causing the problems. This analysis will allow the problems to be designed out of existence. It will also allow the team to recommend performance measurement in different activities to monitor the build of any potential problem from its possible initiation point. This technique allows the team to build in an early identification capability with defined mitigation activity.

There is a time to get into a lengthy discussion of a problem and then there is a time to move on, and not dwell on the problem. Teams can get caught up in trying to understand and assign blame when problems arise. Problems need to be recognized and then a solution needs to be identified and put into action. Debating who is at fault in a problem is like watching a house burn. While it is important to recognize that in fact the house is on fire, watching this for more than a few moments wastes precious time. Recognize the problem, move to devising the solution, and then to corrective action … quickly.

If the elimination of a problem or group of similar problems, will have a big impact, it should be given a high priority in the design and possibly spin off an effort to take immediate interim action. If a problem has a low impact, the team should ask if it is worth addressing at all – it is easier and less expensive to allow some very low impact problems to remain. Remember, the operation will never be problem-free because the business is dynamic and new problems will be introduced in the future. Deal with what is most important first and ignore that which really is unimportant.

Create an opportunity matrix. This matrix will list the opportunities and the business activities as the "As Is" model is analyzed. The team will then note improvements that can be made. Some high impact, low effort improvements become low hanging fruit – "just do it" changes. Others become opportunities for improvement in the new solution design. As with problems, opportunities for improvement can affect multiple activities and thus have a fairly large impact. The opportunities can also, at times, be combined to have a serious impact on the operation. These should be added to the opportunity matrix as they are discovered.

When evaluating the opportunity matrix, include your business partners in the assessment. They have valuable insights as to the degree an opportunity will provide value/benefit to the operation.   In addition, having them part of the discussion will ensure that you gain their commitment to implementing a solution.

Problems at the activity level should break down at the task level and the step level to form a complete view of the problem, what it affects, how it affects it, and the cost in lost opportunity, raw material or component loss, error-related rework, etc.

Volume, timing, staffing, number per unit of time, error rate, cost per transaction, and other metrics, should be identified with the business user, as defined in the data collection standards for the company.

If it is being formally collected, performance management data is likely to be rudimentary. It is also probably incomplete relative to future monitoring and measurement needs, and may not be part of a formally agreed upon performance management and data collection approach. However, any performance measurement program in place is a start and simply needs to be expanded and evolved. Creating a performance management program should not be delayed until every aspect of how it will work and the data it will use are formally agreed upon and become standards. Any start is a good start – get something going and then work with the business areas to improve it and make it more meaningful. Do not fall into the perfection trap and do nothing waiting for the managers to agree on things they probably do not want to do anyway. Remember, people don't like to be measured and it will take time to eliminate the fear that the measurement will be used against them.

3.9 Build ("As Is") simulation model and performance baseline

To have a point of comparison to determine real improvement, it will be necessary to have a clearly defined starting point and a performance baseline that is agreed upon. Without this, you may hit project targets but you cannot prove how much you have really improved the business.

If volumes, quality information, scrap, activity timing, hand off timing, rework, etc., are not being measured today, it will be worthwhile to begin working with business management and staff in the business areas that are in scope to put performance data collection activities in place. This will begin with selling the reasons for collecting the information to Business Unit managers and obtaining a formal commitment from executive management as to the purpose of the measurement and performance management. This move to performance management may be part of an internal change management program from HR or a BPM CoE and the team should coordinate activity on change management with the appropriate group in the company.

The next general step is to define the exact measurement formulas that will be used and identify the information that will be needed to drive this measurement. This information will then be aligned to the points in the workflow where it may be collected and any quality mitigation actions defined. Working with the managers and staff in the area to be measured, design and create collection procedures and begin to collect baseline data. This will be analyzed the same way the future performance information will be evaluated and the same reporting will be produced.

This will provide a test run for the information collection, analysis, evaluation, and reporting, and allow it to be adjusted to make certain it provides the guidance management is looking for. Because this is simply a baseline, the data collection and analysis can be manual. However, if it is automated as a learning process, the business and IT teams may create a better long-term measurement solution and become experienced in the use of the simulation tool that is recommended.

In many companies this will be the first time that anyone is attempting to actually measure baseline activity, let alone performance. In these cases, you can expect excuses and resistance. People seldom like to be measured – they don't trust how the measurement will be used. To help control this natural fear, the project sponsor and managers should do all they can to convince both line managers and staff that the information will NOT be used against them in their performance reviews. If any punitive action is taken based on a measurement of current performance, management will lose the trust of everyone involved and further or future performance measurement will be meaningless. Measurements may be manipulated and any results will be bogus. This is a critical point. It is worth arguing about and standing firm. If this is not used in a positive way, the project will fail in the long run – regardless of what is delivered and its initial results.

The data that is collected should be entered into an automated simulation modeling tool. These tools may be part or the BPMS or they may be separate. If separate, while the tools are inexpensive, their use requires the separate duplicate entry of certain information – unless the two tools can exchange data through either a common or constructed custom interface.

It is likely that the team will need to go through several iterations of this model improving the data and the way the simulation tool is used with each iteration.

Each characteristic of the performance baseline must be a unit that can be quantified. The characteristics must be observable and there must be a defined level for each. Use of any performance measures that are based on opinions should be avoided.

Buy-in regarding agreement on the measures and the levels set for measures should be obtained from business managers and from staff carrying out activities. Buy-in is critical when new measures and/or new levels are established. Obtaining buy-in should be deliberately planned as part of change management activities and must be sequenced properly so that it fits into the flow of the project. Reluctance on the part of managers or staff may be an indication that measures need to be re-examined rather than just resistance.

The simulation iterations will be run using factors defined when the "As-Is" model is being designed and employing data that has been vetted as consistent with the enterprise or project data dictionary. Instead of building actual connections to legacy data for "As-Is" simulations, "Stubs and Drivers" can be put in place using extracts of actual data. Such extracts will need to be subjected to the same validation and verification steps that will eventually be taken as the actual connections are built. Each data element must be obtained from the exact field and file specified with the exact formatting required. The contents of the fields should be inspected to determine if the entries are uniform. If anomalies are found in the field contents, they must be documented because the same anomalies will affect actual operations and steps may be needed to include corrective actions in the overall solution.

The capture and entry of the necessary factors such as steps, business rules, event probabilities, time, costs, etc., are all human activities and as such are prone to errors. It is necessary to verify and re-verify the accuracy of the factors with managers and users. This verification should take place step by step. Sending out a list and asking for an OK should be avoided.

Operational simulation is available through iBPM tools or through separate simulation modeling tools. It is not available through traditional BPMS tools or through traditional application programming.

At the start of the "As Is" business operation discovery work confirm what information will be needed by the company's simulation modeler to run a valid simulation of the current business operation and its performance. This may be available on a company standard, but unless the standard has been modified to meet the needs of your company's simulation tool, the team will need to also check for information needs with the tool vendor and then update the company standard.

Create or modify a standard data collection template and define each data element that is required on a separate but aligned and referenced dictionary. Make certain everyone on the project team uses the same templates in the same way.

Create a manager and staff presentation to kick off the performance management baseline effort. Give this presentation several times to make certain everyone sees it. If possible, video tape the presentation and put it on the company or team website.

As interviews are held and workshops are conducted, make certain that for each activity all information needed for the simulation and its analysis and evaluation is collected. This is a quality check the project manager must take responsibility for. If collected during interviews and workshops, the team will not need to bother the business managers or staff multiple times. Also, make certain that the information collection is properly orchestrated to eliminate different groups asking them the same questions and collecting the same information. It should be collected once and then made available to everyone.

The information that is collected should be formalized from notes and then sent to the people who were involved in the interview or workshop and confirmed.

When the first workflow model is complete, check for information availability and if it is in the model, run the simulation – following the procedures outlined by the simulation tool vendor. Analyze the results and create specific directions for focusing change in the next iteration. This technique will reduce the number of iterations and move the iteration process from a series of improvement guesses ("I think that will improve X") to a formal review and evaluation based on the findings of the simulation modeler.

When the simulation runs no longer point out significant problems, the design is as close to optimal as it needs to be. However, at the project manager's discretion, the simulation can continue until no issues remain.

This will prove the design is efficient. To prove it is effective, you will need to generate the applications from your BPMS and then build "Stub and Driver" programs to link to the interface points in the generated applications. It should be noted that a "Stub" is designed to receive a specific data packet from the generated application when it is run and a "Driver" is designed to pass a specific data packet to the generated applications when it is called. This technique can be used with BPMS-generated applications, or with applications that are custom built in-house.

Work with iBPMS vendors or developers to prepare the business process/business unit workflow models for simulation. Move the models and needed files into the iBPMS simulation module and assign access and control rights.

Run the "As-Is" models through the simulation tool and iron out any bugs. Use this as a learning tool for the team.

Confirm the results with the project team, the sponsor, and the business managers in the area in scope and IT. Make certain that everyone has a "say" and everyone is heard.

Make any changes to the project's performance measurement approaches, standards, analysis/evaluation techniques, and data collection that are needed to improve the business design and performance measurement process in the future for this project and others.

3.10 Analyze current state business operation simulation

The results of the simulation at this time will create a clear understanding of the places in the workflow that can be improved and the ways the workflow can be streamlined. In addition to providing a set of opportunity requirements for improvement requirement definition, the analysis of this information can often show places where simple changes can be made immediately and provide significant results.

This analysis will likely be iterative as performance measurement formulas are evolved to provide the exact information that will be needed to evaluate "As Is" and "To Be" operating performance. This is important because these formulas will be used to determine real benefit and operational improvement – as a delta between the "As Is" and the "To Be" performance numbers. It is critical that all participants agree on these formulas and the approach that will be used in these measurements and the sources of the data that will be used. If this is not done, the people being measured may disagree with the results and the team may not get the right credit for financial, operational, or quality improvements.

The analysis of this information should be the responsibility of a combined team of collaborative partners, team members, and IT.

Keep in mind that the simulation will run on the basis of model design, business rules, data, event probabilities, time measures, cost measures, or sometimes estimations for factors such as time and cost, if hard measures are not available. Each of these factors will affect the outcome of the iteration and each of these factors must initially be entered somewhere and then may also be edited as the iteration is configured. As a consequence, a "sniff" test is valuable, particularly in early iterations. If any of the results are unexpected or seem to be way out of line from what common sense might predict, the factors underlying the result should be verified and validated before it is assumed the model must be re-designed.

Business requirements should be formally challenged to gain additional insight into the problems they are meant to address. Each requirement challenge should include questions on:
- Why is this needed?
- What will happen if we drop it as a requirement?
- What will happen if we leave if for another project?
- How does this requirement affect the business processes and the operation?
- What parts of the business might be involved or affected by this requirement?
- How many people are affected by this requirement?
- What is the business benefit of this requirement?
- Who is behind it – sponsor, business manager, manufacturing production manager, IT, customers, collaborative partners, legislative requirement?

This list of questions is not a complete list – it does not contain everything that you may want to ask. However, it is a good starting point and all of these questions should be answered for each requirement.

Analyze the reports from the simulation in team workshops to train them. Make any corrections to the business process models or information working with the business managers or staff.

Performance measurement approaches, techniques, tools, and standards (such as KPIs) will also be aligned to activities in the workflow to determine where and how performance will be monitored and measured.

Once the current state model is created, cost information will be added to the workflow to support its analysis. This includes loaded staff cost (salary plus benefit), general and administrative cost (usually an allocation of corporate cost), and other cost – identify these costs with the Finance department to make certain all cost categories are considered. This information will point to high cost areas and help focus initial improvement work to deliver improved ROI.

The quality of cost and operational information is important because it will drive future simulation modeling in the new design and in the continuous evolution of the business area and IT support. The actual data that will be captured will be determined by BPM simulation tool data requirements.

Once the business operation is fully understood, the team should move on to defining and analyzing the quality and adequacy of the work's IT support. This includes the IT infrastructure (hardware, storage, web service, social mobility, and data storage/access), the applications available to the business unit(s) involved in the project, the quality of the interfaces, and the quality of the data in the applications.

All performance, quality, and other measurements will be captured and approved by business unit managers at this time. This data represents the real baseline of the operation. All change will be measured against this baseline.

Data quality and content problems must be noted and mitigated if the applications and their reports are to be trusted.

There should be formal governance of data quality and there should be a validated data dictionary in place to ensure accuracy and consistency. If the company does not have a formal data governance mechanism, one must be created and can reside in the BPM CoE.

If performance and other measurement values that will be used in the future are not available, the team should work with the business users and IT to create realistic estimates. These estimates will then be tested against reality in the simulation. If the performance is considered to be off, adjustments to the estimates can be made until affected managers agree that the metrics are as realistic as possible. This may require several iterations of this task group.

The Current State simulation is designed to build a baseline for improvement comparison. The initial simulation metrics can be an educated guess by managers. This will be followed up with tests to confirm or change the estimates as the remainder of the project is being executed. The goal is to make the baseline as complete and accurate as possible recognizing that this may be the first time managers are estimating volume, error, time, etc. So it will evolve during the project.

The Current State simulation also serves to prove out the identification of data sources and steps taken to ensure that data accurately reflect what is intended to be captured and that the results remain consistent.

Once the "As Is" baseline simulation is completed, the team and management will have a basis for comparison to determine the real savings and the value that the project provided. This will be a comparison of the current against the future design and then the complete, deployed new solution. This can also start a monthly trend analysis that will grow in value over time.

3.11 "Low hanging fruit" change modification/deployment

Every business operation evolves and as it evolves it is modified to address specific needs. These changes are focused and seldom consider anything beyond the activities or tasks that they must. This allows workflows and activities in business units to become inefficient and possibly ineffective over time – creating opportunities to find and implement simple changes that re-streamline the operation, improve quality, or save time and money.

These are generally fairly small, focused, quick hit types of improvements. They may or may not have a high value associated with them. The value of doing them is that they don't cost much or take much time to build or implement and they can relieve problems. Low hanging fruit changes are temporary if the team is looking to make serious improvements. The team should not stop at low hanging fruit improvements but should move on to find and create significant improvement in the business operation, its quality, and its performance.

Potential low hanging fruit changes can be found in many process or business unit workflow tasks. They are usually obvious because they simply don't make sense when you look at the workflow and the work. These include duplicate actions, over-complexity, wait places in the work, largely manual work, high rejection, high human error, inadequate automation – the list goes on. If you ask yourself "why in the world would they do that?" you have found a place where a quick fix (low hanging fruit) project can help.

The best candidates for low hanging fruit projects are simple fixes that have a high return. They exist because no one questions them or tries to remove them from what a person must do. Many times these issues were created years ago and the current staff has no idea why it is done or what it provides.

Always follow these four rules:
- Do no harm
- Do that which is most important first
- Concentrate on the high value changes
- Question everything – take nothing for granted

Do not allow the quest for low hanging fruit changes in any "As Is" business model to cause you or the team to lose focus. It is easy to get mired down in these quick changes and let the project schedule fall behind.

When ranking low hanging fruit changes, first focus on those that solve problems or improve customer interaction.

4.0 Future state – "To Be" – business design

Once the "As Is" or current state business operating model is completed, business and technical requirements/program specs are defined and vetted, and an "As Is" performance baseline has been put in place, the project team will be ready to redesign the business operation, manufacturing activity, and related IT support.

The focus will be on the redesign of the business operation with the resolution/mitigation of problems and the expansion of the technology available to the business users and customers. In manufacturing, shop floor control and other specialized capabilities will need to be considered and added to the normal business overview operation.

As this activity starts, it is recommended that project team, collaborative partners, and IT jointly define all constraints that will affect the design along with all current technology support capabilities that will be available to the group for the new solution design. This will allow the team to look more effectively at customer interaction, customer buying experience, supplier interaction, sales agent interaction and support, and a variety of other topics that will contribute to operational modernization and market share improvement.

There are two basic approaches to this redesign. One is to start with a "blank sheet" and create a design assuming there has never been a company – design the company from scratch. This design can then be modified based on the constraints and realities of the current operation and IT capabilities. In this approach, a design that cannot actually be built is created and a series of design steps are used to create an evolution over time to this future target operating model. In this approach, it is necessary to make certain that the capabilities that are needed today are delivered in the early changes from design/construction/implementation iteration. This target design and the steps to building it will need to be modified on a regular cycle to adjust it to the reality of business operations, market changes, and technology changes. This is a type of long-term strategy and allows the business to control its evolution better.

The other approach is to start with the current state or "As Is" model and then, using the requirements list and constraints/capabilities list as the first guides, redesign the current operation as a series of changes until all requirments have been met. In this approach, the team will first adjust the business and IT support to deliver all required capabiliites. It will then need to go back through the design and streamline it, eliminate any redundancies, analyze and improve all decisions and rules, ensure that the rules are vetted, adjust legacy application use, define new applications and ways to interact with customers and partners, design business operation management applications, and embed performance measurement, compliance management, and reporting.

Both approaches have pluses and minuses, but both can provide successful results. The approach to choose is based on company culture, the willingness to try new approaches, and the urgency of the change that is needed to improve the process or business area.

Applying simulation modeling to guide the iteration of the "As Is" model is a new component of the BPM concept and is part of a newly evolved change to BPM called iBPM – the "i" stands for intelligent. With the use of simulation, the solution can be checked for optimization and improvement made and proven. However, the use of model simulation is fairly new and not yet widely adopted. We have included it here because we have found it to be very helpful in reducing iteration time, improving the design, proving that it is efficient, and allowing a comparison between the "As Is" operation and the "To Be" operation model. If not automated, we still recommend that a type of manual walkthrough simulation be conducted to check the design workflow and capabiliites.

In addition to simulation, the current BPM concepts and tools can be used to make a significant difference in the probability of success at lower overall cost. These differences are related to methodology, collaboration, and rules management. The BPM concept is firmly rooted in iterative design, collaboration, and the use of rules to guide and control action. Iteration has been discussed. Collaboration is different. It is based on the inclusion of people from multiple parts of the business, with different disciplines, perspectives and knowledge in the projects. These people bring their own ways and specialty methodologies. All this must be blended into an approach and methodology that will properly direct activity. We term this "orchestration" – the movement of people, skills, and disciplines into and out of the project at points where they need to be applied. This movement is controlled by an orchestration methodology. This methodology sits at the center of a group of methods that others bring with them to the project and directs when each will be applied and what it will control. This allows different specialty methods to be moved into use and then pulled out when the project steps change. Examples of specialty methodologies include:

- Zachman Framework
- TOGAF®
- Change Management
- Data Management
- Agile

The important fact is that there are different approaches that can each deliver successful results. The BPM group should begin by building or licensing an orchestration/execution methodology. This will link with the various specialty methodologies in the company to form a unique combination that provides guidance and governance while recognizing the strengths of specialty methodologies.

Note: An example of an orchestration methodology is the Wendan Consulting Architect, Design, Deploy, Improve (ADDI) methodology. See www.wendan-consulting.com for information.

Following the aproach above, the methodologies will be easily modified to meet the capability, cultural, and preference realities of the company. This will allow a company standard approach to be built through trial and evolution so that the teams are comfortable with it and is proven in the company.

Collaboration will also play a significant role in the creation of the future state transformation solution. Care should be taken in building the future state design team to identify the capabilities and skills that will be needed at different points in the redesign and testing process, and then to find/assign them, build them within the staff, or contract for them. In this way, the strongest and most creative business and IT application design teams possible can be built.

As the new business design is nearing completion, the design specs can be used to drive the initial investigation of their impact on the IT environment and of the new technology that will be needed and then be built to support the business solution. This will allow IT to get a timing jump on the construction phase of the project and prepare for it.

Creativity is key to innovation and it should be promoted in any BPM-based project. This is probably the most important and yet the most stifled talent in many project teams. Part of the reason is that many projects don't have time to try new things and many companies frown on pursuing ideas that may not work out and consume time and resources. We believe that this is the foundation for a learning organization. We also believe that this is the foundation of building a flexible business operation that is nimble enough to use change as a competitive advantage.

Confirm the roles, the people, and the access rights that will be built into the BPMS or Business Process Analysis tool suite and make certain the tool's security and the company's application access security are set up to allow these people the access they will need.

Confirm the capabilities that will be needed to redesign the business operation and its IT support. Define roles and assign people based on their skills and competencies – people can play more than one role, but they can only play one role at a time.

Determine staff member strengths and weaknesses and consider these characteristics when planning the "To Be" design work. If people do not have the skills that are needed, consider either replacing or training them.

Limitations are constraints. Constraints must be identified, defined, and analyzed. This is a critical step. Constraints are important in the design process because they can totally negate any design or activity. Failure to consider them can therefore send the design back to the early stages and make all work in the unconstrained design moot.

Constraints can come from many sources both internal and external to the company and may include (but are not limited to) factors such as:

- Budget limits
- Hiring limits
- Limits on hardware purchasing
- Government mandates, domestic as well as in foreign countries
- State, local, national and international regulations
- Labor contracts/employment contracts
- Quasi-governmental standards and requirements (ANSI, NFPA, ISO, etc.)
- Standards and requirements from entities issuing industry approval seals/certifications
- Physical plant limits

- Talent pool limits
- Internal purchasing requirements, RFP standards, etc.
- Outsourcing requirements and policies
- Immigration/Visa requirements

Guidance needed to define constraints must be sought from Finance, HR, Legal, Compliance, IT, and Facility Engineering (for changes in the building) at a minimum. Identifying and defining these constraints is critical as they will reduce the number of solution options available to improve various tasks and activities.

Two approaches can be used in the new design process. The first is bound by constraints and supported by capabilities from the very beginning of the design. The second is more "green field." With a green field approach, no constraints or capabilities are considered and the business operation design page is blank. The team is free to create the best possible design. It needs to be recognized that this design will never be built, but it will be a blueprint for innovative ideas and creativity. Once this design is complete, the team will then need to work with management and IT to see if any constraints can be removed. This will possibly change the way the constraints will be applied. Next, capabilities must be considered. Again, the team should work with management to see which of the capabilities that are needed by the new design are not available but can be approved for funding and then created. The capabilities then are applied to the design as a type of limitation and the design is again modified. This method promotes creativity and innovation and through the process of applying constraints and capabilities, the design is made realistic. However, it is still a concept and will need to be run through the simulation process and optimized. The exact approach that is taken will be dependent on time, funding, team creativity, and management flexibility.

Formal project team status review meetings should be held every day. These should be 15-minute meetings focused on sharing status, problems, constraints, and technical issues that have been encountered and if eliminated, what was done to eliminate them. The primary purpose of these daily sessions is to share problems and to find help in resolving them. A secondary purpose of these status meetings is to help the project teams better prepare for the next 24 hours of work.

For projects that span multiple time zones due to multiple locations, when these meetings are scheduled is an important factor to consider. To the extent possible, status meetings (as well as other important working sessions) should take into account time differences since this factor can be both an impediment (some participants might have to be available during non-business hours) and an asset (the ability to hand off work to a team that is just starting their workday as one team is finishing their workday, reducing the delay in project/task completion).

An approach that we do not recommend for most operational improvement projects is starting a redesign with a "blank sheet of paper." This approach is fine to look at what could be a model in the fairly distant future; however, every company has current operational momentum (cultural, IT, and other baggage) that must be addressed. No firm can just start over. It should be noted, however, that true transformation level projects are not really common. With that said, there are instances where in some transformation level work, you have the option of ignoring current baggage (with regulatory and legal requirements being an exception) and can start over. For these projects, you have a green field view – virtually no limitations. In these scenarios, you need to start by identifying government restrictions and compliance rules and then adding in other constraints. This will likely produce a design that cannot be moved to in one step – it usually requires significant IT and manufacturing capability investment, and a move across two or more business design implementations as they lead the business to a new operating model with new IT and manufacturing capabilities.

First define changes, eliminate problems and impediments, and then address any quality issues, rule issues (decisions), staff knowledge issues, and customer interaction issues. The team will then streamline the business to optimize the work and check the possible impact of change as it ripples upstream and downstream.

After the completion of the "As Is" review, the list of participating groups should be confirmed along with their activities, what each will provide to the project, when they will be involved, what they will produce, how that will tie into what others are producing, and the roles that will be filled by each participating group. This may affect the list of who is participating, when, and what their role will be.

The multiple business managers and professionals who participate in the project and who follow different disciplines should be contacted, engaged, and should follow prescribed governance protocols.

Involving relevant business managers, discipline experts, and SMEs should be approached proactively and should seek to foster ongoing dialogue. One of the important roles of the project manager and the project sponsor is to be the cheerleader. If key people only play passive or worse, grudging roles, the success of the project can be seriously jeopardized.

Beginning to foster engagement and dialogue should be approached with a deliberately planned workshop for key participants. One dimension that clearly needs to be addressed is the informative track where the overall project intent and structure are addressed. A second and equally important dimension is to begin to build a sense of excitement and have participants understand their value to the project to foster their commitment.

There may be key participants who appear reserved or even reluctant to support the project. It may be necessary to meet with some participants one-on-one to address concerns, provide assurances, and otherwise seek positive and active engagement. Such one-on-one conversations often go better when scheduled as a lunch or dinner or some other activity outside of the routine hectic work environment.

In rare instances, despite extraordinary efforts, a key participant may still choose not to engage and not to support the project. If this occurs, senior management must either decide to remove the individual from the project (and insulate them to avoid sabotage) or consider terminating the project.

The methodology that IT will use is strictly up to IT as long as it does not prove to be a deterrent or constraint to the success of the project. The same is true for change management, Enterprise Architecture, Business Architecture, Data Architecture, etc. Each of these disciplines will have preferred approaches to solving problems, executing tasks, etc. The overall project methodology should be structured to leverage the strengths of these approaches and should avoid forcing these disciplines to abandon their specific methodologies. It does require effort to identify and resolve any issues about how the various methods, disciplines, and techniques interface and fit together, so that the ultimate project is as seamless as possible.

4.1 Confirm project goals and outcome characteristics

Time will have passed since the initial project request was approved. Because the business operation is dynamic, it will have changed. This step is a checkpoint to avoid building a solution that no longer fits strategy or direction.

At this point in the project, the team, the collaborative partners, the business managers, staff, and IT will have learned a great deal about the "As Is" business operation and how it is supported. As a result, concepts, opinions, and ideas may have changed and new capabilities may now be considered to be critical parts of the future state solution. The same is true for project goals and the way management envisions the new operation to work – outcome definition and its characteristics.

The start of the design phase of the transformation solution is the time to pause and check with the project sponsor and affected managers to see if the requirements defined in the "As Is" analysis are still complete and still accurate. Based on possible changes in knowledge about the business activity and management perspective, holes in the requirements, changes in what technology will be used and how, and changes in the way the company will interact with customers, the team can now review requirements and make needed changes.

This review and update are critical. As managers and sponsor knowledge and perspectives change, their concepts of a new business operation can also evolve. A checkpoint here is needed to avoid building a solution that meets the initial but now out-of-date requirements.

Solutions that meet out-of-date requirements are unfortunately common. BPM originally tried to address this problem through iteration of the design and solution. This approach creates a loop that never ends and seldom delivers an optimal solution.

As with the new design and requirements, any changes following the approval of the "As Is" models/requirements should be formally presented to the project sponsor and affected business managers and approved.

In confirming project goals and outcome characteristics, particular attention should be paid to external changes such as new laws or regulations, changes in market dynamics, newer technologies and new competitive products. This review also needs to look over the horizon for changes that may be occurring over the next several years. While one overall objective is to build a change-ready enterprise that can rapidly adjust for future developments, it will likely take several years to mature to that state and changes will occur during that period.

Confirmation of project goals is not a passive sign off; it is an active endeavor that should include requests to identify any changes that have occurred since the project began at all levels including those who perform the activities and tasks.

Goals should be actively reconfirmed from the senior executive level down to managers to ensure that they are current and accurate and that there is still a consistent understanding among all participants.

If any goals are modified, the modifications must track back to current enterprise strategies and be consistent with and can be shown to support these strategies.

If there have been any changes to scope, the entire project team must be updated and there must be a consistent understanding of the revised goals and the impact the changes will have on the work of the overall project and the individual team members.

4.2 Orchestration – setup and control participation

Larger projects today are best staffed with specialists from multiple business areas and multiple disciplines – from IT to manufacturing, to customer experience, and change management experts. The makeup of any project is dependent on the scope, complexity, criticality, business activity, technology that will be used, and legal compliance issues that must be considered. This creates a core project team of business and IT people and an extended team of collaborative partners.

However, all of these people will not be needed full time throughout the project. Their competencies and skills will be used at different times and thus must be carefully scheduled and managed. This creates scheduling and commitment management problems as the priorities shift in their various business areas and they may become over-committed. This is where project and staffing orchestration comes in.

The project manager today must be skilled at not only identifying the skills and roles the project will need, but also in negotiating collaborative resources and then managing the availability of these people with their business unit managers. At times this includes enforcing commitment to the project. All of this is highly political – adding an extra dimension to typical project management political concerns.

As if this were not complex enough, to save costs, many projects have both onshore company staff and offshore contracted staff. This introduces language problems, time zone problems, and problems with the offshore resources living up to commitments.

At times this situation is further exacerbated with the addition of newly licensed large-scale integrated groups of applications, new technology tools, a variety of legacy and current programming languages, and a conflict between business and IT approaches. These types of factors may require new skills and introduce unknowns into the project.

The ability to juggle all these parts is becoming critical as transformation projects expand the scope of typical business and IT projects. There are multiple dimensions to any project – business operation optimization, Business Architecture, Process Architecture, business analysis, simulation modeling, change management, requirements definition for BPMS/traditional programming/interface with legacy applications, social mobility application development, data management, and more. All must be coordinated and all must be leveraged at the appropriate times in an environment that combines multiple approaches, methodologies, and disciplines.

It is important to consider time zones when setting up meetings or calls with collaborative partners. At the same time, time differences can be exploited to produce an ongoing extended project workday by having coordinated project team members located in different time zones. For a US only company that has team members on both coasts, there is an automatic 11-hour day. For a Berlin-based company with operations in Philadelphia, quitting time in Berlin is before lunch in Philadelphia.

Becoming a project team member is really accepting a significant responsibility. Anyone who joins the team as a collaborative partner will have to accept this responsibility. People may be appointed to the team and have no choice. But, regardless of how they become team members, they need to accept this responsibility. This should be done through a workshop where everyone must sign a commitment agreement that details what is expected from them. This should include full time team members as well as collaborative partners.

While projects will require most participants to put in a significant amount of effort, the importance of the project to the enterprise as a whole should be stressed. Clear steps should be taken to encourage participants to view their efforts as an honor rather than a burden.

The company should elevate the status of team members and make it known companywide that they have been selected to participate in a major corporate initiative. Such recognition will help cement commitment and dedication, while at the same time serving to offset any pressure to do regular work at the expense of project work.

Managers and supervisors must be made aware of the importance of the project and a commitment to support the project, and team members should be obtained. The project manager must be vigilant for signs that a team member is being pressured to treat project work as a secondary responsibility and address any such potential situation with the team member and applicable manager immediately. If necessary, the project sponsor should be involved.

4.3 Prepare to redesign the business operation

Once the project staffing model is in place and the project manager is prepared to move staff (skills and capabilities) around in the project (orchestration), he or she can turn his/her attention to preparing for the actual work of creating an optimal new operating model, with new process components, improved business functions, streamlined workflows, and vetted/modernized business and technical rules to control work.

Preparation is critical to avoid what we call "technical successes and business failures."

> *Note: Any set of requirements can be built to support the business operation's work in a lot of different ways (workflow and interaction of internal activity) when the IT developers are free to take them and design the solution. Some of these solutions will be really good. Some will be OK and some will actually hurt the business. All impose a new way of doing work and new workflow on the business staff. It is very possible for a solution to deliver all of the requirements on the requirement list and impose a new way to work that is not acceptable to the business managers and staff. This is a technical success – it*

works. It is also a business failure – the business would have been better off without the improvement. Real collaboration is the BPM approach to avoiding this situation.

Statistics vary on the percent of failed IT projects. Some go as high as 80% - defined as over budget, taking longer than the estimated time, dropping functions, and/or producing results that the business is not happy with. The good news is that eventually, through iteration, the solution can become beneficial and improve the business. But while this is possible, business management often grows frustrated and is seldom kind in discussions about the project. While all of these problems can be managed with the right methodologies and project management skills, most could be avoided to start with if time was taken to properly set up the project to succeed.

From experience in the trenches as practitioners, we know that the time to adjust is before the project building phase starts. We also know that at times this adjustment is just not accepted by the sponsor and by business management. These are hard lessons on what to have included in the initial project planning and estimation, but we believe that if the experiences of the project managers are combined in workshops, the majority of things that have caused issues can be identified and adjustments to the project estimation and planning activity can be made to reduce downstream problems.

Following this line of reasoning, we recommend that anytime a project manager deals with something new, he or she find people in the company or through associations, internet professional groups, etc., that are experienced with the technology or whatever is new that they are dealing with. Education is needed and is good, but it is not experience. We believe that both are needed to be successful.

Preparing for the business redesign is an important task that should not be avoided if running late. It sets the stage for open communication and sets expectations. This should begin with a workshop to confirm all requirements and make certain everyone has a common understanding of what they are and what will result from them. As a safety valve, see if any requirements are low value and can be moved to a second development phase. Do not accept any unreasonable timing, content, inclusion, or constraints as being part of the project. If you do, you will likely fail. This is where negotiating skills come into play. However, we have seen absolutely unrealistic demands and we know the results. If this happens, it is better to go to a higher authority and present your case – but be ready to back up your reasons for your opinions.

It is also recommended that the team interact frequently with the business area managers and staff and solicit their opinions on every aspect of the solution design. It is better to get these people on your side and give them a say in the solution design than to try to convince them after the design is completed. This includes considering business and IT involvement in solution simulation modeling and analysis, and in KPI/CSF evaluation. Extra communication at this point in the project is time well spent.

Just because the project team works really hard on something doesn't mean it has a lot of value. Always keep the goal in mind and focus activity and solution development toward those ends. People will work hard and keep polishing an apple well beyond the point that incremental value is being gained. In addition, there are those who can become fixated on developing a very "cool" solution that leverages technology/process in a very unique way that adds little or even negative value to the ultimate solution. Be on the guard for time wasters like this and be vigilant in holding people accountable for solving the problem, not admiring it!

Now, on this slide, may I direct your attention to the flashy animation and cool transition effects... because I worked really, really hard on them.

Whenever a user needs to reach out to the support center, a vital design consideration has been missed. When designing a new solution, seek to understand the common types of support that are being provided today for various processes/systems so that they can be designed out of the new solution. Examples include calls to a support center to create new or different data views, provide access to additional information, or the redesign of processes. Each will require human intervention (additional cost) to understand and resolve. Challenge your design team to anticipate these potential issues and design the solution to accommodate them before they occur.

When designing solutions, consider the type of work and worker that will be engaged in the solution. There are three distinct types of workers:

- **Knowledge workers** – tend to be customer facing, ad hoc in nature and lend themselves to mobile solutions. Examples include sales people, engineers, and application designers. Ultimately, these are the professionals who are addressing situations with multiple variables that require the individual to make decisions that have a significant impact on customer experience/costs/profit
- **Task workers** – are employees in roles that tend to be well defined and by their nature are repetitive. These roles rely on employees to be trained in understanding the work put in front of them and following a predefined set of rules to make decisions.
- **External workers** – these are not employees of the company, but play an active and integral role in delivering value to the organizations. This includes outsourced vendor partners, consultants, and staff augmentation workers. The relationships can be business to business (B2B) and/or business to customer (B2C) and require processes and access that is unique to them.

When designing solutions, it is important to determine which type of worker will be using the solution that is being created so that it can be optimized for their use.

Any overall approach that is repeatedly narrowly focused will eventually result in damage to the process as the individual changes accumulate to cause a ripple effect that actually begins to harm the process. This is because each small change puts the overall process slightly out of tune with respect to the other unchanged activity. At some point, these small differences add up and cause inefficiency or error.

A narrowly focused approach may force staff to develop workarounds. These workarounds are never documented and because they exist, create a new workflow that is inconsistent with what the BPM models think is going on. With a combined broader view and planned and deliberate testing by actual users and adjustments made on the basis of these tests, the need for workarounds will be lessened and the level of undocumented changes going forward kept to a minimum.

Confirm CSFs and KPIs. Confirm their definitions and components and how they will be measured and evaluated. These can change and result in building the wrong monitoring and measurement capabilities.

For CSFs and KPIs, if the definitions, component parts, formulas and locations in the process are not completely accurate, simulation results may be unsatisfactory because of these factors and not because of design flaws, but this may take a major effort to discover.

Six Sigma is one of several ways to approach performance monitoring and management. Today it is the most popular approach.

Check the "As Is" business model for current Six Sigma or other performance monitoring and reporting activities. Note how performance is measured and tracked today and what information is being provided and not being provided for management. Compare this with the project performance management requirements and determine what can be reused and what needs to change or be replaced. If no real performance management is taking place, work with management and affected business users to determine what level of performance tracking is needed.

Any existing performance targets/goals/standards that cannot be formally measured in a reliable manner must be replaced with criteria that can be measured and that is both valid and reliable. The validity of a measurement is the degree to which it can be proven that it actually measures what it purports to measure. Reliability means that repeated measures come up with the same result. Poor validity and/or reliability often arise when measurements are not placed at the correct point in the workflow or where the measurement is not performed at the appropriate points within the workflow. These errors occur when branches in the process are not tracked to determine possible impact on the measure with sufficient care. Whether or not performance measures have been well designed should become apparent as simulations are run.

Problems with performance measures can result from lack of mutual clarity regarding what is being measured, which could stem from different uses for the same terms. This is why it is necessary to have a company dictionary of terms or at least a project dictionary that is used by everyone involved in a project. Even with this dictionary, it will be necessary to ask clarifying questions to zero in on the best and most accurate measure.

For example, does "Total Number of Widgets" mean everything that runs through the production line including:
- Total defects and those destroyed in process?
- Those that need to be re-run through coating or spot painted?
- Those that actually survive the packaging process?
- Those that make it out of the warehouse?
- All of the above separately or collectively?

The key in applying Six Sigma to help monitor performance in areas is to find how performance should be monitored based on expert feedback of an internal Six Sigma group as well as those managers who are accountable for performance. The points where performance data will be collected can then be identified and collection can begin. Also, identify how the data will be collected, the data source points (and applications), and whether the data will feed any performance monitoring applications. This data will feed the Six Sigma evaluation and will be used to determine operational quality and alert management when the patterns and trends in the data show problems.

If Six Sigma or another approach to performance management will be used, the data collection points should monitor for anomalies and for times when the work, according to the data, is approaching a problem state (i.e., going beyond the performance standards). Minimally, when these situations arise, warning emails should be generated to the specific responsible person. More sophisticated monitoring will have inference logic built into the data evaluation and will also recommend action.

Note: Six Sigma is a statistically based approach to performance measurement. It is used to identify places in a process flow, workflow, or a manufacturing production activity where work does not meet accepted performance levels or quality as defined by the company. As with Lean, it is strongly recommended that the reader look up Six Sigma performance monitoring and reporting, and integrate these techniques into their professional skills.

Lean is an operation and redesign approach. It is based on the fundamental belief that business activity should be made as simple as possible. All work that is not absolutely necessary will either need to be justified and retained, or eliminated. It is the elimination approach that cuts work and staff. In some cases, work is just stopped and in other cases it is automated. Both scenarios will cause a reduction in headcount. This approach has both positives and negatives. While a company can become lean, it can also become so lean that it now lacks the elasticity to support change or do anything other than "heads down" performance of those tasks that are left in the operation.

> *Note: Lean is an approach that is focused on driving out cost in a business or manufacturing operation. It uses value stream identification, modeling, and analysis to identify activity that does not add value to the creation of a service or product. The goal is to use this information to determine where cost can be driven out. It is strongly recommended that the reader look up Lean evaluation and Lean performance management and integrate the philosophies and techniques into their professional skills.*

If your organization has adopted Six Sigma and/or Lean, we highly recommend that readers consider certification in Lean, Six Sigma, and Project Management. This will ensure that your approach to business transformation, project management, et al., is consistent with what is being used by others in the company.

Do NOT reduce staff to the point where people are expected to work "heads down" for 8 or more hours a day. People cannot do that and work quality will suffer. If you do not factor in an acceptable amount of unproductive time (e.g., lunch, coffee breaks, bathroom breaks, or smoke breaks to name a few), you will NEVER be able to maintain performance numbers. You must be realistic in any work standards. This may be dictated by union contracts. If not, it may be dictated by HR. If the company has no standards, work with business managers who will be affected by the project solution and create one. These standards will be used in all performance estimates and measurement.

Always be realistic in cutting work and time. It is very possible to cut too much through unrealistic fervor. Always put yourself in the place of the people for whom you are redesigning the work. You can cut to the point where too much work is piled on too few people. When this happens, quality will be a problem and people will leave and take their knowledge of how the job should be performed and the way rules should be applied with them. The fact is that people make the business work. They make poor business designs work. They provide the flexibility to adjust to change. When the more experienced people leave, the company suffers. So be careful what you cut and how deeply you cut.

When dealing with a business unit, start by looking at what it must provide to others – products, services, reports, etc. Are all of these things absolutely needed by those who receive them?

Eliminate any that are not really necessary. Then look at how the business has divided work – are there really lower level business functions or are they really just aggregation of work. If they are functions, they should be treated as individual groups of work and workflow. Again, determine if all are needed and define why they are needed – who relies on what the function produces and can they do without it? For all functions that are needed, confirm timing, content, quality, standards, etc., and identify problems. You are now ready to redesign the business area.

The use of simulation with the "As Is" model will help to identify and validate things that are unnecessary. When something becomes a candidate for elimination, verification that it is not needed elsewhere in the process must be carried out to ensure upstream or downstream steps are not negatively affected. If the "As Is" model is not complete from beginning to end, then this is a particular risk that must be addressed.

Look for places in the work where operational problems have been encountered. These are "break points" in the workflow or at a higher level of a business model or processes, and are points where a quality problem is first identified. The root cause might be unknown at this point, but you will be able to identify where the problem is first discovered and be able to define what to look for in the work or products. In other words, the characteristics in the data or workflow that lead you to know that a problem has occurred. If problem identification at this point is missed, then look for "break points" at different areas downstream. If "break points" are found, these should be linked together to form an identification chain. The team should then follow each characteristic back upstream in the workflow to identify its root cause and design it out of existence.

Handoffs are particularly vulnerable to "break point" problems and, as a result, the steps where handoffs occur should be specifically checked to determine if there are current problems. If metrics do not currently exist for handoffs, they may have to be created manually to see if there is a problem, and if so, the scope.

Find any Lean or Six Sigma standards that the solution will need to embed or follow. Confirm their use and how each is intended to be used, noting each time a standard is used. This will show compliance with the standard.

Document the places where a standard, compliance requirement, or reporting requirement is used in the "As Is" models and where they are applied in the "To Be" design. Enter this into the automated modeler with a note on the business workflow model or in comments in the activity's supporting data each time a standard is applied. This can also be accomplished by making the standard a rule, then noting the use of the rule, just as you should note the use of all rules.

Every process, sub-process or functional workflow in a business unit must be able to deliver the capabilities required to meet the needs of the business or services. These capabilities will be delivered through one or more business units. Capabilities are the "what" the activity must be able to do and can be delivered as part of one or more workflows.

Capability descriptions are not business cases. Capabilities are created through the combined work in multiple activities. For example, you want the ability to walk across the street. In order to do so, you must be capable to use your legs to stand, use your vision to look for oncoming traffic, and use your motor skills to walk forward.

Business cases should represent specific business situations, events, interactions, or deliverables.

There are many situations where a business case also addresses a specific customer segment. This may occur, for example, for a business case for carrying out a retail transaction via a mobile channel. Different capabilities will be required for carrying out the same transaction via a phone call or a website. Each should be addressed for the specific customer segment even though there can be considerable overlap in the overall activities. Customer segments may also be served by separate business units, but may merge with other segments upstream and downstream.

The redesign must create a framework for the project. This is the identification, definition, description, and interaction among different execution level business functions.

Identify all the data elements that will be used in each task and list them by application system. If the application will be generated, list them by the workflow activity or, at a lower level of decomposition, the activity's tasks, or the task's steps.

All projects are intended to change an aspect of the business for the better. Whether the intent is to reduce costs, streamline processes, improve the customer experience, or put in place regulatory or compliance requirements, all projects inherently deliver a change. How this change is designed and the effectiveness of the solution is a function of how well the project team creates a view of the "To Be". The "To Be" defines what the new business environment will be like. It needs to deliver on business objectives and do it better than things are done today. As a result, the team needs to be clear on how to design the "To Be." This starts with:

- Understanding the business objectives and the business requirements of the "To Be" design
- Identifying all assumptions about how things are done today (which may have been constraining the business) and questioning each. Too often deeply held assumptions are not articulated and become "facts" when in reality they are often simply constraints that have evolved over time, and in fact may no longer apply.
- Leveraging the skills around process optimization that are part of the BPM foundation so that a solution can be designed that is both efficient (low cost) and effective (high quality meeting customer experience requirements).

Once you know what data you will be working with, begin collaboration with the company's IT Architect or data administrator.

User stories are a great tool to clearly define the experience that you are seeking in order to create the design of the "To Be". The user story completely captures the desired outcome of a business situation, and is a representation from the end users perspective. The accuracy and completeness of the documentation allows the design team to fully understand the business situation/logic/rules that are to be supported so that an optimal solution can be designed, developed and tested. A user story also serves as a common set of documentation that is agreed to and signed off by the business sponsors/partners, ensuring that there is alignment and agreement around what needs to be solved. User stories follow a standard set of documentation which focuses on capturing:

As a <type of user>, I want <some goal> so that <some reason>

User stories are short and to the point. They can be written on index cards or sticky notes and arranged on walls or tables to facilitate planning and discussion. As such, they shift the focus from writing about features to discussing them. It is in these discussions that the business better describes the use case and it allows the design team the opportunity to fully understand the intent from a business perspective. These discussions are often more important than the text that is written.

Determine who on the team will need to be added to the tool license and how people will be trained. Identify when training will be needed and schedule it.

4.4 Redesign business workflow - future state ("To Be")

Business redesign is the chance to leverage the business transformation team's knowledge and creativity. It is an opportunity to move from an operation that may have serious efficiency issues and inadequate IT support, to a new operating model that is based on modern management practices, with updated and vetted business rules, and state of the art BPMS-generated applications. It is also a chance to clean up data, find better sources of data, improve data collection and most importantly, modernize the way groups in the company interact with customers.

In doing this, everything must be questioned and put under the proverbial microscope to define the value it delivers and how it contributes to the creation of a product or service. Everything that is done must answer the questions:

- Is this really necessary – can we do without it?
- Is this redundant with other work that is being done?
- Is this effective in delivering our service or product component?
- Does the way this is done today, help or hurt the company's ability to provide a high quality product or service and to attract and keep customers?
- Can this be done more efficiently?
- Can we find a way to make the interaction with our customers a better experience for them?

The design team will base the changes to the current baseline model on the requirements and goals in the project request and the requirements list that was created in the "As Is" model analysis. All requirements will need to be addressed. All problems need to be eliminated or mitigated, and all performance issues need to be analyzed and performance improved. In addition to these improvements, the project team, working with IT, must improve the ability for the business operation to change quickly – at low cost and risk. It must also improve the ability of the business to scale work and adjust to changes in volume.

The BPM-based approach to creating a high quality redesign is based on iteration – evolve the design until it is good. This has caused issues because each iteration improvement has been an educated guess as to how to improve the prior iteration. Also, there was no really good way to determine the real improvement of any iteration. This has caused iteration to become a circular activity in many projects – one that just keeps going.

A newer version of this approach, based on iBPM (intelligent BPM), is to create a new business operating design (hopefully, an innovative one) and run it through a simulation tool. This will point out design issues that affect efficiency. The resolution of these issues is then used as the guide in improving the next iteration. This cycle continues until the simulation analysis says the design is optimal – or depending on the company and its culture, until it is good enough.

Note: For most purposes close to optimal is good. It often takes an inordinate amount of work to get the last small inefficiencies out of any process or workflow.

The project team should work closely with the business managers and staff as well as collaborative partners during this design process. All concepts and ideas should be vetted with the business managers and staff. The results of the design's changes should also be reviewed with the business groups that give information to some point in the process or workflow and receive information from the workflow. These considerations will reduce the issues with connections to other process flows and business area workflows.

We also urge that every design team learn what business, manufacturing production, and IT capabilities they can leverage today and in the future so they can be used in the design. This will set the limits on the "box" that the solution can operate within and thus constraints that need to be considered in the new business design.

In performing the activities in the future state or "To Be" design, it is important to keep foremost in everyone's minds the reason that the project is being performed, and who it is being performed for. This means that it is being done to improve the business operation for the benefit of the working staff and the customers. If done right, the value to the business and the improvement in the way the work can be performed will deliver high measurable value, make the applications easy to use, and remove interaction/buying barriers between the company and the customer. The result should be a new, customer friendly, efficient, and effective new business operation.

That is the ultimate goal of any transformation project. Putting in new applications and technology is not the ultimate goal. The goal is to improve the ability of the business to compete and to manage cost and quality. The team's customer is not IT. It is first the end customers and secondly the business unit workers that will need to perform the activities. All barriers to their interaction with the company for any purpose should be removed or simplified in any transformation project.

When building "To Be" designs, the team should make certain that the following are addressed:

- Workflow models that identify each activity that will be performed and the order they will be executed in – this may start at a process level or in a business unit at a workflow level
- These models will be decomposed or broken down, to a task or step level (the two levels below the activity flow level) to show the use of application systems
- Any decision in a workflow may have multiple outcomes. Each of these outcomes is a separate decision exit (result)
- All rules that govern work – rules need to be vetted with business management, HR, Legal, Finance, and in some cases collaborative partners to ensure their accuracy
- All application use and at the task level, data use, data flow, data edits, data transform, etc.
- Workflow, staff workload assignment, work list, issues
- Policy, procedure, rules issues
- All problems and what activities they impact – and how the activities are impacted
- All performance measurement data collection points for monitoring in the workflow
- Quality issues and what they apply to
- Customer interaction issues and where they occur
- Transaction volume, timing, content/quality, problems
- Human resource issues – training, compliance, union, etc.
- Volume issues and timing
- Notes on things that should be considered
- Legal and financial regulatory compliance requirements

As these design elements are considered, it is important to look at them in the context of the requirements that the solution will need to deliver and make certain that any people to people, people to computer, computer to computer interaction is as simplistic as possible.

As the new design is evolving, it is recommended that the changes be evaluated with IT to determine if any changes to the IT infrastructure or new IT tools will be required. These changes should be discussed with IT and the project sponsor and potential costs and impact defined. If approved, the solution design team can move forward. If denied, the team will need to adjust and consider the denied technology as a constraint.

It should be noted that as soon as the new business solution design is completed, the interfaces and all technology modules will be known. Although neither the requirements nor technical program spec will yet be written, it will be possible for IT to begin to define interfaces and data requirements. This will allow them to get a start on constructing the components of the solution that are external to the BPMS-generated applications.

Begin by making certain that you have a list of all the business and IT rules that must be applied to the new design. Make sure that the rules have been vetted by the business managers, Legal, Finance (for compliance), and the extended team – collaborative partners. The rules may affect each of these participants and failure to capture all the rules accurately may produce overall compliance issues or hurt their ability to work effectively and efficiently. Without sound, known, and vetted rules, any new design that the team comes up with may be un-implementable.

Large projects are like rocks, not pebbles dropping into a still pond. They have impacts that will cross organizational, functional, and business boundaries. As a result, it is important that large, especially transformational projects, create a tight link between all of the architectural professionals that inhabit organizations. This includes, and is not limited to, business architects, process architects, technology (enterprise) architects, and organizational architects. Each of these architectural disciplines has a unique set of skills and their own view of the organization and individually, each can be myopic in their view of the organization. For example, a process architect will find a process solution for every business issue or objective, whereas the technology architect will seek to solve things with additional investment in technology systems, and organizational architects will seek to structure, restructure and/or change jobs and roles to solve their perceived view of the organization around them.

Each adds value in their own way. It is the role of a project manager to harness each of these disciplines and leverage them together to build a highly effective team that can develop appropriate solutions that deliver on the projects goals. Harmonizing this set of resources is like getting an orchestra to create amazing music together, initially each instrument will be out of sync with the others, and each will try to be heard as a unique voice. Ultimately, the orchestra leader, or the project manager, will bring the different voices into harmony and, together, create magic. It is with this mindset that projects can deliver truly amazing results.

Pushing the new design envelope can test the bounds of the team's and business managers' limits on creativity and innovation. The issue is, "how far should a project team really go?" It is very possible to create a design that cannot be built, is too costly to be built, or that simply does not have the ability to overcome known or hidden financial or cultural barriers.

Solving for the 80/20 rule. Too often a project team will seek a solution for 100% of all business activities. In reality, a good 20%+ of business activities are exceptions that need to be either eliminated as part of "To Be" business operations design or possibly left alone. This 20% can be addressed as part of a second phase of change. Dwelling on it initially will simply take time and deliver little value.

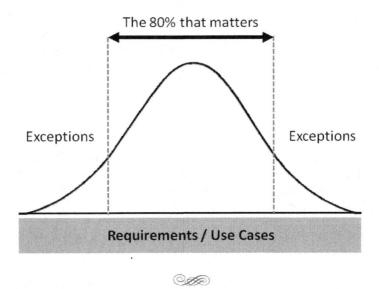

If the 80/20 rule is valid, logic will dictate that pushing the envelope and taking risks should be avoided. In fact, the opposite is true. The project team needs to question assumptions, design criteria, even business requirements as they analyze and develop design considerations. This forms the foundation for designing the solution. With sponsor and business area manager support, the habit of questioning the foundation concepts, ideas, actions, and decisions allows for creativity in design, which is valued by the business.

BPM teams are not necessarily supposed to create the 100% best and most optimized business process. The team should be focused on making the business as effective and optimized as possible within financial and other constraints. This distinction is vital due to the fact that too many teams will focus on solving all aspects of a process, while the business is concerned about the cost of delivering their ideal customer experience. Also, why spend time and resources improving activities that are seldom executed? Why automate work that is seldom performed? So why do we seek to optimize the entire process, including all exception processing? Why not focus on the 80% of the functions that are executed frequently? Business is focused on delivering results.

It is critical that the entire team understand the business operations in scope, how it/they work, why, and its problems. This provides a common base for determining changes, identifying sprints, and the user stories that will be developed. Through this understanding, a design can be created that defines all change, and then structure an incremental Agile-based approach to delivering improvement. In this approach, a high level new conceptual design will be built based on changes in the current operation needed to optimize it.

Never assume any significant technical sophistication in a user. Always design and build a business solution for someone who has never seen a computer. Make any use of an IT tool as simple as possible. Embed as much of the operation into the tool, based on rules, as you can. Do not design things for people like yourself – you know too much about technology to make anything obvious for a non-tech user. Technology is only good if people can figure out how to use it. Have designs tested by non-tech users and gather their reactions, both positive and negative.

As part of the design process for customer facing portions of the new solution, review the types of inquiries and assistance requests that are currently coming into your tech support chat and call centers. These requests often begin to form patterns that can help pinpoint areas that may need attention in the new design.

When designing a solution and conducting User Acceptance Testing, be sure to create mechanisms in the new process that forewarn of gaps or eventual failure points in delivering the customer experience. These are called "customer signals" and provide a valuable means to correct processes/customer experiences before they go wrong. Examples include tracking the amount of time a customer is on a phone call before their issue is correctly identified. If a customer has to reiterate their issue over and over again, or supply the same account number to multiple customer care representatives, it will invariably end in a frustrated customer. Capture these interaction points before they become an issue. Another example is a claim that is processed multiple times because it falls outside of the "normal" algorithm. If a claim cannot be processed correctly, there is a flaw in the solution that should be corrected vs. accepting that the claim will be reworked multiple times. Always design solutions with both the experience and the ultimate outcome in mind.

A short list of key considerations for solution design includes (but is not limited to) the following:

- Rules that govern the process being delivered
- Data types and how they will be used
- Security features to ensure the integrity and access of information
- User interfaces with the process
- Signals/alerts within the process to forewarn delivery/process breakdowns
- Analytics to support the customer experience and to provide information to make better and more informed decisions

- Reports needed to support decision-making and/or measure results (financial, risk, performance, etc.)

Each of these elements needs to be considered in the solution design steps.

From the project definition in the request, project setup, and the "As Is" business analysis, identify all business requirements that the solution will need to support. All must be formalized and reconfirmed with all who will be affected by the project as the new business operating design activity begins – they have often changed by this time, so this is a critical step that is often overlooked.

Any new business design must be outcome focused. The eye must always be on the business results and how new business operation will function. BPMS tools, legacy applications, the IT environment and IT methodology are all enablers or constraints. Do not let the focus move from the business operation to the way the solution will be built or on the use of technology in the design. Both are means to an end – the business outcome.

Do not allow a solution to become technology enablement rich and business operation execution poor. Many solutions have great technical applications, but fail because those applications are difficult to use or fail to make the work, workflow, and tasks easier for the business staff on the floor.

When looking at the order in which the solution will be built, look for what groupings of changes can be built to solve a serious problem or support a strategic goal. Pull these components out of the complete solution design for creation first. These groups should deliver the highest benefit and should be built and deployed first, if possible. If these capability groups can be built first, they can start to deliver benefit much sooner than other capability groups, thereby changing the ROI curve.

Start the business redesign by identifying the high impact processes and address them first. Do not start by identifying business cases and dividing them into Agile sprints. Once you have the whole process or set of workflows in a business unit addressed, you will have the new operational context for the creation of the solution.

Within the group of high impact processes, first focus on those that have a low operational maturity – areas that are largely manual, poorly automated, heavy requirement for paper pushing, etc.

Efficiency is not always the primary goal of process or workflow redesign. At times, the focus will be on building an operation that can respond to change quickly to survive in a volatile market or a heavily regulated environment. At other times, the focus may be on reducing error and improving quality or it may be on customer experience.

Effectiveness should be the first goal in workflow redesign. Doing unnecessary activities faster and cheaper doesn't get you very much. For this reason, efficiency is secondary to effectiveness. The operation must only perform the right work at the right places in the workflow – this can be defined as the activities/tasks needed to deliver a high quality service or product. Anything that does not directly contribute to this product delivery should be questioned and, if possible, eliminated with the goal of removing significant portions of work. Once an optimal effective process has been reached, the design can focus on efficiency.

Be judicious in looking at promoting staff enablement or operational creativity in the business staff. There are places where you want the rigor of a rigid process and places where you want agility. Be able to justify the approach you are taking (flexible or rigid) and the benefit the approach brings to the redesigned business operation. The same is true for IT application support – you don't always need everything to be automated and you don't always want support to be bound by inflexible rules. As the business designer, you have to make choices that will either constrain or free staff, and the way they work within the company and the way they interact with customers.

Simplify the business operation whenever possible. Complexity is simply a symptom of a poor design. Complexity should be put into applications systems where it can be handled behind the scenes.

Multi-tasking – do not build multitasking into a new design. In fact, forbid it. There is a saying that describes multi-tasking perfectly - there is no limit to the number of things you can do poorly. The fact is that people who brag about their ability to multi-task are just kidding themselves.

Placing information on the data elements that are used in each activity into spreadsheets will help data architects and analysts find issues, such as alpha characters in normally numeric fields and vice versa, variable character lengths within fixed format fields, errant special characters, values that exceed min or max, etc. This information will be collected during the "To Be" design. To make certain that the right information is collected, the business solution team should work with the IT data architects before the design is started. It is also a good idea to have an experienced user review these data requirements to identify anything they know from experience that does not appear to belong.

Start with the "As Is" or Current State business model and correct any obvious issues or weaknesses in the work or workflow.

An alternative approach is to begin with a "blank sheet" of paper and start over as if you were designing a new company or activity. This was proposed by Michael Hammer in the mid 1990's and can produce a future target design. The problem is that this future design does not consider current reality and constraints and generally cannot be built today. However, if the team is looking to produce a future target and then a series of design steps that help the company evolve over time to that model, this approach may work for the company.

Using the problem identification in the "As Is" model creation, list all problems and define what is being done to resolve them, mitigate them, or live with them (work around activities).

Eliminate all redundancy and unnecessary work. Cut it out of the workflow tasks, but make certain any business unit or business group receiving something from the redundant work is linked back to the version left in a workflow.

Remove all work that just doesn't make sense. When you understand the purpose of the work and the way the business area works, some tasks will just not make sense – you will ask yourself, "why do they do that?" Check to make certain that the definition that describes the work is correct and then analyze the reason for the work. If it is not needed, delete it.

Eliminate the cause of all operational problems and process errors by redesigning them out of existence. If it is not possible to eliminate operational problems and process errors, wrap their causes in a layer of monitoring to detect the situations that build to the problem and design in alerts.

Strip out all unneeded rules and activity that stop flexibility. You will now be down to basic level workflows. Remember, simple is good. Next, check the work against business requirements and add back in tasks that will be needed to deliver these requirements. Add in all activities needed for compliance monitoring and reporting regulations. Identify how performance will be tracked and how it will be reported. Build performance monitoring, measurement, and reporting into the design (Six Sigma, activity-based costing, standard volume and timing limits, deviation reporting and other checks, can be used).

Compliance and regulatory rules must always be known and fully understood. They can have profound implications on the design and implementation of the "To Be" solution. Be sure to have representation from legal/compliance on the team, especially when the project touches, even to a minor degree, any processes that need regulatory approval.

Evaluate all decisions and their approval/determination rules. Streamline by first eliminating any decisions that are not absolutely needed. Second, eliminate any unnecessary decision rules – especially those that cause delays in the workflow. Automate as many decisions as possible by embedding them in the workflow. Put timers on each manual decision with alerts to keep the decision timing within standard performance specs.

Since handoffs to different organizational units are fertile ground for breakdowns, needed skills should be considered as just as important as which units execute a particular task. If needed skills already exist or can be readily developed through training, then relocation of a task should be seriously considered. Better yet, if the needed skills can be operationalized through business rules contained in a BPMS, the handoff can be eliminated without any additional skill development.

Legacy application changes needed to support the new operating business model will be identified in the new model associated with the activities they support. All legacy application capabilities will be identified and defined first in the business model at the activity or lower task (step) level, and then compared against available application capabilities to see if there are features available but not being used by that business area. All identified changes to currently used applications will then become a decision by the IT application managers. Decisions around changing a legacy application, generating a new one through the BPMS, licensing a new application or building a new application must be reviewed and acted upon. The requirements for any change or new application will be shown in the capabilities listed for each activity. To obtain a complete picture of support, the business analyst and the IT analyst should work together to pull requirements from all the activities (or lower level of detail) and then see how they should be combined to deliver the best mix of application delivery approaches.

When an application is designed, it should be designed not only to deliver the stated requirements for each business activity, but it should also follow the flow of work to support the way people work and the sequence in which they will be doing things according to the new operation design.

Check to make certain that all information that is needed to drive simulations is collected and entered into the simulation model. Next, run the simulation. It will show flow and bottleneck problems.

When looking at exception handling, consider the cost of handling in the redesign – if an exception is hit a few times a year, you need to ask if it is worth automation or even much consideration. Focus on the high volume exceptions and handle those in a manner that reduces work, increases quality and simplifies the operation to reduce human error. This is where the real benefit can be found; it is not in seldom executed exceptions. Leave the rest for another time and create a manual way to handle them. The same goes for low impact problems or ones that are infrequent. Spend time on the big things first and worry about the small things in the future. This approach is seldom considered, but it is much more realistic and cost effective.

Utilizing the combination of compliance management requirements, financial monitoring, customer experience, and other requirement sources, create the first "To Be" design iteration.

Look up and confirm all legal and financial compliance management (monitoring, evaluation, reporting) rules and standards. Work with IT and Legal, Finance, clinical, or whoever needs to be involved to identify the required data, the data sources, the way the information is collected/counted/evaluated, and the format and media for reporting. Legal, Finance, clinical or another responsible manager must formally review the data content, source, collection, calculation, and reporting solution and formally approve it.

Eliminating work can leave holes in the workflow and it can break information dependencies or links to other work. All holes must be addressed and any disconnected work must be reconnected. When doing this, be careful not to build in complexity or unnecessary steps.

In many cases, complete aggregations of tasks will be performed based on a specific business case, document, answer to a question, etc. These should be considered to be "response scenarios". They are executed only when a specific situation occurs or when a specific set of answers is given. These "situations" can become a complex, interrelated groups of scenarios.

For example, in the insurance industry, response scenarios can include questions to further focus activity – such as "what type of insurance would you like to purchase?" The answer to this question will then direct activity and questions/scripts to a specific second level of questions. Those answers may move the conversation to a third even more focused set of questions. These actions will cause activity/workflow branching based on answers to questions. However, once you build one scenario, it can be reused (with modification) for all of the types of insurance that is sold. This will save you time and help you control the reuse of rules and application design (BPMN use).

Iteration is a great concept and approach. However, it must be used the right way. If a simulation tool is used to check the new business design, it will show what to change in the next iteration. This focuses the nature of the new changes. One must remember however, that the law of diminishing results applies here; the biggest improvements are in the first few iterations. After that, the improvements become smaller and smaller. The question is "at what point is enough, enough?" Is a small benefit iteration worth the time and cost of another iteration? This concept applies if the design is supported by manually drawn models or by models supported using a business process analysis tool.

The data models, schemas, and definitions will have been defined during Chapter 3 "As Is" discovery and analysis activities, then confirmed and modified in the "To Be" workflows as part of the new solution design. These data models will need to be used to define sources of information and reporting content possibilities.

Identify how CSF and KPI measurement will fit into a new design. Build the data requirements, measurement requirements, and reporting requirements into the new design at the points where the data is being created/obtained/transformed/edited.

Define performance monitoring support and then link it to activity. Design it into the automated part of the solution and have the application keep track of timing, volume, and other performance information to comply with company performance monitoring standards. Design performance reports to capture the appropriate information of the activity. Also build live, real time alerts into the workflow based on performance measurement. If something is counted, the system can keep track of standards, such as X number over Y time. When it is likely that this will not be met, the system should send an alert to management. When it is exceeded, the system should send a warning to management and take whatever response action management has predefined should be taken. All alerts and warnings should be tracked along with impact.

Define the predictive analytics needed for the workflow and the ways data will build at given points, looking for limits, trends, etc. Build inference capabilities (based on rules) that infer a course of action from the trends or from action historically taken in a given combination of conditions. Use this to drive business intelligence reporting that helps management leverage trends and other operational information in order to determine the best way to mitigate, avoid, or leverage business capabilities, processes, etc.

Ensure that all the information in the business solution models is available and that those reports defined as BPMS-generated reports are built and tested.

Test applications against tech specs, interfaces, screen delivery, data availability and access, business use, usability in the business, and evolve with the user or IT to make the applications accomplish what is required.

There is an old adage, "...don't pave the cow paths." This refers to the risk that the old processes are so engrained in the business that the only possible change is to formalize the old process and even automate it when in fact these old processes need to be completely thrown away and eliminated. After years of walking the same path over and over, a cow may be following a route that is miles longer than if the path were straightened out, providing a more direct access to the green fields of clover that it is headed for. Processes can be like these old paths. They are well known, documented, and work. As humans, we also like the certainty of the old path, and we do not naturally seek a different path when then old way works. In business, this old way can be costing the company significant resources and time. The process may have delays which affect the cycle time in ways that are not immediately obvious. When designing the "To Be," be mindful of the cow paths and the natural tendency to hang onto the old roadmap. As a BPM professional we know that old maps only capture what is immediately known. If the explorers of 1500 A.D. had a complete map of the world, they would have never tried to reach India by sailing west from Europe. Let your business objectives/requirements and clear definitions of business logic/rules define your path forward.

The solution model should include everything needed to build and run the new operation – including rules, decisions, metrics, applications, monitoring, new equipment, and reporting.

Comparative analysis is a useful tool to do a rapid evaluation as well as a detailed analysis. A key in using this tool is ensuring that the criteria used to form the basis of the comparative analysis represent the "To Be" that you are designing towards. For example, if the team has created two alternate solutions, a comparative analysis will help determine which is most appropriate for the "To Be" design. Factors such as costs, process time duration, delays and decision points are all important factors, but there are several that should be considered as priority. These include alignment and delivery of business objectives and delivering on the desired customer experience.

The new business design should include BPMS requirements and BPMN models with data models, access to external applications, access requirements to databases, legacy application/social mobility apps/website interfaces, web services, etc.

During the "To Be" design, make sure that all of the business partners are at the table thinking about alternative solutions. This includes not only the upper management of the business areas, but also the managers and employees. After all, they understand best what needs to be delivered!

Always include IT early in the "To Be" ideation stage. If a solution is too complex, it might also be too expensive to design/deploy/support from an IT perspective. It is better to find this out before the team creates the "perfect" solution, only to discover that the business cannot afford the IT implications.

Establish an idea box on the company website - or the BPM CoE website to solicit input from across the organization. Employees move from job to job over the years and there are always people in other organizational areas that either have history with, or a unique perspective on, the problem your team is seeking to solve. The more people contributing to a solution, the better the design and adoption will be.

When identifying "low hanging fruit," be sure that the opportunity really can be implemented quickly with nominal cost and negligible impact to the business. Sometimes a "low hanging fruit" idea is part of someone's personal agenda and can be very difficult to put in place and risks the reputation of the overall team.

When creating a project prioritization algorithm, be sure to update it annually to reflect changes in the business strategy and associated business objectives.

Establish a business area/IT committee to look at emerging tech and business techniques and determine the potential benefits to the solution space that the team is focused on. However, do not become enamored with the "shiny rock syndrome," that is thinking that the latest technology will be just the ticket for easily solving the business problem at hand.

4.5 Prepare "To Be" business design for workflow simulation

The new design will be built in iterations – a basic part of the BPM concept. Each design will be reviewed by the team for additional improvements. This is generally done manually today as the teams go through the designs over and over looking for new ways to be creative and for improvements that can be made. Each review and set of changes is one iteration. This process relies on the experience of the team to improve the design and eliminate inefficiency over time as it goes through iterations.

We have found that simulation tools greatly improve this process. These tools are fairly inexpensive and can make a significant difference in the time it takes to finalize the design and the quality of the design. However, as with the first time any tool is used, time will need to be built into the project for training.

Simulation is one of the major advances of iBPM over BPM. The goal in simulation is operational efficiency – you are checking workflow for a variety of conditions. The second goal is to save time in the iteration cycle by using the results of the simulation to focus on improvements that should be made to the next iteration of the design. Today, the team moves from iteration to iteration in design by educated guesswork. From experience, teams will find issues with a design and then in the next iteration improve the design. However, they seldom find all of the issues or opportunities for improvement in any iteration and the iteration cycles continue on and on as new issues are introduced in changes made in prior iterations and missed improvements are discovered. This is the real "Achilles heel" of BPM-based iteration – it can get out of hand and virtually never end. This is also a key issue in defining requirements – once the business model is accepted and the requirements for the new solution are defined, they will be used to create the new solution. Changes after this design acceptance and requirement definition can be costly, but they can also be controlled through Agile change control processes.

The simulation tool used will have an impact on the way the simulation must be approached. For example, if the simulation tool is a module in a BPMS, it will be integrated with the modeler and the way applications are generated. If the simulation tool is separate, the results will need to be applied to the solution model in the modeling tool that is being used or the BPMS models that are being created.

If the simulation system is new, the team will need to work with the vendor and IT to have the programs installed and tested. The team will need to be trained and their understanding of the tool tested.

The standards for any BPM project that is supported by a business modeler, business analysis tool, or a BPMS should include standards for the data that will be needed for business design simulation. These standards should be aligned to the simulation tool that is being used and the data it requires.

Regardless of whether the simulation system is old or new, the project manager will also need to work with IT to deal with access security, data storage, and other IT application operations issues. Any team members who are new to the simulation tool will need to be trained – and their knowledge tested prior to their use of the tool.

To prepare for simulation, the team should work with the simulation system's vendor to clearly define all data requirements. If the simulation engine has been used in other projects, the list of data that will be needed should have been available to the team for the "As Is" information collection and analysis. If this is the case, the data will have been collected and it will be available for the team at this time. If not, the team will need to work with the business user to collect the data – or if it does not exist, to help them put collection mechanisms in place as the "To Be" design phase of the project begins. This is done so that some baseline data is available.

The use of simulation will provide proof that the design is optimal when the tool no longer indicates serious errors in the efficiency of the workflow. This is a significant step because without simulation, the design team cannot prove that any design that is proposed will be more efficient than the one in place. It is also important because simulation saves time and reduces risk by focusing the change from one iteration to the next to identify the places in the workflow where improvements need to be considered.

Simulation modeling is the real foundation capability in any move to iBPM. It is the single most important capability - separating traditional BPM iteration (even IT Agile iteration) from iBPM. The key difference is that a full business operation design can be quickly iterated by running each iteration through the simulation tool and using the analytics it offers as a guide to focus the next round of improvements to the operation design. In this way, iteration moves from improvement guesswork to guided improvement. The reports from the simulator also allow design teams to know when a design reaches an optimal state of efficiency – no remaining serious efficiency issues are reported.

Simulation will tell you when a design is efficient. It will not tell you when it is effective.

Simulation, as used in this section of the hints book, refers to the optimization of process flow or workflow. Although this simulation can be done manually, it is an onerous activity. In fact, for most uses, unless you use an automated tool, it is not worth it.

The BPMS simulation module will be used to simulate change and try/test/apply innovative ideas to the business operation model and to IT support. This will help to uncover solutions that are less complex and have a higher acceptance level by the business partners.

One of the major problems historically has been the inability to really test business or IT application designs until the solution was built. Traditionally, each iteration of any design has been reviewed in a process often referred to as "desk checking" by the project team. Improvements are based on experience, creativity and educated guesses. The result is that some improvements are better than others and some "improvements" have actually been catastrophic. But, there was simply no way to tell what the real outcome of an idea would be. Today, with iBPM and simulation, that has changed. Each iteration of a business design can now be run through a simulation tool and the workflow checked for a variety of problems. Volume -related problems can also be predicted along with a variety of other tests. These tests point to the changes needed for the next iteration of the design. The design is optimally efficient when the simulation cannot find additional faults.

To prepare for the operation redesign simulation, the team will need to check that the design is complete. If not, the simulation modeler will tell you. The team will also need to make certain the rules that apply to the operation are complete and their conversion for entry into the rules engine produced properly coded rules. Finally, the team will need to make certain that the models have associated the data the simulation tool requires.

Simulation, volume data, timing data, rate data, error data and more may not all be available. In these cases, work with the business manager to create initial metrics. To improve these estimated metrics, initiate manual transaction counting and other counting to improve the data over time. If you start this during the "As Is" modeling activity, the data will be fairly good by the time the new business operation design is ready.

4.6 Perform "To Be" model simulation - iterate until workflow optimization

The objective of using simulation in workflow redesign is two-fold. First, it will check the design of the workflow to make certain it is efficient. It will tell you where bottlenecks are, where decision mistakes are made, where parallel processing is a problem and much more. Secondly, it will also provide direction to the places where improvements can be made and what those improvements should be. Simulation modeling will not, however, tell you whether or not the design is effective or if it will deliver the targets or goals of the business redesign. Solution effectiveness and the ability of the solution to deliver target goals can be tested in a full solution simulation once the BPMS applications have been generated. See Chapter 4, section 10, (4.10 Conduct BPMS Generated solution simulation and iteration).

The purpose of iteration is to support the introduction of new ideas and new approaches into a design for a new business operation. The benefit of simulation is that it allows you to not only try these new ideas, but also to ask "what if" questions about volumes and test performance in different operating scenarios.

The initial solution model and supporting information will be as good as the team can make them. The first simulation iterations should not be expected to find that the solution is optimal.

An analysis of this information will, however, point to problems and help focus improvements for the next iteration.

All needed data should be entered into the simulation system/engine and an initial iteration of the design simulation run. This will likely point to missing data, misapplied data, model problems, and more. This initial iteration is really a "shake out" run that allows the team to create a real working simulation. The second iteration is thus the real first test of the solution design.

Each iteration that is run through the simulation engine should be formally reviewed and the results analyzed to determine what really improved in the business operation and what should be changed further. This analysis will be the foundation for deciding how and where the next iteration should be changed. This also allows the team to anticipate the results of the change and test for actual workflow/rule/decision improvement.

Once the "To Be" business operation workflow design has been proven to be efficient through an iterative, focused simulation process, it will be ready to be used to create solution requirements and technical specifications (specs).

The "As Is" simulation will have created a baseline of the current operation – complete with data. The "To Be" simulation should begin with this information to test improvement over the current operation. From this point, improvement scenarios can be run to look at changing workload and transaction volumes by categories – such as degree of difficulty or customer preference.

These new volume and other assumptions that define a given future business operation scenario will show how the solution will perform in different situations and allow the team to improve the operation of the solution.

Once optimized, the team will be faced with another fact – the proven efficiency of a workflow improvement does not guarantee that business targets will be met by the solution design. To do this, the solution will need to run through a different type of simulation. This simulation will test the ability of the solution to actually produce results. Here we suggest that a Model Office that mirrors the real operation be built to test activity and response in a semi-live operation.

This approach assumes that the company will use a BPMS tool to generate a set of core applications that support the design. This is the heart of the new operation's capabilities and operating model. Legacy application changes and other applications external to the BPMS-generated applications may also be needed to complete the solution.

No solution will remain optimal for long – it may even be out of date with respect to the business operations and their needs when the solution is delivered. This does not mean that the solution construction should be stopped, and updated with the changed requirements, and then continuously rebuilt. If you do that, you will never deliver anything. Checkpoint the requirements on a monthly or frequent cycle until the solution simulation is completed and then temporarily "freeze the requirements." If you don't do this, you will spend all your time iterating and never deliver a solution. At this point, the solution completion will be a rapid process and the business should not be far out of sync when the solution is delivered.

At solution delivery, the continuous refinement iteration process takes the place of the build process and the solution begins to evolve. This allows the solution to catch up with the changes that have occurred since the requirements were frozen. This is where BPM and BPMS really start to make a difference – solution evolution at this point is very fast, allowing the solution to catch up and stay in tune with the needs of the business.

Optimal is a great target, but be prepared to back off a little. It is possible for optimal to cause a total loss of flexibility and creativity in dealing with real world situations. Be sure to build in flexibility. For example, the number of cases a person can handle will be impacted by a lot of factors outside of their control – such as a power outage, slow network response time, application outage, and the list goes on. Build in contingency processing for disasters and for mini disasters and the normal things that affect work.

Never accept that something cannot be done without an explanation as to why. Then document it as a constraint.

Never accept that something *must* be done without an explanation as to why. Then document the details of the why.

Always question everything and search for the real answer – it is often different from the one you will be given. Ask questions on the same topic in different ways and from different perspectives at different times in any interview or workshop to get information that you can put together to build an understanding of the situation and the real answer to your question.

The final arbitrator regarding how tasks and activities are executed is not what the documentation might say nor is it how anyone says it should be done; rather, it is how those people executing it actually do it. This can only be captured by observation.

The preferred observation approach is to use an "apprentice" role and be taught to execute the task by a person who is identified as the best expert. Identification of the best expert should be determined by peers.

When observing how a task is executed, pay particular attention to steps taken and information used that is not obvious from available screens, forms, etc. Ask, "How did you know that?" "Where did you get that information from?" "Can you show me that?" and other similar questions until you are satisfied that there are no blank spots.

It is recommended that the execution of tasks be observed as they are carried out by more than one individual (although the apprentice approach need not be used for each observation). If activities are carried out in more than one location or on more than one shift, it is necessary to carry out observations for each location and/or shift. These additional observations will almost always identify some variability that may have to be addressed in models. Keep in mind that some variability can be intentional, such as where there are separate locations, but the locations are set up to handle different segments of customers.

If variability in how work is executed is identified, each point where it occurs needs to be specified in some detail. This variability may present an opportunity for some low hanging fruit early improvements.

Where variability is found, the activities where it is found should be carefully reviewed to determine if automation can execute the tasks for consistency as well as for efficiency.

To comply with information collection standards, the "As Is" or current state discovery process should have collected all the data that will be needed to redesign the operation and drive simulation. Check this against what the simulation tool needs. Also, do a "sanity check" on the data. You will now know more about the business and the information. Check for any information that just doesn't make sense. Confirm both the information with the team and its use. If needed, substantiate the accuracy with multiple users because accurate and realistic data is critical.

The importance of data hygiene cannot be stressed too much. Bad data will produce bad simulation results. GIGO is a term that arose in the early days of IT and means "garbage in/ garbage out." As IT has matured over the last several decades, however, it has also taken on an alternative meaning, "garbage in/gospel out." There is a high risk of believing that if information is computer generated, it is accurate and it is the truth. This can be a trap since the input may still be garbage. Each data element should be re-checked to ensure that it carries the desired information in the necessary format.

For each activity, identify the application that will be reused or changed. Identify and design all application screens and data content for each screen. Define how each will be used and why and what edits are needed on the data. Identify all paper forms that come into the activity and all data that may be pulled from email or the phone. List the data elements or items and their sources. Tell how the raw data that comes in will be transformed (changed) in the activity and what it will turn into. IT will use this to create data models and design data bases. The business design team will use this to make certain that the activity has what it needs to perform its tasks and that it is performing them the right way.

Remember that project or enterprise dictionaries of data elements, terms, activities, applications, etc., must be kept up to date to ensure consistent understanding and use. Various participants will infer meanings that, even if consistent within an operation or discipline, are different than what other participants think they mean. Within a project, each of these labels can have only one meaning.

Always look for anomalies in the work being done, the way it is being done, the data, outcomes, etc. When something just doesn't make sense, it is probably wrong.

Do not openly challenge something you believe is wrong and do not prove someone is wrong openly in front of others. You will turn the person off and the whole group will side with them – no one wants to be publically challenged or publically proven to be wrong. Instead, ask leading questions that take the answers in the direction you want it to go. Do this logically until the point you want to make is clear and then move on with more questions. The clever will know what you have done, but many will not and you will not have publically challenged anyone.

If a person you are interviewing doesn't have the information you need, ask a few general questions they can answer and end the interview. They will feel good and you will have confirmed some general things. You do not want to make enemies of those you are trying to help.

One way to facilitate finding the right people to provide you with information is to ask people who are doing the work, who they go to for advice on how to do things and handle problems. This often identifies a few people who can provide much of what you need to know. The people you find using this approach may not always be the same people that managers and supervisors identify, so you may have to use some finesse in getting to these additional people.

The entire team needs to be communicated to often so that everyone understands the status of not only their work activities and those that they have dependencies on, but the overall project. After all, the project is delivered as a team, and the entire team wants to know they are delivering together. This is particularly important when an aspect of the project encounters unexpected barriers, delays, or overruns. By communicating, you can harness the skills and experience of the entire team to build the solution and overcome challenges, as a team.

The new business operating design will be complete when requirements in scope, problems, and ability to change rapidly are built into the new design. The design will be optimal when the simulation tool cannot find significant problems and thus necessary additional improvements.

Each of the factors in the simulation results must be carefully reviewed to ensure that all defined metrics are within an acceptable range. There is a risk of tunnel vision, especially when multiple iterations are run on the basis of small tweaks, because of the tendency to focus on the metric or two that you are trying to improve.

Many simulation engines will generate a very large number of metrics as part of a simulation run. In all probability, only a fraction of what is available will have been defined as a specific performance metric. It is good practice to review all of the available metrics whether designated as a formal performance metric or not. Among the things that might be found are:

- Metrics for component parts and steps that you might be examining at a rolled up level
- Metrics that just don't feel right and should be double-checked; is the simulation configuration correct, is the result unanticipated, is there a pattern across steps, etc?
- Metrics that should be included in formal performance monitoring
- Unidentified flow issues

As you tweak the model to run improvement scenarios, the underlying details that drive the simulation will need to be specified for each and every new, deleted, or modified step. It is a good practice to build and maintain a checklist that captures each change and ensures that the simulation has been re-configured to address each change.

If the process being simulated is a full end-to-end process, you should follow the entire process stream and check associated metrics to be sure that problems have not been created upstream or downstream from the activities you are modifying for an iteration. If the process is really one or more sub-processes and is not truly end-to-end, managers of functional areas executing activities before and after the sub-processes being redesigned should be involved to review whether problems have been created for them.

4.7 Prepare to generate BPMS applications

Note: Control here will be passed to IT project members to be executed according to their specific methodology.

The project manager will now have completed the new solution design, vetted it with the business managers and collaborative partners, and the sponsor. The BPMS-based models and supporting rules, data, screens, reporting, work listings, and other information, are also available and linked to the new business operation model.

Standards for modeling, model content, supporting information, performance measurements, and simulation information should have been created when the BPMS was installed. If they were not created at that time, the team should work with the vendor and IT to create these standards. If they were not available at the time of "As Is" information collection, there may be holes in the data that need to be filled. Review the data needs and fill in any holes in the data that has been collected. Work with the company standards committee to make certain that the standards needed for BPMS application generation evolve as quickly as possible to direct improvements in the standards and the projects.

The information needed for the BPMS application generation was identified and set as a data collection standard, and collected along with the new design information needed to support the applications generation during the initial "To Be" design – and then modified through the iterations.

This includes:
- Workflow models that are decomposed or broken down, to a task or step level (the two levels below the activity flow level) to show the use of application systems
- All decisions and the probability of each exit from the decision
- All rules that govern work
- All application usage and, at the task level, data use, data flow, data edits, data transformation, etc.
- Workflow, staff workload assignment, work lists
- All performance measurement data collection points for monitoring in the workflow
- Quality checkpoints and audit points
- Customer interaction changes and the need to generate social mobility apps

    Note: These information requirements will vary based on the BPMS tool that is being used. The procedures needed to generate the applications will be an IT responsibility, but need to tie to the design delivery.

At this time, the project manager will pass all needed information to the IT project solution developer team manager. This should happen formally in a workshop. Any missing or unclear information will be identified by the IT project manager and obtained/transferred by the business project manager.

The activity that will be performed in IT will be performed following the project task plan using the special purpose IT methodology and approaches that are linked to the core BPM project methodology. Status should be reported weekly to help the project manager understand problems and delays.

The actual approach in constructing the solution will vary from company to company depending on the version of Agile the IT group uses – or the use of an entirely different approach. For example, the IT group may break the new business design into small functions called Sprints and then generate these small components from the BPMS. They may then manually build all components external to the generated applications to have complete solution components before they test. Or, the team may generate the BPMS solution's applications and then break the solution into components. We prefer the second of these approaches because it offers an opportunity to test the entire solution before it is divided into Sprints for the creation of the components that are external to the BPMS applications and BPMS environment.

The generation of the BPMS applications will be the first test of the completeness of the business model. If BPMN coding is in error, it will show up in the attempt to generate the application. To help avoid major issues, the business design should be walked through by the business and IT team members who designed it. It may also be helpful to have others sit in on this walkthrough for a new perspective. If there are any major business design issues, they will likely be identified as a result of the walkthrough.

The generation of the BPMS applications will also test the way business rules were coded in their entry into the BPMS rules library or engine. Rules are generally decisions and are stated as IF "X" then "Y". They can be strung together in a list:
IF "A" then "X",
IF "B" then "Y",
IF "C" then "Z",
IF "D" then "E"
In reality, rules become much more complex as variables are added to the decision.

It is recommended that rule coding be checked before the design is turned over to the BPMS Developers for application generation.

Rule coding is also a place to look for application performance improvement.

Make certain that all business model standards are met (including the entry of supporting data) before the models are turned over to the BPMS Developers.

The business analysts should walk through the design, the supporting information, the project request requirements, the rules and the performance criteria, including embedded performance reporting and inference analysis/reporting with the technical (BPMS) developers.

The business analysts should work closely with the BPMS developers as they create realistic business requirements from the business process models and translate the business designs into technical requirements and specs.

The business project manager and the IT project manager should work closely together to ensure that the solution's technical architecture and the application's user interface have a high probability of functioning as per the requirements from the user base. This cooperation will significantly increase the probability of end user acceptance

4.8 Generate the BPMS applications

BPMS applications are generated by the BPMS tools suite from models, rules, data definitions, and screen designs that are incorporated in the tool suite. These generated applications will run in a type of operating technical environment that is created by the BPMS tool. Any other IT support is built manually and these components both reside and run outside of this BPMS environment. These applications are built separately and linked to the applications that run in the BPMS environment with data feeding back and forth across interfaces.

The generation of the BPMS applications will require that the project team create models that show workflow, the improvement of workflow, activity, business rule coding, data use, and data origination definition. The actual information and its entry will be driven by the BPMS tool that is used. For this reason, standards for information and the way it is entered should be available in the IT group. Once this information has been entered, tested, and evolved to reflect the future state of the business operation, it will be used to generate BPMS applications and provide requirements and technical specs for external applications, interfaces, web services, and data management.

Data handling must include designing what data will reside where and how it will get there. This requires work from BPMS developers (specialists in the use of your BPMS) and Data Architects.

The actual generation of BPMS applications should be a joint activity between the business project manager and the BPMS administrator.

In some companies, this step breaks the business design into Business Stories or Use Cases and each is built following an IT Agile approach. These construction components are called Sprints and each is designed to address small groups of work steps. However, this approach, while common, is not universal and other approaches can be used. The actual approach that is used should follow your company BPMS application construction standards.

The applications that are delivered in this BPMS application generation are generally not complete. They require the construction of interfaces, external applications, modifications to legacy applications, and modifications to web site applications to be complete.

Confirm that all the information identified by the BPMS vendor as elements needed to generate an application in the BPMS environment (also called a platform) has been collected and verified as being accurate. Correct any information or data issues.

The models and supporting information will be used to identify and define business requirements (i.e., what does the new solution need to support, how does it need to support it and what does it need to deliver?). These requirements should align to the future state business design. They should also address the difference between the "As Is" model and the "To Be" model.

The business requirements will need to be numbered, given a name and defined for the BPMS developer. They should be shown on the business model and aligned to the activity that they apply to. This alignment may be at a low level of detail (the task or step level).

The business requirements are converted into technical requirements by the BPMS developer working with the business analysts. This may take a couple of iterations to get right because the two specialists speak different languages (business vs. technical) and they each look at the solution from very different perspectives. But with a little patience and respect, they can get past this gap and create solid technical requirements.

The technical specs and technical design should be reviewed by a committee of the BPMS developers (as a quality checkpoint) and approved before the solution is generated.

The applications will be generated by the company's BPMS developers. These are technical staff that have been trained and certified in the use of the BPMS and in generating applications through the BPMS suite. Go over all the information with the BPMS developers and obtain any information or definitions that are needed. Once the information is complete and clean, turn the application generation over to the developers.

The BPMS will generate error messages on the models and information. These errors will be corrected by the business analysts who created the models and collected the information, working closely with the BPMS developers. Application generation is normally an iterative process until all solution generation errors have been corrected.

Once the models and information fully enable application generation, the new solution will be generated. At this point, the BPMS developers and the business analysts need to check to see that each activity's support provides the needed functionality as defined in the business process models and the supporting information.

Keep the business users in the information loop. It is better to have business users involved as much as they are willing to participate than to keep them out of the information loop and risk the loss of their acceptance. Make them feel that they are part of the team and that the solution is theirs. If you do, the probability of their acceptance of the solution is much higher than when their involvement is at a minimal level.

The design must be tested for effectiveness to ensure that it produces the needed support based on the expected results and delivers the expected project goals/performance targets. For this set of tests we again turn to simulation. However, the simulation for this second design testing must include business use as well as the IT components.

Once the simulation tool has shown a business model to be optimally efficient, the supporting applications can be generated by the BPMS tool. This process may take a couple of iterations as business rules, user interfaces, data, and logic are cleaned up. It should be noted that these applications are generated from the BPMN symbols and other information put into the business design model. This process can be complex and the generation may require some model and rule clean up.

During the time that the BPMS developers are preparing and adjusting application generation, the IT team members should be defining and confirming all places where external legacy or ERP type applications and their data are called, where data is sent to the external applications, or where processing is temporarily transferred to them. These are the interfaces. In regular BPMS support, this list of interfaces will include social mobility apps and web apps, which are generated in iBPMS tools.

The designed solutions can now be run in a type of simulated production or business operation. This simulation will be used to check solution effectiveness. If the simulation is not effective, then the business design can be adjusted and once again simulated for efficiency and then simulated again for effectiveness. Since the iterations are guided by the simulation (efficiency and then effectiveness), the number of iterations is controlled. This allows the solution to be proven before it is fully built, therefore reducing risk and overall costs.

Remember that there must be validations of both the model and the configuration factors entered into the simulator to ensure that iterations, that do not meet all standards and goals, are not missing targets due to inaccurate and/or incomplete information rather than design improvements that are needed.

Confirm that the simulation baseline metrics have been approved along with measurement formulas, compliance reporting requirements, and data elements/with their sources. Confirm acceptance of the approach that will be used to measure the simulation results.

There are multiple types of simulation that may be required. The first is the creation of an "As Is" or current state operating model, utilizing a simulation tool to simulate the current operation and create a performance baseline. The second type is the use of a simulation tool to guide the "To Be" or future state design iteration. This is what will prove design optimization when the simulation tool cannot point to any significant workflow issues. Later in the development process, once the BPMS applications have been generated, a third type of simulation that deals with application interfaces will be recommended. A fourth type that is used at the end of the solution development is used to evaluate how the solution actually is used. This will guide iteration of the user interface. All must be considered when designing the approach to creating the solution.

When modeling a business workflow, be sure to document the various aspects of the workflow, including associating application systems that are used when the actions or steps in a task are performed, identifying the screens that are used in the task, and noting the data and source of data that is on each screen.

BPMN symbols fall into two basic groups – a business group and a technical side group for application design, and in the case of BPMS tools, application generation. The symbols for each area are different and it is generally not productive to have business people, who do the workflow design, also figure out how the applications should work and enter the technical side application definition symbols.

4.9 Conduct BPMS generated solution simulation and iteration

The BPMS applications were generated in Chapter 4, section 8. If the project manager has decided to break the solution into components and generate the BPMS in parts as components in a series of Agile Sprints, this simulation might not be performed.

In either case, this is a technical activity that will be performed (or not) depending on the approach and standards used by the IT group. We recommend that this simulation be conducted because it proves the solution and saves iteration and rework time.

The goal of a full simulation is to test the end-to-end solution. This test is to make certain that the solution will deliver the stated project targets.

The applications will have been generated and if a simulation model was used, the solution will be known to be optimally efficient (or as close to optimal as the design team wanted to get). However, both the interfaces and the external program modules will not have been built at this point. Further, social apps, website applications, and the reuse of legacy applications will also not have been tested as yet.

Dusting off an old application development approach to simulate complete solutions so the delivery of project targets and performance goals can be simulated in testing, we recommend that the team consider breaking with more traditional IT approaches. Instead of building everything needed to deliver a use case, consider completing the use case solution using "Stub" and "Driver" modules that simulate the way data is passed to and from the proposed solution. This may or may not be possible in any given company – depending on its application development and testing standards.

This involves:
- Building common "Driver" modules that pass data across a simple interface to the BPMS-generated applications. These program modules will link to the BPMS applications following BPMS interface standards and be customized for each link by specifying the size, format, content of the data that is to be sent. "Drivers" can be designed to simulate differing workloads to test for scalability.

- Building common "Stub" modules follow a similar logic to "Driver" modules, except "Stubs" receive data and test that it is in the right format. In simulation, these modules each are customized to look for a specific type of data in a specific format. "Stubs" can also be designed to look for certain timing and other conditions as they receive the data from the given point in the defined BPMS-generated program.

When all "Stubs" and "Drivers" are built and attached to the BPMS-generated solution, the full solution simulation test can be run.

Since the data passing to the solution is known, "Drivers" can be built to pass the specified data representing a given condition. This data is then used to initiate activity within the simulation. Further, since there will be multiple points were the data drives processing, the use of multiple versions of the "Driver" module will be required. These can be similar versions of the same code, each just accounting for differences for data formats and content. The same is true for

"Stubs". They can be built to accept data in certain formats and attached to the part of the new solution's applications that send data outside the BPMS-generated solution.

This requires that the technical solution construction stop for a brief time while these modules are customized to simulate all needed interfaces. This allows the team to run the fully generated applications to test for effectiveness in meeting the goals of the project before time and cost has gone into building the programs external to the BPMS-generated application. It also allows interface requirements to be confirmed or changed before they are built – saving time and cost.

If performance measurement was built into the workflow design (recommended), it will now be used to measure the results of the solution. This will also allow the solution to be tested under simulated load and for the resulting applications to be tested to ensure that the project's targets are hit.

The construction of the applications external to the BPMS-generated applications by IT is addressed later in this Field Guide because it is performed separately from this simulation. This section of the Guide is focused on preparing for the operational simulation BPMS-generated applications. The next section of this Guide addresses the actual simulation.

The business project manager should work with the IT project manager to confirm that this simulation is acceptable under corporate IT standards. If it is not, the simulation may be cancelled. If this is the case, we suggest that the business project manager recommend to IT that this simulation testing be allowed. This simulation should be performed before the business design is divided for construction using Agile Sprints or any other application development approach.

The real purpose of the simulation is to:
- Prove the generated BPMS applications actually work the way they should
- Prove the generated BPMS applications will deliver the project's targets as stated in the project request
- Point out needed improvements

The key point here is that this simulation will point to any changes that are needed before the solution's programming for external components is performed. This saves time, money, expectation issues, and rework, while improving solution quality and acceptability.

The BPMS-generated solution programs will need to be reviewed to identify all points where data enters the solution to drive activity, where data is sent to call/execute external services, or when data is sent to an interface. In many of these latter cases, data is sent outside the BPMS environment and data is returned in response. All of these "touch points" will be identified, mapped to the solution's programs, and defined (what will be passed to the solution programs and the format of the data, and what will be passed from the solution and its format). Any timing or other considerations for these interfaces will also be noted so the "Stubs" and "Drivers" will be able to simulate real operation. This review is an IT application developer task.

For each interaction or touch point identified in the interface review of the BPMS-generated solution, determine exactly what data is expected, what its receipt or sending will cause to happen, the timing and the format of the data packet (a data packet is a technical term for what is sent in any electronic communication: the data, its ID, its source, its destination, time sent, and possibly some encryption code).

Identify exactly what should be expected of each interaction point and how the "Drivers" should initiate work in the generated BPMS solution's applications. This is the foundation for the tests.

Once the generated applications are "cleaned" and functional, the IT team members can build "Drivers", small applications that when called or invoked will pass a specific transaction in the format specified by the new generated application. The IT team members will then build "Stubs", programs that pass information to and from, or are called by the BPMS-generated application. This now simulates the whole solution, all without yet needing to build custom IT parts. This not only reduces risk, but produces increased savings in expenditures and time.

Before work is started on the creation of the full solution simulation, the team should understand what will be done and why, and what each "Stub" or "Driver" is looking for.

The technical design that is created by the BPMS developers should show each interface point to legacy applications, social mobility apps, web apps, external databases, etc. These will be used to guide interfacing and to guide the creation of "Stub" and "Driver" modules if the project manager will include the step of proving that the solution will deliver targets before traditional programs are built. This is recommended but is often not done using the reasoning that skipping this step saves time and expenses – except, it really doesn't save anything. Take the time to do it right and improve the chances of the solution being accepted and even promoted as being a great improvement.

In most cases, IT will use Sprints to develop specific components external to the BPMS, such as interfaces with legacy systems, web support, app support, etc. As a result, there will be a series of steps where "Stubs" and "Drivers" are removed and real connections can be tested. It is good practice to re-run the simulation as each of these pieces becomes available to see if there are any problems. Any needed corrections or changes can be made on an ongoing basis. By the time the final pieces become available, the vast majority of components will be in place and already tested and proven functional.

Build the "Stub" and "Driver" modules and attach each to the point in the generated BPMS program. Run the solution in the test environment and test against expected interaction outcomes. Modify the BPMS-generated applications' models and rules and regenerate.

Before the "Stubs" and "Drivers" are populated, validate that the data will be drawn from the exact fields specified in the project or enterprise data dictionary. In some cases, this may include specification of a particular system as well as the fields and formats.

Run the full simulation again iteratively until the solution is both operational and provides the expected target outcomes.

The results of the full solution simulation should be used as input into the design of all interfaces to and from the BPMS-generated solutions programs.

When looking at operational simulation results (using "Stubs" and "Drivers"), particularly for early iterations, make sure the metrics are properly defined and located at the correct points and then double-check. Where unexpected or counterintuitive results appear, it is necessary to rule out model and configuration errors before investing in redesign efforts. Missing information can have as much impact as erroneous information. The quality of a simulation is only as good as the quality of the business process model and the quality of the data and its associated activities.

4.10 Run/test/iterate the BPMS-generated "To Be" solution to simulate

This section of the Field Guide assumes that the applications generated by the BPMS will be tested in simulation using "Stub" and "Driver" program modules. If this approach will not be taken, this section of the Guide can be skipped.

In previous section introductions, we introduced the concept of a full solution simulation before money is spent on building the solution. As noted earlier, this is dependent on the openness of the IT group to support this approach. It involves the generation of all BPMS applications that will be part of the solution and the identification of all places where the work or automation that supports the new business operation is external to the BPMS-generated applications. At each of these points, the team (with the help of IT) will need to define exactly what is passed to and from the generated part of the solution's applications. For future use, the team may also want to identify where it is passed to, when, why and any rules that govern the interaction. This information will allow the technical team to build simple program modules called "Stubs" and

164

"Drivers" that attach to these points and either provide anticipated data or take anticipated data. This data will all be controlled for testing purposes.

With these "Stubs" and "Drivers" in place, the entire solution can be run in simulation using test data and results compared with solution targets. The results can be analyzed and used to direct improvement iteration. This iteration will evolve the applications until they deliver all targets.

The solution applications that will be generated by the BPMS should be based on complete, comprehensive models. This generation can be broken into component parts following an Agile development approach, but we recommend that it first be generated as a complete solution to check for context, inclusion, execution and other problems. The development of any applications or interfaces external to the BPMS-generated applications can then be effectively developed following Agile or any other approach your IT group uses.

Once this BPMS generated solution simulation test is completed, the solution team can define the first version of the solution support requirements and build the technical program specs with IT. Collaboration is needed to make certain that all requirements are understood and all specs are written to conform to IT standards. These specs should include:
- Interfaces
- Data use – data flow models, schemas, data bases and places to find needed information
- Legacy application changes
- New applications
- Social Mobility apps
- Website changes and new website applications
- Document management
- And all other considerations required by company IT standards.

At this point, IT will be in a position to initiate further construction activity and build parts of the solution while the solution is refined in. However, the final solution will not be determined until the Model Office test. It is thus possible for additional changes to be needed and for IT support requirements and program specs to change. The ability to get a start on building the components external to the BPMS should thus be weighed against the possibility that changes will be needed.

The BPMS environment is deliberately focused on being able to make changes rapidly and run quick simulation iterations. It may initially sound like heresy, but the objective is to use that speed to identify changes that are required and then to generate the changes themselves. As a result, there does not need to be 100% accuracy of requirements and specifications before the design is tested. Use the simulation results to identify where refinements are necessary or desirable. This is not, however, an invitation to be sloppy since every single problem requires a redesign until it no longer exists.

The simulation approach is actually quite beneficial to IT, because as the design is refined the ultimate requirements become more and more accurate and each will have been tested before IT has made major investments in executing the technical changes needed to integrate legacy systems with the BPMS. For most in IT, this may be the first time that the specifications actually are accurately addressing exactly what is needed.

The simulation run should be using every single factor, step, connection, etc., that has been entered into the BPMN model as well as every value in the configuration editor. For initial iterations, it is suggested that simulation results be reviewed from a wide view as a starting point. Areas where there are problems must then be examined in more detail begin to separate design flaws from errors in the model and underlying details. Errors will eventually become apparent, although it could take several iterations before some are completely addressed. The BPM simulator will execute exactly what it is told. It may be an iBPMS, but it cannot simulate what you thought you were telling it to do.

Similar to the way steps, tasks, and activities must originate within the applicable work unit and be vetted by people actually doing the work, the values utilized in the configuration editor should arise in operational areas for the most part. Not all needed values will be something that has been regularly tracked. There may need to be sampling studies to either validate information from operating areas or to produce values directly. Sampling studies, however, must still be given a "sniff" test by knowledgeable staff in operating areas.

The first iteration of the simulation will produce a list of errors and problems. These point the way to improving the operational design. The business operation design at this point will contain all of the activities that will be performed by the business unit staff (or at a higher level. the people in different business units performing the work in the process). The business design will focus on activity, workflow relationships, decisions, and performance metrics. The simulation will probably not consider IT applications, problem resolution, error rate reduction, and benefit calculations.

The simulation model results from the prior iteration will give the team a list of things to consider in the next design iteration. This will continue until no significant activity, decision, or workflow issues are found in a simulation. The key here is that only the first iteration of the new design is based on what the team thinks will work. After that, the improvement is based on model review results from the simulation. As the design is iterated, each iteration should take less time than the one before.

When the operational simulation iteration testing redesign no longer produces a list of significant activity, content, work flow, or performance problems, the business and performance measurement parts of the solution will be completed and certified as delivering an optimal new business operating model.

As simulation iterations are run and problems diminish, it is important to periodically take a step back and inject a reality check into the design components and simulation results to rule out any possible problems that might arise from factors that are beyond what is being simulated. For example, a design may shift activities into a different operational area. While such a shift may have been cleared in design stages, simulation results may shift more work to the new location than was ever contemplated. This could result in overtime costs, stressed employees, delays, etc., when implemented. The operational staff who accepted the shift will probably never see the detailed simulation results, and the iterations will show success. The project manager in particular and project staff in general must be alert for such buried differences from initial thinking and discuss these with relevant team members when they are discovered.

We recommend that the "As Is" model be simulated as part of activities early on. The results of the "As Is" simulations should be consistently available and used as a benchmark for "To Be" simulation iterations. Normally, you should expect every "To Be" simulation to have better overall results than the "As Is." Iterations that are not better or are only marginally better should be carefully examined for underlying errors before assuming that the design is bad. Errors can and will occur in the BPMN model itself, the values entered for configuring the simulation, and the data contained in the "Stubs" and "Drivers".

Making changes and running a simulation iteration can be executed rapidly. Before there can be Model Office testing, however, the selected user representatives will need to be trained in the use of the solution design. Therefore, both testing and training should be planned in advance, so that the critical need for input and feedback does not delay overall progress. The most important training should be in conjunction with very early iterations and will need to address new flows, new or changed steps and tasks, and the new UI for each set of activities. Subsequent iterations will normally only have incremental changes and the amount of training is usually small and can directly precede line lab sessions.

If parts of the solution design will have customer touch points, and a Model Office is supported, you should begin to set customer usage testing in motion. You will need to identify all customer segments that will have UI changes where the segments might include role (consumer, supplier, shipper, etc.), channels used (web, mobile app, call center, etc.), and demographics (age, language, geo-location, etc.). Begin by determining what the various customer segments both expect and desire keeping in mind that all segments are becoming increasing sophisticated at an accelerated pace. Also be concerned about what the segments do not want to see or deal with.

The importance of customer service for each of your customer segments cannot be overstressed. The BPM discipline is all about customer focus, but it is easy to lose sight of that as you wade into the business and technical details. It really is not possible to focus only on internal operations and think there will be no effect on customers. In the end, the effectiveness of a solution design can only be measured in the context of a customer interaction. Efficiency should not be gained at the expense of customer experience. For example, the number of customer problems fully resolved is a much more important metric than the number of customers disposed of in a given hour. The determining factor in measuring success should be overall revenue growth and increase in market share. This cannot be determined until the solution has been live for some time, so care must be taken in the design and refinements to continually ask what impact changes may have on customer experience across all segments.

4.11 Identify IT infrastructure changes needed to support the solution

At this point in the project, the new business solution design will have been tested and will deliver expected results. The design may include change requirements that impact the current IT application inventory and/or the IT infrastructure, and thus the IT Enterprise Architects and the Chief Technology Officer will need determine the impact of these changes and their potential timing and cost.

New IT capabilities are often a foundation consideration for business operation improvement or transformation. These changes can be related to increased communication bandwidth, increased data storage (on the cloud or internally), upgraded servers or mainframe computers, more capable PCs (with things like touch screens), mobility app generation, etc. The use of these capabilities may require changes to the current or planned IT infrastructure and computer device inventory.

It is also possible that the new business solution will require additions to the company IT application or tool inventory. These additions will also require an evaluation from IT to determine their potential impact on the technical operating environment. Costs and impacts should be defined and added to the project's plan and cost model. Actual changes will be dependent upon project sponsor and senior management's approval.

If the changes are denied by senior management, the project team will need to return to the solution design and come up with a new approach. However, the changes should not be denied if approached properly. They should have been identified early in the new solution design and discussed with the sponsor and IT. Potential costs and impact should also have been discussed before the solution is finalized. This will avoid the potential problem of having IT infrastructure changes rejected.

The acquisition and installation timing for obtaining and integrating these new technologies should be negotiated with the vendors and with IT. The timing for these technologies and for training IT and project staff will then need to be either built into the original project schedule or built in as a modification to the schedule.

In addition to leveraging these new technical capabilities, the project team may discover a potential requirement for additional changes to the current technical environment, application inventory, or automated tools. These changes should be rare, but it is possible that new technology may be discovered that will be a "game changer" in how the company may function or how it may interact with customers.

These changes represent a new request and must be cost justified. The request will then likely go through the company's budget and procurement processes – significantly slowing down the delivery of the project solution. These changes will probably first need to be approved by the company Chief Technology Officer, then by the Chief Information Officer, then by the Chief Operating Officer, and possibly the Chief Executive Officer or the board, depending on the scope of the change and the cost.

As the new business design is created, the design team will need to involve IT technical services professionals to look at these issues and recommend innovative ways the new capabilities can be used.

Evaluate the business, noting all application touch points and the required characteristics of those applications. Work with the design team to define the conceptual future state business model and what it will take to move from the "As Is" state to the "To Be" state.

Work with the data architects to determine the data storage requirements and the requirements for moving the data from all the sources and creating transient data warehouses. Note the implications for hardware (computing scaling, communications, middleware, and specialty software).

Work with tech support to look at load balancing, PC and other computer capability, and software needs. Jointly determine what will be needed and when.

Work with Computer Operations to determine if auxiliary data center space will be needed.

Work with tech services to determine if backup and recovery capabilities are adequate or will need to change.

Determine the approach – cloud vs. traditional in-house computing support. Combine the information from the various computing requirement studies and determine if new hardware, communications, middleware, or applications will be required, and if the technical requirements (specs) for this IT infrastructure need to change.

Work with IT to align acquisition schedules with "just in time" infrastructure changes.

IT will determine actual infrastructure changes, the timing, and the investment costs. This will need to be presented to the project sponsors, especially if it was not in the project budget. If the investment was not in the project budget, this will become a go/no go decision point.

4.12 Build "To Be" solution Model Office simulation environment and run simulation

A Model Office is a testing environment designed to simulate the way the finished solution will really work. This testing environment will be built at this point, but will not be used until IT has completed the solution components that it will build – external to the BPMS-generated applications. It will thus be ready for the completion of the Chapter 5 IT construction activities.

Once IT has completed building all solution components that are external to the BPMS-generated applications, a final optional testing can take place. At this point, the solution will have been tested for technical support operability – it will work. All BPMS-generated applications will have been tested in simulation and all solution components external to the BPMS-generated applications will have been tested by IT. This test is for ease of use and it is designed to make certain that the solution is both a technical success (it works) and a business success (it actually improves the business operation).

A Model Office test environment mimics the actual way the business will work. All business changes and all application/IT changes are built into the creation of this simulated business operation. The purpose is to test the solution in a type of live operation. All documents, transactions, emails and time initiated work that drives activity in the real version of the business unit will be copied to drive this operation. The goal is to come as close as possible to creating a parallel real working business unit. The solution will be tested as a parallel operation and all screen use, data use, and workflow will be tested and improved. This is the final test before the solution is implemented.

All issues related use and efficiency will be identified and resolved as quickly as the IT team and the business solution team can react. These changes should be small but important in improving the way work is actually performed. Performance management, work listing, and other management aids can also be tested at this time.

Because this test is time-consuming, it is suggested that it be used for complex, mission critical business solution changes. It may also be appropriate to use for customer interaction changes to test customer experiences and improve them. Simple operational change does not require this level testing.

At this point, the business workflow design will be optimal. The technical side of the solution will have been completed and proven to deliver the targets and goals of the project. The interfaces and other technical components that are external to the BPMS-generated applications have also been completed and tested. However, simply because the solution works, does not mean it will really improve the business operation or the way people do their jobs. That can be tested in one of two ways – live production or a Model Office. In live production, if the solution does not really support the way people work, changes will be disruptive and the impact can be significant. If it is tested in a Model Office test environment, there will be no impact on the business operation and the final solution, when implemented, will be proven to actually improve the business and deliver value.

Simulation begins with the creation of the detailed business operation model with BPMN-based applications generation design embedded. The technical BPMN side of the design should be developed jointly between the business and technology team members to avoid technical design rework. This approach provides a close sharing of background and concepts between the two groups.

Run the new design in simulation, either using an automated simulation tool or manually through a detailed walkthrough. The new design should be iterated in a controlled iteration process that continues to refocus each iteration to specific issues based on the last iteration. To avoid delays, iterations must be closely managed with each iteration being tested. An automated simulation is recommended.

It is recommended that people who will actually be using the new design begin to look at it and provide feedback for considerations such as flow, ease of user interface, intuitiveness, general look and feel.

In many cases, the move to e-commerce (electronic commerce) means that actual users will include not only customers but multiple customer segments that will have differing needs and expectations. To address these needs and expectations, not only should customer input have been obtained way before the new design was created, but ongoing feedback from customers should be deliberately planned for and obtained throughout the project. Feedback must be obtained from all customer segments.

In defining relevant customer segments, at least three dimensions must be considered:
- Role. Is this person an end consumer, a broker or agent, a supplier, a wholesaler, a shipper, a financial intermediary, etc.?
- Channel. Is this person being serviced via a website, snail mail, mobile app, automated phone service, call center, etc.?
- Demographics. What is the country, language, age, etc.? Are they represented by a group, are they loyalty members, etc.? Are there access, vision, or hearing issues?

While this may sound like a lot to address, if an enterprise intends to generate income from any of these segments, then addressing their needs and expectations becomes a necessity. To update an old customer service rule of thumb, an extremely pleased customer will often tell no one, but someone who is annoyed will tell the world and in the age of social media, word can spread quickly.

4.13 Evaluate the probable impact of the project's solution

The solution can now be evaluated for performance and the delivery of the project targets. The performance can now be judged and the project's success measured.

The initial simulation will have proven that the business workflow or process design will be as optimal as the project sponsor wants it to be – for timing, the team may stop short of actual optimization. While optimization sounds like a good thing, it may not be justifiable based on cost vs. additional return. This level of optimization will have been decided during the "To Be" business design. The value of the new business operating design will have been proven as a review of the "As Is" operation simulation vs. the "To Be" simulation results.

The solution is now ready to test in a Model Office once IT has delivered the components of the solution it is building – it is complete and it is fully tested at the conceptual level (the entire solution will not yet have been built, so any test must be considered to be conceptual). The solution can now be used to determine the changes that will be needed in the IT operation and infrastructure. Will new PCs or other hardware be needed? Will specialized mobility devices be needed to monitor and control social media apps? Will the company website need to change? Will current communications capability be OK or will it need to be expanded?

To help in this review, it is suggested that the project team work with IT to identify the questions that will be addressed, all of the technical decisions that will need to be made at this point, and what data will be needed to make those decisions. This data may all be available in the simulations that will have been performed. This will be especially true if the business design will have performance and other metric data collection at places in the flow built into the models and thus generated as part of the solution.

This information can now be analyzed with the IT team to determine probable impact on the business area's IT support, on the applications, on the IT infrastructure, and on the business operation. This evaluation should be considered to be a check point in the project and used to make certain the solution (business operation and IT support) will be adequate or will need to be changed.

The IT impact will be determined by IT; however, the project manager should structure the assessment of the impact so that it includes hardware, software, facilities, staffing and resource needs for interfaces, SOA, etc.

172

The impact on the business operation needs to be traced all the way through the initiation of the process until it has reached its final endpoint. This assessment must cross all functional boundaries, even if it currently appears that there will be no or only minimal changes within a functional area.

The assessment of impact on business operations should form the foundation of a formal change management plan that addresses, at a minimum, both the planned timing of changes and the specific changes that will take place in each functional area, and may be further refined for specific roles in functional areas in some cases. The change management plan must then lay out a schedule of training activities and define training materials and modes that are key to the specific changes.

When designing training, two dimensions should be kept in mind at all times - skills and attitudes. While you clearly want to develop skills, the approaches taken should also try to foster positive attitudes. Consider setting up the training outside of the normal work dimensions and think about things like:
1. Close by, but off site
2. Breakfast or lunch or snacks
3. Casual attire
4. Come in an hour later or go home an hour early.

When planning for both information sessions and training, there should be deliberate thought about appropriate group size. Initial thinking may be to hold one large session, so that training can occur once and everyone gets the same information. While the information may be identical, what people "hear" will be quite variable. Experience has shown that small groups are often the better choice. They tend to be less formal and much better at promoting dialogue which not only improves clarity of understanding but also commitment. Some additional benefits are seen around resourcing. If smaller groups are used, then normal operations can continue with only a portion of the staff being available.

Training materials as well as project communications may need to be translated into the common terminology in each functional area. While the team will have used a common vocabulary and data dictionary to carry out project activities, these may not be exactly the same as used by people actually performing the work. Functional areas usually have a common understanding of the terms they use and trying to impose other terms may lead to problems. Rely on team members from each functional area to identify any translation needs because as team members they should be conversant with both sets of terminology.

Do not underestimate the motivational power of small tokens like a special lanyard or a pin for the ID tag. Experience has shown that such little things can be much sought after. These can also be used to reward staff who identify problems or suggest solutions or participate in testing, etc.

In its natural habitat, change or even the possibility of change often produces fear at the negative end and frequently only manages to produce apathy at the positive end. The first line of defense for the project is to deploy a good offense in the form of constant, accurate, and consistent information. This information should be made available to every potentially affected individual or even to the company as a whole. The second step is to deliberately sell the changes and what is positive about them both through dialogue and through positive packaging. Constantly check to make sure you are doing things with people not doing things to people.

If there are indications or even intentions that changes will result in some people losing their current positions, this will need to be discussed with the sponsor. If possible, try to obtain executive commitment for reabsorbing all of the quality people elsewhere in the company. If that cannot be supported, this topic should be part of the overall change management plan.

4.14 Define the final "To Be" design solution's IT support requirements

After the application requirements are created, the IT group could have started their construction of some of the solution components. But it could not finish them because the design was still evolving. The design is now finished and the BPMS applications have been generated and iterated. IT and the solution team now need to create the solution's technical components requirements (outside of the BPMS environment).

Many of the applications that are needed to support the new business design will be generated by the BPMS. However, the BPMS-generated applications will need to be augmented by external modules, interfaces to legacy applications, external databases, web services, mobility apps, and web site changes. These will have been identified in the solution design simulation and refined in the BPMS-generated solution "Stub" and "Driver" supported full simulation.

The results of these simulations will be a comprehensive, vetted solution design. This is the design that will be used to identify and define the final version of all business and technical requirements. In this way, all requirements will tie directly to the business design and its application support needs. All of the applications that make up the solution will also be shown in their execution sequence with data flow and transform defined.

From the business process design models and the requirements, the business members of the project team and the technology members should now work with IT to clearly define all interfaces, legacy application functionality changes, all database schemas and designs, etc., and create program specifications (specs). These specs should be vetted to make certain they support the business design as it was provided to IT. IT should not create either the requirements or the specs without the business design for operational reference or the people who will use the solution.

This collaborative team will be responsible for ensuring that the requirements and specs are accurate and do in fact lay out the right workflow and apply business rules in the right places and in the right ways. This is also true for data use.

It is recommended that the proven business process design and the BPMS-generated part of the final solution now be used as a complete picture of the end outcome of the project. This design can be divided functionally into Use Cases/Sprints for the creation of the additional capabilities that are beyond the BPMS-generated applications. This provides the context of how the solution can be broken apart and how it will be recombined.

The final step in this turnover of the requirements and specs will be a formal workshop to explain each workflow, each activity and decision, and how applications will need to support the work in the business unit. This turnover team will also need to review and OK the detail in the IT project plan to make certain the appropriate checks are in place to ensure success.

Requirements identification and definition will start with the project request. That will be enhanced as the "As Is" business process models are defined and analyzed. Constraints will also be identified and used to limit certain requirement approaches, content, or scope. At this time, the new "To Be" business design will be complete. The team will now be ready to confirm past requirements, validate goals and create new requirements needed to define the changes in the new solution. This will create a list of requirements that is complete and comprehensive and that defines the changes needed to deliver and support the new solution.

Exactly who *must* review the operational "To Be" simulation for approval will vary from company to company and will have been defined at project setup. Typically, it will include key managers and/or executives from each of the affected operational areas. Who *should* review the "To Be" simulation is another matter and may be a wider group. Since buy-in is critical, it is a good idea to also seek approvals from other team participants at least down to a reasonable level of responsibility. While managers and supervisors may have approved components as the project proceeded, it would not hurt for them to see the entire solution in action.

During the review process, revisit performance metrics to ensure that everyone is still on board with the measures and expectations. The simulation will generally show that the solution delivers the metrics, but there may be concern about how the metrics will look when the operation becomes live.

BPMS-based solutions will have a part that is generated by the BPMS and run in the internal BPMS environment as well as parts that are built and run external to the BPMS operating environment. To generate the BPMS applications, the team needs to work with the BPMS developers to create the specs. Separately, it is critical to create the specs for all external parts of the solution. These external applications will be called from the BPMS application and will be controlled by the operating environment. However, execution of tasks and other maintenance will be handled by the external applications.

These external parts include:
- Changes to legacy applications
- Changes to and new application interfaces
- New databases – within the applications and totally external to any application
- Social media-based applications (may be generated by some BPMS tools)
- Document management applications
- Website applications and separate web applications
- Various web services to move data among other things
- New applications for specialty activities, like compliance reporting and Business Intelligence Reporting
- Internet use – internet of all things
- Cloud-based applications

All of these external applications require specialized design and development approaches that must be considered as well as integrated into the solution specs and the solution development approach.

Working with the BPMS Developers and IT project managers, identify all parts of the solution that will need to be outside of the BPMS environment and custom built. These should be listed and defined along with the data that will be needed for each and the way that data will be used/transformed. From this list, define the technical requirements and specs for each external application. Also, make certain these external applications and changes to legacy applications are planned and coordinated as part of the core solution definition and development. They also need to be tested in all full solution tests.

In certain scenarios, it will make sense to pull required data from several sources into one place for storage and access. The data can refresh into this new database on a cyclical basis to keep it up-to-date and it can serve as an interim data store for data coming from the BPMS application. This allows the BPMS-generated data to be collected and merged in different ways to send to other systems and parts of the business. This is a multilayer database design.

Scenarios are an aggregation of activities that does one thing and can be predicted. For example, you can have the solution set to execute a given set of activities for each type of call that comes to a call center. This can be based on rules, which may be fairly complex, but once the situation is selected, all the activities will be executed in the same way, using the same applications, the same data, and the same rules. These scenarios can be built separately from a specifically designed set of technical specs.

External applications need to be built to replace the "Stub" and "Driver" modules that were built to simulate data passing to and from the BPMS-generated applications.

There are two main aspects of these external parts of the solution. The first aspect is the program(s) that will deliver the external applications and their capabilities. The second aspect is the interfaces to these applications. Both, the applications and the interfaces, need to be defined, planned, designed, built, tested separately, and then tested as part of the full solution.

For each rule, review the current rules library and determine if it is close to one that already exists. If found, modify it to meet the requirements of the new version. If no similar one exists, a new rule will need to be created. The key is to try to find existing rules to avoid duplications or conflicting rules.

The technical specs for each type of application environment will be different and each must follow the standard for that environment. Examples are web services, social mobility apps, website applications, cloud applications, etc. Each is very different and will need to be described differently with special terms with specific concepts being leveraged. For each of these, content, format, inclusion, language, etc., requirements should be specified as standards which the solution design team should follow in defining the needed external application and which the IT team should follow in building the applications or interfaces.

If standards for external applications (applications that are custom built but are not generated by the BPMS) are not present, the team should create them and vet them with teams from other BPMS-enabled BPM solutions. These standards will evolve and become more complete, but it is important that the team provide the same information, in the same format, for all parts of the projects. This is critical in creating a foundation for model, data, and information reuse.

4.15 Revise project plan and estimates as needed

Now that the project requirements are known, the technical specs for new applications external to the BPMS-generated apps, are known, IT infrastructure changes have been identified and costs estimated, and the scope of changes to the business operation have been approved, it is time to revisit the project plan to see if changes need to be made. The initial estimates will have been a guess. An educated guess based on known and assumed factors, but still a guess. Depending on the real state of the current business and IT operations and other factors that may not have been visible to the project requestor, sponsor, and business managers (such as business rules, root causes of problems, and pending legislative compliance needs), the original estimates may have been either overly optimistic or pessimistic.

Now that more is known, the estimates may or may not hold and the approach, the staff skills and mix of disciplines and methods, and more may need to be changed. This is a tough position and it is one that often kills project quality and scope as project managers are afraid to be open and honest with sponsors and business managers about the changes that are needed.

Consulting companies deal with these unknowns by including assumptions in the estimates. If the assumptions are wrong, the estimates change. That is a good rule to follow when setting expectations and later when talking about what the project team is uncovering.

> *Warning: Do not simply try to force the project into the original time frame or costs. Re-estimate and provide realistic updates now that you know more. The sponsor will now make a go/no go or scope reduction decision. This is important. Many projects simply try to conform to the original estimates and follow the original approaches because the project leader is reluctant to make changes – even though he or she knows that the scope and other factors have to be changed. This may be based on internal company culture and a fear of changing the project at this time. However, if this step is not performed, the risk of the eventual failure of the project will increase.*

Once the possible scope/functionality has been justified and approved, the project team will be in a position to finalize the design scope and the comprehensive full solution design. Based on the scope, difficulty, risk, staff availability, and other factors that will be known at the completion of the requirements and spec definitions, the project manager and sponsor can now re-estimate the remainder of the project.

It is important that this discussion with the sponsor and the business managers happen immediately after the IT group estimates the cost of making changes to the IT infrastructure and the IT group responsible for building all components external to the BPMS applications completes its estimates. The business project manager should also confirm/modify the estimates for the remaining parts of the project that are under his or her control at this time. A complete picture of the needs of the project can now be built from these separate estimates.

At this point in the project you have much more information about what the needs are for the rest of the project than you did initially. There will also have been multiple changes and adjustments to team members, time commitments, purchases, sequences of activities, time needed for completion of steps, and so forth. If this is the case, then it makes sense to formally adjust the project plan and estimates based upon what you know now. Project sponsors and senior executives need to be kept informed so that their expectations are managed and unpleasant surprises are avoided.

When reviewing the initial plan and estimates at this point in a project, it is very common to discover that there are components that are already over time and over budget and perhaps even the entire project. Experience has shown that it is not a good idea to commit to making up lost time and/or adjusting expenses going forward to make up any overages and thereby avoid updating the plan and estimates. A fair and honest appraisal of where things stand and how they are likely to proceed going forward is a far better approach.

If your review results in any significant revisions to the plan and/or estimates, invest some effort in identifying the main factors that contributed to the needs for the revisions. Next, examine whether these or similar factors are likely to have impacts on future activities and make additional adjustments to the plan and/or estimates as appropriate. If any of these main factors identifies specific resources or actors that are tied to delays, budget or estimate issues, these circumstances should be discussed with the project sponsor to determine if there are any actions that can be taken to prevent further problems. For example, if there is a vendor that consistently does not deliver SLAs (Service Level Agreement terms), does the contract contain provisions that would support pressuring for remediation efforts?

A good practice is to check into how much time team members are investing in the project rather than simply relying on entries in planning and forecasting tools. Under estimation and under reporting of time is common. When used to estimate time going forward, such under estimation and reporting will seriously distort results.

Most people hate requirements to report time and often make hurried guesses when time reports are due. Draconian pressure to comply with reporting requirements may only add pressure to the team, so there must be a balance between getting accurate information and how to best approach the need. One alternative is to simply have a conversation with key people to determine how much time they are really devoting and then adjust estimates accordingly.

The cost components of the plan and estimates must be updated with current information that incorporates known costs of software, hardware, equipment, physical plant changes, etc., and replaces former estimated amounts. Look for costs from contractor change requests, specification modifications, vendors/vendor support, rate changes, and similar factors that may alter ultimate costs. Use the known amounts to adjust estimates going forward. Readjust estimates as more values become known.

Obtain updated compensation information for those employees whose costs are to be included in the project and check periodically to make certain the information has been updated to reflect raises, promotions, etc. There may also be overtime that needs to be factored into the rate calculations, including current trends and any planned or estimated overtime as part of the project. A small percentage increase can aggregate to significant dollar amounts across large organizations. Check and confirm planned versus actual overtime usage, if applicable, and adjust estimates based on these actual values. There may be instances where compensation amounts also include a "load" for benefits associated with the individual. Although it is uncommon to include the benefits load as a project cost, be sure to update these amounts as well if they are part of the project estimates. In addition, when using consultants or contractors, obtain updated rate card information and include their costs accordingly.

If project estimates include projected savings resulting from staff reductions, you will need to base the projections on accurate information. Projections are not just linear amounts obtained on the basis of the number of bodies times some fixed guess on average compensation. Rather, the estimates should include factors such as payouts for accumulated leave, any post termination factors such as a buyout, early retirement, continued benefits, any union negotiated factors, relocation costs (if applicable), etc. It is also good practice to factor in a cushion for increased overtime that may arise until new activities have become routine or may arise from cutting too deeply. Be aware that overtime can be a planned component for a project, particularly for transition periods, since the overtime costs will normally be less than adding an FTE; however, overtime costs must be factored into estimates if they are applicable. These factors should be reviewed and updated, if necessary. If initial estimates did not include these factors, new estimates may have to be prepared.

Large organizations often have functional units that routinely carry a number of vacant positions that persist over time. This can be a result of ongoing turnover and the "normal" level of vacant positions should be considered in estimates for staff reductions. If vacant positions are eliminated, there are no reductions in current personnel costs.

Some projects will result in increases in staff. Estimates should be revisited and adjusted if necessary, once simulation results are available. Estimates should include not only the personnel costs, but all associated costs such as workspace, software, work stations/tablets/laptops/smart phones, communications, infrastructure, etc. If any of the projected additional staff require specialized skills and/or are expected to be within higher compensation bands, there may also be recruitment costs which can be substantial and may also have to be factored into estimates.

4.16 Define and eliminate political concerns for the solution implementation

Corporate culture and internal politics are a fact of business life. All potential political concerns and all changes to corporate culture will need to be defined once the solution design has been proven in simulation. This should be done in parallel with the creation of solution requirements and technical specs.

As cultural changes are being considered, it is suggested that the solution team involve the business area managers and staff. This will create barriers to innovation in some cases, but innovation is really not worth much if it is rejected by the managers and staff who will need to implement it.

It will be critical to pre-sell as much of the solution and its benefits as possible to all the main managers who will be affected. This collaboration should be part of an ongoing incremental approval of the solution's concepts, component changes, and impact assessments on both the business area's managers and the staff. This presale will likely need to be based on both benefit to the company (quality, cost savings, competitive improvement, etc.) and personal benefit (lighten the workload, increase the value of the work and thus job security, help everyone meet their performance targets, etc.).

Even though the business area managers and staff will have been involved in the "To Be" solution design, it will still be necessary to make certain they support the solution. In planning for this sales effort at the end of the "To Be" design simulation, the team will need to identify the best way to approach each manager who is involved and help them understand the solution's benefits and why it will be low risk with high returns. This follow-up is critical for all innovation. Everyone involved will need to not only accept this innovation but promote it.

This involvement will need to begin with the new design and continue through the installation and implementation of the solution to deal with fears of operational disruption, staff adjustments, and unflattering internal information staff gossip.

> Note: Staff adjustment will need to be approached with HR change management specialists to make certain that the activities are approved by the company and that any issues are handled properly.

It is unfortunate, but the project manager must be constantly aware of any existing or building resistance to the overall project and the redesigned operation. Most people do not like change and many people are afraid of change. That is why there must be a professionally designed and operated change management plan throughout the project. This will mitigate much of the potential resistance and should be designed to build buy-in and support instead. There will, however, usually be a few people who continue to attempt to thwart the changes.

Some of those who resist will be overt and vocal. Each of these needs to be discussed with the project sponsor and plans put in place to eliminate the resistance. If each person cannot be brought around to a position where they support the project, senior management may be forced to take steps to insulate the person so they can no longer affect the project.

More difficult to identify are individuals who are quietly resisting and often using passive aggressive modes of resistance. The project manager must be alert to possible signs such as missed deadlines, missed meetings, complete lack of input, etc. The project manager must, however, distinguish between these signs being resistance as compared to being evidence that supervisors or managers are not allowing time for the person to carry out their responsibilities. If it appears that there are indeed resistance issues, the same must be followed with the project sponsor.

In addition to addressing political concerns regarding key players, attention must also be given to building a favorable environment within the company as a whole, or at the very least, all the functional areas that may be affected by the project. The change management plan is the foundation for creating this environment and the plan and results to date should be reviewed on an ongoing basis to determine if adjustments may be needed.

At this point in the project, representatives of those people actually performing the tasks and activities will have been brought into the project team to provide information, validate understandings, review flows and models, test and refine user interfaces, and otherwise support the project. These individuals should be deployed back to their functional areas as "evangelicals" for the project. They will have had direct experience with contemplated changes that their coworkers can only speculate about. Speculation, rumors, and filling in the blanks with imagination can build deadly and nearly silent resistance that can create big problems as the project proceeds. This direct experience should be leveraged by having the team members keep their coworkers informed about the project and the progress being made. There should be specific assignments and time allotted to update staff on an ongoing basis.

Team members who actually perform the work in functional areas are the team's eyes and ears for early warning about any building problems that might impair project implementation. These problems can include details that need to be taken into account for redesign as well as concerns and fears that might generate resistance. Any issues identified should be taken seriously and input from these team members should be actively and regularly solicited rather than waiting for something to be brought up. This information does not have to be solicited in a large group setting; sometimes one on one produces more candor.

The change management plan should include deliberate project orientation as part of overall new employee orientation, at least for those at the supervisor level and above. If there are new executive level personnel, the orientation must be more than just a project overview and should address project goals and objectives, current status, team activities and dynamics, role responsibilities, and fit with corporate strategies at a minimum. New personnel in key roles must be up to speed almost immediately.

Be alert for routine personnel changes, especially at the manager and supervisor levels. While key individuals will often be part of the team due to their roles, there can be changes in other staff that may be off the radar screen. The workforce is not static and new people may have an impact, particularly if they are from another company or from an area within the company that does not play a significant role in the project process. They may make changes in the way steps or tasks are executed and they will not have been part of the change management activities that have been fostering a positive attitude regarding the project. There is also a risk that new people will be less flexible regarding team member participation. When there are personnel changes, teams members from the functional area should be actively asked for any input that may impact the project.

When considering alternatives in the future state "ideation" stage, be sure that the team and the business agree on what alternatives will be prioritized. Create a prioritization algorithm that is signed off before evaluating one solution vs. another. This will save time and frustration as different people vote for and try to influence solution selection. Key variables in the algorithm should include ROI, time to value realization, risk to implementation, risk of not using the solution, degree of change needed to implement, complexity in solution creation and, of course, the level of senior leadership support. For example, if the CEO has a solution that he or she believes is correct, all the analysis in the world will not make much of a difference in swaying his or her opinion.

5.0 Build the solution

Note: The IT application development team can begin to define interfaces, look for data sources and more as soon as the "To Be" design is completed and confirmed through simulation – as discussed in Chapter 4. This will allow the IT group's participation to begin before the full solution simulation and the creation of formal support requirements and program specs – a benefit, as discussed in Chapter 4. The driving factor is that the BPMS-generated applications will be created and tested as in Chapter 4 as a collaborative effort between the business and IT members of the design team. This leaves the applications that are external to the BPMS. The IT members of the business solution design team will then be responsible for making certain that the information needed to drive the overlap between the design and construction activities will be robust and final enough to begin IT infrastructure and interface development work. Also, before the requirements are finalized, if the IT developers will follow an Agile approach, it will be possible for them to begin working with the solution design team to divide the completed business design into functions and then further into business stories/use cases and built as Agile Sprints. The actual development of new applications and solution components (legacy application changes, databases, web services, social mobility applications, web site applications, etc.) will begin once the design support requirements and application specs have been built in Chapter 4. See diagram below.

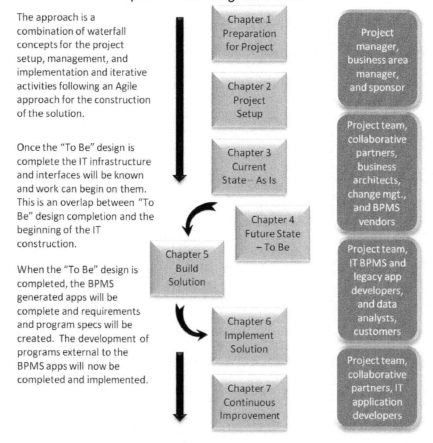

The final business operation design will be tied to the IT infrastructure changes that may be needed. As decisions on these changes are made, constraints and capabilities will be identified and the solution design and application requirements can be refined.

Once the solution requirements and program specs are ready for use, the business area team members are responsible for working with the IT program designers and developers and the BPMS developers. Their goal is to make certain that the programs that will be built externally to the BPMS-generated applications fit with all other solution components and actually improve the business operation.

The development of the solution will require a coordinated effort between both business and IT professionals. If manufacturing is involved or in the case of healthcare, where clinical activities are involved, representatives from these areas must also be part of a solution build committee. This committee must direct the overall solution construction, focusing on what is to be built and _how it will work – not how it is to be built_. The "how it will be built" is clearly the realm of the IT group, but the programming construction team can easily misinterpret the real meaning of the activities in the business design and the related technical requirements (specs). Any set of requirements and their technical specs can be built to deliver services in a wide range of actual support approaches. Some may work well and others may actually impede the workflow. This committee should make certain that what is constructed changes the activity in a way that actually improves the execution of work.

In addition to internal programming, many companies outsource some/all of their IT development projects to leverage inexpensive offshore resources. Dealing with outsourcing firms requires a different approach than many companies are used to. While any direct interaction will be managed by IT, business analysts should be part of requirements interpretation discussions on how the screens will be designed (user interfaces), how the system functions will fit together, and how the systems will flow from task to task. Business analysts do not typically attend these meetings to advise the offshore applications developers – but they _should_ in order to reduce the risk of creating a solution based on language misunderstanding or spec misinterpretation.

The chart below shows the levels that we recommend in any modeling. These levels are the ones we refer to at various places in the hints. This helps divide any information into components and shows the relationships between these components. In reality, the actual modeling levels and names that guide your information decomposition may differ from the ones in this chart. Most companies have their own model decomposition hierarchy. However, most BPM modeling structures start with Process and do not contain Business Architecture or Business Capability levels. We add these levels because it is important that transformation level changes consider the impact of the changes on the ability of the new operation to support strategy and deliver the capabilities needed to deliver strategic goals.

The important thing is that whatever model hierarchy you follow in your company should be commonly referred to in all BPM projects, and it should clearly guide the successive breaking apart of information to lower levels of detail. This creates a common framework for the models and supporting rules and information to be deconstructed into lower levels of detail and then easily reconstructed summarizing the information at the lower levels.

BPM Model Levels

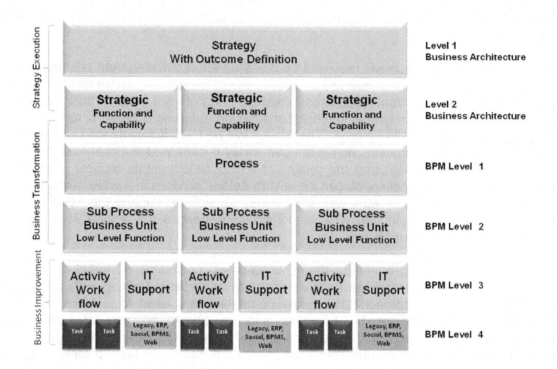

In this hints section, the focus will be on creating the IT applications, interfaces, data uses, user interface designs, and then testing the overall IT side of the business improvement or transformation solution. The hints will NOT be directed toward IT developers since they have specialized guides for the BPMS tools and programming languages being utilized. This section of the Field Guide is meant to help the business and other non-technical project team members to stay engaged and to direct the creation of the content of the applications and the way they will operate.

In this discussion, it is assumed that a BPMS or a Business Process Analysis tool will be used. Business analysis tools are great for creating graphical models, but provide minimal assistance in the automatic generation of the applications that form the core of business improvement or transformation solutions. Generating these applications is the focus of the BPMS tools – with the better tools generating business transaction applications, workflow management applications, and social mobility applications. For this discussion, we assume that business operation tools will support the construction of solutions in the same way that is recommended above. This includes the ability to:

- Graphically model the activity and its flow through the business operation
- Align application use with activities
- Decompose process to sub-process to workflow/activity and on to the task level and that this hierarchy can be clearly followed in the tool
- Collect and associate information with the activites they support
- Simulate workflows with a variety of diagnostics that help identify inefficiency and problems
- Design new screens and associated screen sets
- Identify all data and edits on a given screen

186

- Associate problems with activities and define them
- Add notes to comment and show opportunities
- Embed performance measurement into the workflow of applications at given checkpoints in the operation.

Regardless of the method or tools that are used, the project will reach the solution construction phase. If a BPMS will not be used to generate applications, any hints related to BPMS will not apply. Readers may, however, find that there are many hints that are more general that will have value.

5.1 Determine how the solution will be built – divided or big bang approach

Experience has proven that the best solutions are built from complete, detailed, comprehensive, business operation designs that provide the background information needed to let the business managers and staff, the collaborative partners, those affected by the solution, and those who will build the solution, have a solid understanding of the business operation, what it does, how it will function, and how it will be evaluated. This information must be provided to the BPMS developers and the IT staff who will support the project (e.g., data architects, UI architects, SOA and other interface developers, mobility device/social media application developers, website developers, new IT application developers, and legacy application modification developers).

The solution design is the picture of the new operation and shows the outcome that is expected from the project. It defines what the operation will look like in the future. When looked at as an interrelated set of functions (what the business does), it can be easily compared to the "As Is" model to show differences. The "As Is" workflow models' activities can be aligned to these functions along with the data that describes each activity and the hierarchy of detail that each activity may break into. These functions may be able to stand alone or they may require the addition of another function or functions to form a complete deliverable, but that can be determined by what activities need to be combined to get a specific part of the overall improvement delivered and deployed. These components can be built separately and then combined – as long as the team has an understanding of the big picture, how it breaks into component parts, and then how it can be recombined to form the outcome pictured by management.

By associating costs and benefits for the changes to each business function, a picture emerges of the real advantage that changes to each function will provide. This allows the team to pick the high value functions for early development and implementation to obtain an ROI model that allows the project to literally pay for itself while it is being built.

This process of evaluation and division allows teams to break the overall solution development project into components and allows the transformation or improvements to happen as an evolution of the business operation. This approach can be used to guide the solution's decomposition and division for construction as Agile Sprints. Because the "To Be" business model shows all relationships between activities, the team will have a clear guide for constructing the final version of the solution from the parts that are built following an Agile approach.

187

It is recommended that the workflow (activity and work steps) be used to guide the definition of the business operation changes and therefore guide the activity transformation or modification. The changes to IT support will also be defined by analyzing the technology infrastructure required to support the business operation shown in the "To Be" models. The result of this analysis will be a list of requirements for the changes that can be looked at in the aggregate or in separate business functions for construction as Sprints.

This approach allows the business and IT members of the team to work together to make certain that there is a clear definition of what is needed, what will be produced, how it will be built, and how the solution will build from delivered business function to business function until the entire solution is reconstructed and delivered.

For small narrowly focused or problem resolution projects, the normal approach most companies take with Agile works fine. This is interviewing business users to find and define use case or business stories, which in turn become Sprints. The outcomes of these Sprints are narrowly focused modules in what will become a final aggregated grouping of modules to form a solution. Because each of these modules stand alone (built separately as Sprints), they can be modified quickly in solution iterations. For large transformation projects, we recommend that the team take a different approach. This approach marries both complete and comprehensive solution design to Agile. In these larger projects, the identification of business activity interaction is important. This complete design provides a type of puzzle picture of the full solution, since activities are all shown in relation to one another. Tying problem and improvement benefit analysis to these activities produces a complete view of the workflow's outcome. It is possible to determine the sequence that these puzzle pieces will be built in. The actual construction can be through Agile Sprints. The key is that this approach controls the order in which the solution will be built and the way the output of the Sprints will be aggregated to form the entire solution, or in other words, the construction of the entire puzzle. This approach improves understanding of how the entire solution will work, guides the construction of the solution, and provides a map on the aggregation of the Sprint components that form the delivered solution.

Every effort should be made to have realistic timelines and milestones. It is far better to manage executive expectations than to lose key team members mid-project due to high frustration levels or burnout. While confronting reality may be uncomfortable, trying to explain why a major component is not properly functioning or is significantly delayed will be much more uncomfortable.

The creation of a new business operating solution in a "big bang" single project, single IT application build, has been proven to be high risk and high cost. Do not do this unless you have no choice.

A traditional Agile approach is typically far better than a "big bang" approach, but also has its drawbacks. Another alternative and a fairly new methodology is called "Wagile". Wagile is a combination of Agile and Waterfall methodologies. It combines the flexibility of Agile with the control of a step-by-step approach (Waterfall). This was initially tried in IT to overcome some of the main issues with Agile, but it was not well accepted by IT specialists. However, when applied to the business side of the project, it allows the control and activity predictability needed to manage all the different parts of the project while allowing IT to follow an Agile approach for the creation of applications, interfaces, etc. This is an important issue because the approach forms a solid basis for managing the way the project will be performed.

A Wagile approach will also support the various tools and approaches that are common to disciplines such as Six Sigma, Lean, and Kaizen by creating the complete picture that each of the participants can keep in view while applying the specialized tools that each would normally apply.

When the solution involves manufacturing, the approach taken in creating the solution is a blending of business, IT and manufacturing considerations, along with technology considerations for the current IT infrastructure (e.g., "how do we integrate Six Sigma into the construction of the solution?" or "can true collaborative design and development be supported by the network?"). Most things today are interrelated and drawing an arbitrary box around a part of the interrelated work in a process can cause a great deal of harm. This type of thinking is one of the main reasons that BPMS projects fail. The approach that is used to build any solution should consider the impact of true collaboration and the inclusion of concepts and tasks from the different disciplines involved.

The project team must work with IT to determine the approach that will be taken to build the solution. In all likelihood, IT will follow the Agile approach. However, a business approach is needed to provide solution context and organize the work. The business solution design team should build a complete composite picture of the solution and then divide it into functional components, noting what passes between each component, utilizing the main question points of what, when, where, why, how, and to whom. This allows the components to become one or more IT Agile Sprints, while providing a complete picture of the solution to guide the assembly of Sprints into a working solution, business function by business function.

Business redesign will provide the foundation for defining business changes. Determining the automation support that is needed should be based on the full new design, not on a part of it that is isolated to become an Agile Sprint. The full business design provides the context for the way the business will operate. When you focus on a business case, a single function or some other isolated subgroup of work, you lose sight of the big picture. When that happens, the business design will provide requirements that are too focused and are essentially a box full of isolated activity, without operational context. These activities then become the foundation for technical requirements and technical build specs. When the technical design and specs are created without consideration for the broad context of the entire solution, it is very possible to deliver a solution that meets all the requirements, but fails the business operation. Any set of requirements can be delivered through a lot of different technical designs, each of which affect the business differently. It is, therefore, possible for narrowly focused solution components to actually cause operational harm and to fit poorly together, causing more work and more error. In short, be sure to consider the broader picture of the business operation and how all the technical support components will be used, and how everything needs to fit together and work cooperatively as you design the separate components.

Technical specs can be interpreted differently by different groups of IT application developers. Even if interpreted the same way, the way the specs are reflected in programs can be very different and each variation can produce a different workflow, different way of dealing with source documents, different way of dealing with data and user interface (screens), and produce different business operations. While all variations may achieve the same goal, some might be more beneficial, while some might cause unintended harm to the business. Only the business manager and staff can determine which one of these outcomes the design of a program or group of programs will produce. So a close interaction (not typically done) with the IT team members in the development of the solution is important and should be insisted upon. The business analysts are not part of this stage to tell the IT professionals how to write programs. They are there to make certain that the way the programs work provides an optimal business solution.

Once the full business design is in place and approved, it can be broken into parts like the pieces of a big puzzle. In this way, you have the context and you know both what each part needs to do and how it fits into the big picture. You also know how it needs to interface with all the other parts around it and how it will build into a whole solution. This allows the technical part of the team to build an Agile-based plan for the components – prioritizing them and building them in a low risk sequence.

Once this development plan is approved, the IT members of the team can follow the company's version of Agile to build the individual components. However, in constructing the components, the team must follow the detailed business design to make certain the activities are properly understood and supported, and the applications support the workflow in the most effective and efficient manner possible – in the opinion of the business managers and staff.

The IT technical team members will need to work with the business analysts to prioritize and properly sequence the build of the different components of the solution. Eventually all the components must fit together seamlessly or the IT application side of the project will fail. It is imperative that the technical design be comprehensive and taken to a detailed level. This is a departure from the way many technical team members view Agile – jump in and start doing use case Sprints that reflect job level activity. The problem with this is one of a lack of context – the big picture of what is being built, so it all fits together to provide optimum business support.

The solution is all about business improvement. It is not about the technology.

Any approach should provide a BPMS-based outcome with parts that can be added to a functional inventory and reused. It is also recommended that the components of the solution be defined in the BPMS, that all parts of the solution outside the BPMS are documented following company documentation standards, and that the documentation be linked to the BPMS model activities. This will allow reuse and enable changes to take place faster and for improved accuracy.

While the Enterprise Architect will define and carry out IT related changes, it falls upon the project team to clearly define and test through simulation all of the components, including all of the user interfaces, channels that must be supported, required data and the current systems that contain defined data elements, flows and much more. Any lapses in defining these capabilities and characteristics could potentially result in faulty infrastructure design.

Historically, IT has had to take incomplete and poorly defined requirements and specifications presented to them by business users and then refine, re-define, adjust, and modify to create workable requirements for devising solutions. This approach has generally evolved out of necessity and is part of the way IT approaches projects. In BPM projects, such refining, and redefinition, can be very problematic, since when properly executed, the methodology is both designed to produce very precise requirements and specifications for IT to use and is dependent on that precision being carried all the way through. Buy-in regarding the methodology and the necessity for precision should have been gained much earlier in the project. However, such buy-in does not eliminate the need to track each of the details through the IT support and back to validate that BPMS and legacy components use identical specs.

It is not uncommon for IT architects to insist that detailed requirements and specifications be clearly defined prior to embarking on assessing and designing the infrastructure. Up to this point, project activities have been executed within a context of capabilities, concepts, and goals. Only in this phase do the detailed requirements begin to emerge. Depending on the current infrastructure and the scope of the project, the potential impact will range from minimal to significant. There should be a head start in gauging the potential impact well before the details become available. For this reason, the IT architects should be involved with the team from the outset of activities and there should be deliberate ongoing dialogue about how the capabilities and concepts might impact infrastructure needs going forward. As the project proceeds, the level of detail will continuously evolve and the thinking of the architects should evolve as well.

Despite early involvement and ongoing evolution of requirements, sometimes there are infrastructure needs that far exceed the planned investment because software, hardware, facility, and/or staffing needs cascade well beyond what was initially anticipated. If this situation arises, there must be an immediate review of how the infrastructure needs can be met and the project sponsor should be brought in immediately. There are really only four choices, although the first three might be used in combination:

- Secure additional funding from the executive level
- Scale back and defer until later one or more components of the solution
- Revise the solution using simulation to identify the best workaround option
- Terminate the project (given the investment to date, this should be the last resort option)

Devising a roadmap to compensate for the absence of necessary infrastructure must involve both the business users and IT staff.

5.2 Create the technical IT program build plan

You now have a completely vetted set of solution requirements and technical specs for modules, new applications, legacy application changes, application interfaces, data base designs, website changes, and social mobility apps that need to be built outside of the BPMS environment and then linked to the BPMS-generated applications. The vetting process will have included both directly and indirectly affected business managers, collaborative partners, IT BPM and traditional applications designers, and the team sponsor. The scope will also have been confirmed or changed and the solution capabilities will now be final.

In this phase, the components of the solution that are outside of the BPMS-generated applications and the BPMS operating environment will now be built and linked to the BPMS applications to form an operational solution that can be implemented.

In reality, this construction could have been started as specs became approved in the previous phase, so it is very possible to have phase 4 and 5 activities overlapping. See diagram below.

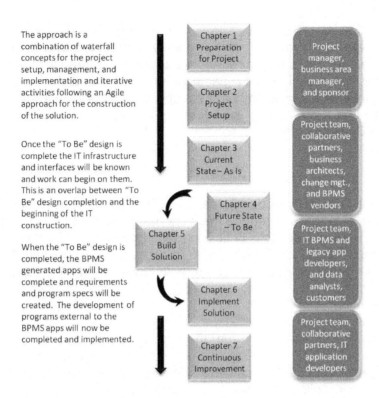

The approach is a combination of waterfall concepts for the project setup, management, and implementation and iterative activities following an Agile approach for the construction of the solution.

Once the "To Be" design is complete the IT infrastructure and interfaces will be known and work can begin on them. This is an overlap between "To Be" design completion and the beginning of the IT construction.

When the "To Be" design is completed, the BPMS generated apps will be complete and requirements and program specs will be created. The development of programs external to the BPMS apps will now be completed and implemented.

The decision on the timing to start will be made between the business solution project manager and the IT project manager. If the two project managers decide to overlap the development of the technical components (applications, interfaces, data use, etc.) that are external to the BPMS-generated applications, time will be saved in the project's development and implementation. However, delaying the start of the technical side of the project work will not negatively impact the quality of the deliverable. Whatever approach is agreed upon by the business and IT project managers for the project will determine how the work is scheduled and staffed in the technical solution development plan. This plan should align with the business side of the solution's development and drive the solution's delivery and implementation dates.

This phase is really an IT phase and it will be planned and managed by an IT project manager. However, in a BPM-based project, business redesign team members will serve as consultants to IT and the technical project(s). Their role will be to provide guidance on how these "external" solution components should function and how they should fit into the business design. The goal of this collaboration is to avoid creating automated solution components that fail to actually improve the way the work is really performed. It is also to help the technical teams understand performance monitoring/measurement/reporting, so the data captured at different points in the workflow can provide optimal information.

As with all major project components, the IT project team will create a project plan for their work. It is important that this project plan be linked to the master project plan used by the business project manager. The technical component plans should follow the IT methodology – Agile or whatever discipline the company is using. The ties to the main business solution project plan will need to align both plans for dates, deliverables, tests, etc. This alignment will need to be reviewed by the project sponsor, the business managers who will be directly affected, and IT to ensure that it is doable and will provide the desired results.

Technologists love the latest hardware/software that eager sales people are touting as the solution to all business problems. While technology can solve many problems, typically with lower costs/higher reliability, it is important not to become enamored with the latest and greatest solution. Businesses need reliable and repeatable solutions that deliver consistent performance and value. Ensure that your technology partners and design teams are focused on creating and delivering solutions that work, rather than looking for an excuse to try some new toy just delivered under the Christmas tree.

Business transformation, especially during the build stage of the project, may easily lose sight of the fact that technology is there to reduce the work that people have to do; therefore, making it easy to interact with the applications is critical in meeting this goal. This interaction is also a key element for reducing waste and increasing performance. The big mistake that is often made is that even though the technology staff does not really understand the business, they make user decisions in the technical design and change the way screens are presented, used, and supported by the solution.

The issue is that they often build from their perspective, and not the business user's perspective. The result can be solutions that are difficult to use and may make the business operation slower, more error prone, and more frustrating for workers than it was before the change. Be careful and collaborate closely with the business user staff throughout the build process. This begins with the division of the solution into functions and then the functions into use cases for creation as Sprints. This is the underlying foundation for the technical side project planning.

We have found that many BPMSs do not live up to the "ease of use" claims made by the vendor. We solved the problem by dividing the design between process architects/business analysts and BPMS developers. We made certain the BPMS developers understood the business process models by starting their work at the point where the business design is augmented with necessary BPMN application symbols to support the BPMS application generation. We didn't make this technical augmentation a hand-off. We overlapped the two teams' work to ensure interaction between them. Once they agreed on the business and technical designs, the IT application developers got involved to help design and build interfaces and modify legacy application functionality.

Construction must orchestrate multiple disciplines and be partially done in parallel with future state design finalization.

During this phase of work, there should be strong representation from IT on the team. Once identified, work with this person to divide the overall new business operation design into separate, but related business functions. These functions can then be broken into one or two lower levels of detail that will eventually be able to be built separately as IT applications. As you are dividing the business functions and their operational designs at the workflow level, keep track of the way each of these sub elements of the business operation are related to one another (data, control, rules). This will allow you and the IT people who will build the solution to know how to reconstruct the solution.

Identify all of the business functions or lower level components of the "To Be" solution and determine if there are dependencies between them. This will help you and IT to understand how the components can be built as well as identify the order to build each component.

IT will have a methodology that they will want to follow in building the BPMS and/or traditional technology applications. It is important that this methodology must be tied to and aligned with the business transformation methodology that is being used, and not become a separate and distinct methodology apart from the overall project. Part of this alignment includes the standards that must be followed in defining business and later, technical applications development requirements. This is critical, as poor requirements equal a poor solution. All requirements must tie directly to activities or at a lower level, a task and the application support should address entire workflows.

Any business design should include multiple support elements. These include:
- BPMS-generated applications
- Constructed new applications (following traditional IT approaches and built in the preferred programming language of the company)
- Application interfaces
- Social Mobility Applications
- Web services
- Databases with data movement (probably following a Services Oriented Architecture (SOA) approach)

These support elements should include identification of the required new computer hardware, printers, communication needs, etc.

Monitoring and reporting compliance requirements, both at the local and federal levels, may apply to any application system. The same is true for financial reporting. Considerations for these mandatory requirements must be included in any group of technical specifications for final solution build.

When following the approach used in IT for application construction (usually either Agile or Waterfall methodology), identify the major activities and what each activity will provide. Make certain there is a design that ties the IT support design to the business operation workflow models. Both areas must be clearly aligned with specific support. Constraints must be identified for each place where automated support will be used. Failing to create this alignment is a typical issue. However, without this alignment and definition, risk is increased and an ability to tie support seamlessly to the business operation will likely not be fully exploited.

Offshore and outsourced staff can contribute significantly to any application development project. However, unless they are able to deliver all business analysts on site at your location, they should not be considered for business redesign work. The reason is that while most offshore firms can provide competent people, it is extremely difficult to interview business people remotely and to have the level of communication required to reduce risk when significantly different time zones are involved. Face to face meetings invariably produce better information and remote interviews should be avoided even if outsourced staff is not used.

If an external contracted vendor is retained to build the solution, a portion of the vendor team should be located on site with the other members of your solution development team. This will help avoid misunderstandings and allow the external staff to gain a feel for how the business operation really works.

Consider insisting in any contract with an outside vendor that the same people be assigned to the project until it is completed, unless a reason arises that absolutely requires their replacements. This reduces the need to constantly on-board new people, bring them up the learning curve, and integrate them into the team.

Proper management of offshore or remote teams is difficult and requires considerable attention from both the project manager and the senior business design team members. The transfer of the work should be based on a formal and a fairly detailed solution development plan that has defined deliverables tied to specific dates. It is also important that status checks be carried out at regular intervals so that adjustments can be made well in advance of final deliverable dates.

External teams should be given a plan that shows specifically how any significant deliverables will be built and how they will be integrated into the final product. This evolution should be tied to a defined and accepted timeline. It is important that at least portions of the solution be proven to have been created on a continuing basis.

Progress is often difficult to judge with external contractors, especially if the development of a solution is fully outsourced. This has caused delivery timing, content, and quality problems that could be avoided. For this reason, expected progress should be defined in greater detail that might otherwise be specified and status of actual work products should be determined on a regular basis. It is not unreasonable to take a look at progress, as well as potential problems, on a weekly basis.

Status meetings are really not sufficient in outsourcing situations. All progress should be shown in specific deliverables that are designed to evolve, so the team can see exactly what is being done, and evaluate the quality and progress before a problem becomes difficult to fix.

It is wise to have a Plan B when outside staffing will be used for the construction of the whole solution or for significant parts of the solution. Any contract with external resources should have a back out clause for failure to perform or deliver on time. This should carry penalties, and criteria should be simple and easy to prove to avoid legal contests.

Do not lose visibility of what is being done by any outside contracted support. Status reports can be misleading. Be sure to do spot inspections of the work being done to ensure that quality is being maintained, progress to goal is being achieved, and deliverables are consistent with expectations.

It is important that external resources be given copies of company IT development standards and that their compliance with these standards be monitored.

Following an Agile approach for application development allows the project managers (business and IT) to keep closer track on the construction of the solution. This is important when frequent solution component delivery is needed.

5.3 Build the new business operation business and IT support

This section of the Field Guide includes hints on building the business operation, generating the final versions of the BPMS applications, building applications and other technology components external to the BPMS, and integrating them into a single solution.

In approaching the technical side of business transformation and generating or building software applications, there are a series of basic questions that should be considered when starting the development activity. These questions include:

1. Will a traditional BPMS-supported BPM approach be followed or will an iBPM approach be used? There are differences in approach, philosophy, and capabilities between these two approaches that should be considered.

2. What BPMS/BPA analysis tool set will be used and can it export models/information to other tools? This is critical if separate modelers, rules engines, simulation tools, etc., will be used.
3. Will a Model Office testing environment be built and used for a "simulated live" full solution test?
4. Will the development of the solution applications/interfaces be started as soon as the full business design is completed, or when parts of the design are completed, or when the design is fully tested in a simulated operation (using "Stubs" and "Drivers" – small interface modules that pass or receive information and control to the solution), or when the business and application requirements and the program specs have been completed?
5. Will changes to the existing hardware and technical software environment be needed to support the new solution? Have changes been approved?
6. Is all the right technical staff available for the roles they will play in the project?
7. What standards must be followed?
8. Will an Agile approach with focused Sprints be used to build the solution components external to the BPMS? Will Agile be used in the approach to BPMS application generation?
9. How will the deconstructed business design be put back together once the applications have been built?
10. How will application functional quality be determined? Who will be responsible for certifying that the applications have been tested and that all requirements have been met?
11. And more ....

When using an iBPM approach, it is recommended that the business solution be run in simulation before any business requirements are finalized or any technical requirements (new applications, application modifications, interface designs, etc.) are fully defined. This is, however, optional.

In a traditional BPM-based business operation redesign, business modelers may be used that do not support application generation or the types of rules use, data use and definition and other capabilities that are offered through formal BPMS tools. This means that the business designs must be supported by applications that are built manually, following traditional application development approaches, using those application programming languages in use in the company.

This section of the Guide will provide hints from a business perspective dealing with BPMS application generation, new application development, legacy application changes, interfaces, and data use.

Today, every company using a BPMS or iBPMS has a hybrid technical environment. Some applications are generated and some are legacy. Further, some are "packages" (integrated groups of applications) and some applications are newly custom built. This mix requires that the BPM design team work closely with multiple disciplines within IT to leverage capabilities and avoid constraints. In addition, most companies have a mixture of IT technology that has been used. This fact is neither good nor bad. It simply is the way technical environments have generally evolved over the past 50 years. This environment includes:
- Multiple programming languages
- Old applications that are running in base technical environments that are no longer truly supported by the vendors

- A mix of technology that often does not really work together that well
- A mix of high quality and poor quality data
- Mostly poor application documentation
- Largely undocumented data flow between applications and interfaces between applications that, while generally operational, can be "finicky."

These and related factors are what makes the IT side of any solution difficult. When the current drive to do everything faster is added to the mix, it is easy to underestimate what it will really take to build adequate, high quality, well tested application support with a sufficient communication, data storage, and operation infrastructure. It is also why in some cases testing can only be partially completed and the possibility of the infamous IT ripple across applications and data bases is a concern.

The requirements and technical specs that have been provided have now been fully vetted and designed to help make certain the business operating design is adequately supported by the applications that will be built. These requirements and specs need to conform to the standards in place in IT to ensure that all needed information is available. Based on the business design and these requirements, IT can work with the business project manager to create a comprehensive picture of the new solution – including IT support. From this picture, the IT project manager can understand and define all components that need to be built and estimate the time and resources needed for their construction and testing. This estimate needs to be aligned with the original project estimates and a final negotiated estimate created. From this, IT can create a comprehensive solution development approach and project plan.

In planning the solution construction, it is strongly recommended that any division of the business model into business stories or use cases be done with the involvement of the business team members who designed the business process models. This will improve the quality of the Sprints and help in the reconstruction of the Sprints into solution components.

IT will build all application support in this section of the project. This will include BPMS application generation and all new applications, changes to legacy applications, interfaces, social mobility applications, data bases, etc.

All Sprints and the solution components that are built will combine into the applications that support the business solution. These should be tested following formal IT testing standards and their accuracy certified by IT. This should include:
1. Capability function testing
2. Normal and high load work – what transactions, when, how many (stress test – daily time differences, seasonal, product special sales) - the data load's effect on key decision points
3. Regression testing
4. Data use – screen and report build, data flow, data transformation, database usability
5. Interfaces/load testing – when will the load cause failure? What happens when each of the apps fail?

Note: This list provides examples and is not a complete list of all things that must be considered. The real source of this list must be the company's IT testing standards. Care should be taken to make certain these standards are followed if testing is outsourced.

Using an iBPMS tool will allow the project team to generate at least components of the business solution as part of simulation modeling and analysis driven design iteration. Using programmed "Stub" and "Driver" modules, the majority of the final solution will also have been defined, tested, and iterated until it delivers needed support. This approach will have created a solution design based on application generation that defines all application construction requirements external to the BPMS environment, along with directions on how the generated and external applications will fit together. The basic conceptual design that was created early in the redesign process is now finalized showing all business activity and how each is supported by IT.

The BPMS or iBPMS application developer is a specialist in the use of the BPMS tool and the environment it creates and operates in. These specialists will be responsible for ensuring that all data, models, rules, relationships, etc., required to generate a high quality set of applications from the business solution design are documented. The data and the business process models needed for this generation should follow adopted standards for the team and the information should have been collected during the "As Is" discover and the "To Be" design. However, it is still possible that additional information will be needed.

BPMS application generation has two sides, a business operation design side and a very technical side. The business operation design side is meant for modeling, simulation, data collection on a wide range of information areas (they should be defined by company and BPMS standards), and rules identification/definition/coding for entry into the rules library or engine of the BPMS. The technical side is focused on generating applications. The BPMS tool forms a type of separate operating environment where all generated applications run. This environment tracks a lot of varying information and offers significant development shortcuts for developers. However, to drive application generation, the BPMS designer uses a specialized set of symbols that follow a standard called BPMN.

Today vendors are on the second version of these standards, referred to as BPMN 2.0. These symbols are used to identify program code modules that are accessed and placed in sequence according to the models during application generation. These code modules have blank spaces in them that are filled by the rules and data that are associated with the symbol in the workflow model. Once populated and sequenced, the code modules are ready to be executed as directed by the BPMS in actual business operation. The BPMS developers are generally responsible for the technical entry of the BPMN symbols, the definition/coding/linking of rules, and the generation of the applications. These generated applications do not, however, deliver a complete support operation. There are external components including external applications, modification of legacy applications, the creation of interfaces and data edits, and more. These external components are the responsibility of more traditional IT application developers.

Generate BPMS applications: In the application generation process, the business analysts, the BPMS application developers, and the IT application specialists must work together to create an integrated solution design, and then a plan that guides the activity and orchestrates the involvement of all three groups. This may also include data architects, enterprise architects, and user interface architects. The project managers and the business analysts on the project team should make certain that this part of the project is collaborative and that all potential technical and business aspects of the solution are involved in solution design and planning meetings.

Generate BPMS applications: The technical team will use the BPMS models and information to generate applications. These applications will not be fully functional because they will not have interfaces to legacy applications or access to data that is not part of the BPMS-generated solution. The technical team will identify all places where the BPMS-generated applications must pass data to an outside application or data source or receive data from an outside source. They will also define what the data content must include and what formats must be followed for each interface. They can now build "Stub" programs to accept data from each of these exit points from the BPMS application and for each entry point where data is passed to the BPMS application from an external source "Drivers." These "Stubs" and "Drivers" will allow the solution to be simulated and run with all embedded performance and analytics reporting. This is a full solution simulation, conducted using the BPMS-generated applications in an operating environment that is as close to the real technical operating environment as can be created.

BPMS application generation: The business analysts will need to hold a turnover meeting with the technical BPMS development team. The turnover will include a review of key notes from interviews, rules, application use, data use and flow, mobile apps, web services, website apps, customer user requirements, and any other relevant information. This will result in an ongoing review cycle, which should include business managers and staff, collaborative partners, and IT developers.

BPMS application generation: All rule coding should be reviewed and changed as needed. In some cases, the rules will be coded by BPMS developers and in some cases by rules coding specialists. In both cases, the rules should be vetted before they are put into live use.

A comprehensive solution technical architecture should be created to guide the design and creation of the applications that will support the solution. This architecture is a design that shows all the solution components and how they fit together. The interface designs should show not only what passes, but acceptable values, timing, volume, and any error conditions that should be tested. The business project leader should work with IT to ensure that this architecture is built and that it serves as the guide in designing and building the solution.

The solution design should address the entire business operation that is within the scope of the project. This design may be at the process level, the sub-process level or at a lower level of business operation – business unit function workflow, business function task or task step. The level of detail is important and may vary depending on the needs of the change design. However, the scope must at a minimum, be the entire business unit function workflow. This design should include all components (e.g., generated applications, new applications) that will be custom built in a traditional programming language, legacy application use and changes, interfaces, social mobility apps, etc.

The aforementioned design forms a context for the construction of component applications, business activity, and IT infrastructure change. It is especially important if an Agile approach is used. This breaks any business design into low-level components, usually at the task level looking at how a person does a single task in job or activity. It is important to note that the Agile approach, like the BPM approach, is implemented differently among companies. The concepts are often adhered to but the way they are implemented does vary. In many cases, the IT analysts start by identifying business "use cases." These are generally low level descriptions of a specific task or job that is being performed. The goal is to build these separately and then release them to deliver some improvement quickly. Eventually, these individual components will be combined to form a solution.

This level of division can create serious construction issues if it does not have a complete business or application solution design to guide the reconstruction of the components into the solution. Designed separately, these components often don't fit together as well as people would like them to. This is a problem that causes support, time, cost, and quality issues. However, it can be avoided if the use cases are actually defined by first creating a full solution design that integrates all parts of the business operation and then dividing that into components or business use cases. This method allows the team to understand the context of the business operation and how everything will fit together before they divide it into use cases.

Legacy application changes will be identified in the new business operating model. All application capabilities will be identified and defined in the business model at the activity or lower task or step level. The information that will be needed should be developed using a company standard to ensure that all teams will collect the information needed for this activity as well as other technical and business design steps.

If an Agile approach will be used, it is recommended that it be modified for its use in BPMS-supported BPM projects. This includes looking at the scope and then dividing it by Business Stories that will address a specific single action in the workflow. These "Use Cases" will become Agile Sprints. This approach requires the creation of a foundational understanding of the business area.

New application development requirement specs will be driven by the new business operation design. Each business activity in the business operating model will reflect applications and their capabilities, if not on the model, then in supporting information. Combine these capability requirements and work with the business analysts and the staff who will use the applications to map the flow of information through the new business model and the why the applications are used. Create a capability use matrix with the capability on one axis and the activities on the other axis. Show every activity that uses each capability and in the intersection of the capability /activity columns, list the way the capability is used. Align capabilities with use in the business operating model and consolidate business rules for each capability. Data use and its flow can also be defined at this time. This will allow the business capabilities to be translated to requirements and allow the IT applications designers to determine the best way to support the business needs, generate an application, build changes to legacy applications, license an application, or outsource the whole business function.

Sample Capability vs. Activity matrix

Capability Matrix						
Business Capability - Sell Over Internet Sales Channel						
Capability/Activity Matrix						
	Activity Name		Activity Name		Activity Name	
Task Name	Used in this Activity - yes/no	How used?	Used in this Activity - yes/no	How used?	Used in this Activity - yes/no	How used?

Sample Business Activity vs. Rule matrix

Capability Matrix						
Business Activity - Sell Over Internet Sales Channel						
Business Activity/Business Rule						
Task	Business Rule	Business Rule	Business Rule	Business Rule	Business Rule	Business Rue

Sample Business Activity vs. Data Elements matrix

Capability Matrix						
Business Capability - Sell Over Internet Sales Channel						
Activity Name	Activity/Data					
Task	Data Element	Data Element	Data Element	Data Element	Data Element	Data Element

If possible, DO NOT let the BPMS developers try to interpret the business operation models and create business or technical requirements without the business analysts and process analysts who created the new business process models.

Do not allow the BPMS developers to reinterpret business rules or how they fit together to support decision making or to guide work. Any questions or problems should be taken to the business project manager for resolution.

If possible, DO NOT let the BPMS developers start to identify "business cases or stories" by independently interpreting the business process models or going directly to the business managers and staff. BPMS developers typically focus on the technology needs and have a difficult time understanding the real business operation. The business cases need to be selected from activities, or possibly the activity's tasks, with the help of the business analysts or process analysts that created the design. This interaction is needed to explain the concepts and needs of the business operation depicted in the model and supporting information.

Any compromise in the business design due to technology limitations should be reviewed with the business managers and those indirectly affected by the business design change. If possible, the changed design should be run through the simulation again and treated as another iteration. The simulation will again point out any efficiency problems with the new changes. This provides the team a chance to make certain the changes will not impact the overall efficiency of the solution design. The key in the business design is to reach a design that can be proven optimal before it is built. That is still the objective regardless of when a limitation/constraint based change needs to be made.

Most interfaces should have been identified and defined in the new business design as part of the current application use identification phase. Those that are "behind the scenes" in the way applications interface and data travels should also have been identified by IT as the business support requirements were analyzed. This analysis is the foundation for decisions about legacy application modification, new application construction, and application licenses. As these decisions were made, the IT team should have identified/confirmed the interfaces that would result and the data that would pass across each interface. The actual interface identification and definition is an IT team responsibility with the business redesign team providing data and support use guidance.

IT should have current data interface diagrams for all applications, data flow diagrams that show how data moves between applications, a data architecture model, a data dictionary that defines data and its attributes, and data edit documentation for each application. If they don't, additional care must be taken in considering interfaces. If this information is not available to the IT interface team, the risk to the project is increased and additional testing time should be built into the project.

It is better to take the time to make certain that everything in the new solution works. To rush to meet a deadline and deliver a product that does not function properly is not a good approach and will end up delivering a solution that functions poorly.

Before interfaces are built, check and recheck to make certain the specifications include each of the relevant data dictionary definitions associated with each data element. Then define the performance and data transformation quality testing with IT. This will spell out clear expectations. IT will then be responsible for building the interfaces between the BPMS-generated applications, the legacy applications, as well as both newly built applications (including web applications and social mobility applications), and licensed applications.

Each interface should be modeled to show what passes in each direction, when, why, and under what control. All expected data transformation should also be part of interface modeling so expected results coming back across the interface can be tested to avoid garbage passing in either direction. These models should be used to design comprehensive tests. These tests should be used to certify the operation of each interface.

Interfaces are a weak point in most solutions and should be carefully tested in a variety of situations. Make certain all parts of the solution work. Consider negative testing as well in order to see what breaks them and then if the situation is likely to occur, make corrections to the solution.

Data is the thing that drives any business operation as it is created, collected, and modified when it moves through the business operation. Its quality is critical as is the way it is used and the way it transforms from activity to activity. Control of this flow is very important as is control over the way it is edited and used. This flow and editing should be mapped in a dataflow that aligns with the workflow models of the business.

An iterative approach is often used to design and construct solutions. This is good and bad at the same time. Unless iteration cycles are controlled through a focusing approach, such as a simulation modeler, the changes in each iteration are a guess as to what will make the business operation more efficient and/or will improve quality. Using a simulation tool, the workflow can be evaluated by the tool and changes focused onto the parts of the operation that have flow problems. This refocusing of change in each design iteration reduces the number of iterations needed and thus the time and cost needed to create an efficient new operating design. This approach however mainly tests for efficiency but not effectiveness (i.e., doing the right thing at the right point in time to maximize value).

Construction of business application support is clearly an IT developer role. With a BPMS, this role is different from traditional application development. However, both BPMS and BPM developers are needed to create a full BPM solution. This is because the BPMS will require specialized BPMN (Business Process Model and Notation) symbol use that will be based off of the work that is done with the business analysts to define how the generated applications will be designed and constructed. The BPMS developer will also be responsible for the coding of business rules and the definition of how each will be used. Further, the BPMS developer will work closely with traditional IT application developers to ensure the proper construction of components that are external to the BPMS-generated applications so that they are able to be executed within the BPMS environment.

The role of the business operation designer during the construction of the application support phase of the solution development is to support the IT application developers by offering business design and operational background interpretation and helping to explain term definitions. Where the business requirements hit IT constraints, the business designer will work with the appropriate business managers and staff to redesign the operation around the constraint. The same is true for design changes required to interface properly with external partners whose IT applications will be part of the solution or generate the data that will need to be transferred (such as the federal or state governments).

As the component parts of the designed business solution are built, each must be tested following IT testing standards. This is a specialized technical job that should follow a specific plan for testing each component of the solution and then as they combine, the combined parts of the solution. This testing will be used to prove the applications, interfaces, web service, web sites, and social applications function properly. This should be the foundation for testing, but it should also be expanded to include break testing, identifying whatever can go wrong, and then doing something to handle the problem. This is necessary because it is not acceptable for predictable errors to cause applications to fail and crash.

Traditionally, IT has been responsible for testing without much input from the business managers or staff. This has caused failures since IT may think something is working when it is actually causing problems. This is typically blamed on requirements definition issues. To avoid any potential disconnect in considering a solution success, testing should be reviewed for completeness by a combined group of business managers and staff, project business team members, and IT developers to make certain that the applications, interfaces, etc., function as envisioned and produce correct results, including performance monitoring, measurement, and reporting.

5.4 Run interface test in the Model Office

At this point, the BPMS applications will have been generated and tested. The interfaces and applications external to the BPMS will have been built, the data schemas will have been designed and the databases built, the social mobility applications will have been generated or built, and the web site changes will have been made.

The technical support to the solution should be fully operational at this time. But the solution will not have been tested in a simulated full operation with the target business staff using it. This simulated business operation is called a Model Office environment. Without this live test, the solution may still be a business failure and if implemented, it may be rejected by the business managers and staff as causing more harm than good. For this reason, we recommend that a simulated business operation be built and used to test the solution in this Model Office environment.

Construction of this environment takes time and increases the cost of the project. As a result, the Model Office simulation is often omitted. It is our belief that omitting this step increases risk and leads to unhappy business users and potentially customers. It is simply a question of the level of risk that a solution team is willing to take.

This test will first require a place near the actual business operation for the simulated business operation to be built. The construction will include running communications lines for PCs, printers, phones, etc., to this new work site. It will next require that additional PCs, printers, etc., be obtained and installed in the Model Office along with desks, tables, etc.

In addition, the security/access (to the Model Office, the PCs, the applications, application features) will need to be planned and Model Office staff will need to be trained. Once these people complete the Model Office test, they will become trainers and mentors for the implementation of the solution. The preparation must also include planning for all forms, letters, emails, work lists, etc., that are used today to be duplicated and used to drive work in the Model Office. New work drivers may require that forms, etc., to be manually built to form samples. The actual numbers of documents, etc., that are used in the simulated operation will need to be determined by company IT testing standards.

> Note: There are many articles on using Model Office simulation tests on the internet. For readers who are uncertain as to what a Model Office really is and how to build one, we suggest you do a search on the term Model Office and conduct a personal study.

As the Model Office is built, it is recommended that interfaces between all applications be tested. This will be the first time some of the solution's technical components may be tested in the full solution. Because each application will have been tested following IT testing standards, they can be assumed to work properly. At this time, all interfaces need to be tested as well as the flow of data with edits and transformations.

Once the business design is proven to be optimal (using simulation modeling), the BPMS applications have been generated (with the performance monitoring and measurement activities/applications built in from the business solution design), the performance of the rules (rule coding makes a difference in the way the applications can run) have been tested, the interfaces between applications (and the flow of data and its transformation) have been tested and certified by IT, and the solution has been proven to deliver the project's target improvements, it will be fully functional. At this point we recommend that another step be added to the testing.

The solution is now a technical success, as it has been proven to work. But it is not yet a business success. The next step is one used in the past by many software vendors to ensure the solution is accepted as being operationally acceptable to business managers and staff. This final testing is for usability and it offers IT a final iteration opportunity. This test is in a Model Office environment.

A Model Office is a fully functioning duplicate model of a business operation. It is used to test new business operations and their support as well as to train managers and staff. In many cases in the past, Model Offices have been used to deal with complex operational changes and test the quality, scalability, and use of the solution in a type of live environment. The tests and work are initiated using the same forms/data/timing rules that are used in live business operations. The staff in the Model Office will then process the data as if they were doing so in the actual operational mode. Results of both the new and old operations will be compared and if the savings or targets are capable of being realized, the project will continue with the rest of the people in the business operation.

Actual solution operation testing by those who will use the solution is critical and should not be avoided. It does add time and cost to the original estimate (unless it was already built in), but it also reduces the number of construction redesigns and iterations, and leads to a better solution.

Never rush to simplify or shorten the interface operation, business operation live simulation tests, or their impact evaluation. This evaluation looks at the refocusing of each design and build iteration and user acceptance steps in a project.

Make certain that the team fully understands all interface points between the solution that is being created and associated technology environments. Today's systems' architecture is often complex and not fully understood, let alone completely documented. Design implications can have unintended consequences to the solution being developed and the native environment that is in place.

The Model Office test should immediately follow the training of a select group of business managers and staff. This group should be a mix of senior or experienced business staff and fairly new staff. Once trained, the people should run their operation in the Model Office. This environment will take all the mail, transactions, timing triggers, etc., that initiate the business unit's activity and process it as they will in the new version of the operation. This testing should uncover all serious operational issues, including screen use, data flow, and inefficiencies. The results of the actual work should be checked against the expected outcome of the processing to confirm that rules are being used properly. Any problems can be fixed easily in this operational testing environment. The result is a solution that is acceptable to the people who will use it. This makes the solution a business success. It is now ready to be implemented.

The BPM project should be led by a business-focused project manager, while the solution development will be led by IT project development managers. In the design stage, the IT project manager or staff on the project team will play a supporting role. In the development stage, the business project manager and staff on the team will play a supporting role to the IT project manager. In the Model Office test, the business and the IT project managers will be co-managers and will work closely together to deliver the final working solution.

5.5 Simulate the business solution – live Model Office test

The Model Office was built in Chapter 5, section 4, and all application interfaces were tested. The team now has a fully functioning Model Office to conduct a complete test of the solution by the people in the business area who will use it. This is a live, but parallel business operation test that is designed to evaluate the workflow and the usability of the solution.

The purpose of this testing environment is to go beyond the IT application functional tests, the interface tests, the web services (SOA) tests, and the social mobility application tests. These types of tests are technical tests that are designed to check the operation of the computer programs and ensure that all technical requirements/specs have been met and are functional. While this testing is critical, we recommend that testing for a BPMS-enabled BPM solution go beyond this traditional IT testing.

This Model Office test may uncover errors in the applications. However, this test is designed to simulate the way the solution works and identify problems in the way the applications support the work, workflow, and the human/machine interaction. The solution must be intuitive to use and limit human error.

As noted in Chapter 5, section 4, the creation of a business operation that mimics the business area's actual operation is driven by copies of live documents, emails, etc. Once any document, etc., which initiates and drives work is put into the front of any workflow, members of the business area staff will process these transactions/cases the way they will be processed in the new solution. Results between the current and new operations can be compared and use issues can be identified. All issues with workflow, application use, screen group content and flow, etc., will be open for discussion and improvements jointly designed between the IT developers, the BPMS developers, the business designers on the project team as well as the collaborative partners. This is necessary to avoid "ripple" problems since changes may affect upstream or downstream work.

It is very possible to have a technical solution that has been tested and is fully operational but is rejected by the business managers and staff. Any set of requirements or specs can be built following a variety of usage designs. Some requirement fulfillment designs will be much more beneficial than others – and some designs can actually cause the solution to be worse than the business operation before the project. These issues can make or break the acceptance and thus use of any business transformation solution by those who will use it.

The goal is therefore for those who will perform the work to use the solution and recommend improvements to the technical team. These improvements will then be made to optimize the acceptability and usability of the solution. A final testing should be an extension of this Model Office test that looks at any customer facing social mobility applications, website applications, and human interface activity. Focus groups may be used for this review.

If this is done, risk will be greatly reduced and corrective action can be identified and taken immediately to eliminate use issues – in both internal use by business managers and staff, in customer use/interaction. Usability will become more and more important as each market moves ever closer to requiring companies to evolve to digital enterprises.

Time and budget pressure can cause leadership, sponsors, and even team members to seek to shorten activities associated with full and complete solution testing and to cut testing costs. But testing will ultimately be done – either in a controlled environment or in live operation where performance may be harmed.

Always ensure that the test environment or "sandbox" is current and contains the most up-to-date solution. Too often the test environment is out of sync.

It is expected that users will have been involved throughout the project and provided inputs that are incorporated into the design. The users will not, however, have been able to test the full solution for flow, usability, efficiency, etc., until this live solution has been built. Therefore, once the Model Office solutions are available, this should be tested by representatives of end user groups to check the design, as well as to obtain input regarding any changes or modifications that should be considered.

Since there may be multiple functional areas that should test the solution in the Model Office, any proposed modifications must be coordinated to ensure that UI changes do not negatively affect other users upstream or downstream.

To run a Model Office scenario, actual input information that is used in normal "As Is" processing should be captured in sufficient quantity to be useable. Since the Model Office runs outside the current production system, it can be used in the simulation without affecting production. Actual information is preferable to trying to generate a fictitious data set since it reflects input from the real world.

If any parts of the solution have end users external to the company, such as consumers, brokers, wholesalers, suppliers, etc., representatives of these groups should also test the solution in a Model Office environment. For consumers, this testing is critical. While employees can be told they must use the solution, consumers may avoid a company if the solution is difficult to use or does not meet their needs and expectations. This can be accomplished by incentivizing representatives (will vary depending on the nature of the business), having them test the solution with the types of transactions they would typically carry out, and then interviewing at least some of them and having a questionnaire completed by all of them. Access can be via a web or mobile link and/or by having groups assemble at convenient locations.

The "Model Office" allows staff, who will be executing the steps and tasks in various operational areas, to work with the UI design that applies their responsibilities and become acquainted with the features, functionalities, look and feel. Such testing identifies positives as well as potential problems that may slow down work, contribute to errors, or be seen as cumbersome. For most BPMSs, making changes to UI screens is quick and easy. It is very important to use these hands on testing environments to refine each UI to make the workflow smooth and to eliminate opportunities for errors to occur.

5.6 IT infrastructure improvement

While the computer applications for the solution are being built, IT senior management can be evaluating the needs for infrastructure expansion/enhancement. These two activities can thus be performed in parallel. This will include the generation and testing of the final version of the BPMS applications along with the construction of all IT solution components that are external to the BPMS-generated applications.

Technology infrastructure improvement design and implementation requires several specialty IT technical services and operations to build a functioning new technology environment. These specialty services include:

- Interface design – SOA, web services, EDI
- Data Architecture – data schema design, data modeling, and database design
- UI (user interface) design
- Communications network architecture
- Etc.

This is not easy. People representing these specialty areas in the company should be consulted first when the new conceptual business design is being finalized, and again at the time the business operation design is almost ready to be finalized and technology support requirements defined. This review will allow these technology specialists to determine if any changes to the current IT infrastructure will be required. Once this is determined, IT can define what will need to change, the cost and the required lead time. These definitions by IT may significantly change the cost estimate for the project, making this a mandatory step.

Computing needs, data storage needs, web site use, web services use, and other needs will be evaluated by the company's Chief Technology Officer or Enterprise Architects and used to define any impact the project solution may have on the current IT technology infrastructure. This impact may or may not be accepted – it will likely have hardware/operating system/middleware/data storage and staff costs and disruption charges, as well as timing and other constraints. If accepted by senior management, the Chief Technology Officer can work with the project business and IT project managers to align his/her acquisition/implementation plan with the project solution development plan and the IT application development plan.

The identification and definition of actual component activities of any infrastructure change plan will be the Chief Technology Officer's responsibility. The tasks will vary based on the changes to the technology infrastructure, but the plan should be formal and it should be detailed.

If it was possible, these changes and costs will have been considered in the business operation redesign cost estimates in the project proposal. At this point in the project, the costs will need to be reconsidered to determine if they will cancel out the value the project will provide. The approval of any refinement of these estimates may require a careful look at the solution's technical side and a revision of the cost benefit analysis for the project. The project may run into cost trouble at this point. Cost estimates will be much more definite. If a simulation tool was used to optimize the workflow and the solution was tested to determine realistic benefit (performance testing using "Stubs" and "Drivers") and iterated to maximize the solution's benefit, the benefit estimates will also be much more solid at this point. This gives the project a much better chance of meeting goals and providing a real ROI.

In all cases, these infrastructure changes, once approved, will be responsibility of the IT department. The schedule for these infrastructure changes should be aligned with the business solution and IT application construction plans and timing. This will help to ensure that all parts of the project's solution construction come together at the right times.

The business operation solution design team should contain an IT representative. This person will represent the IT department and be responsible for determining the impact of different business design choices on the current or planned IT infrastructure. Infrastructure here refers to the hardware (i.e., computers, data storage devices, document management system hardware, communication switches, etc.). As it is very possible for a new business design to have a significant impact on the available capabilities of the IT infrastructure, it is important that each design component that relies on computers, applications, communications, mobility devices, electronic registers, electronic manufacturing controls, etc., be discussed with IT. Failure to do so will cause issues with the solution and may result in the inability of IT to support the solution without significant new investment.

If the IT infrastructure will need to be changed, the project manager will need to work with IT to determine the cost and time impact on the projects estimates. Any necessary adjustments will need to be brought to the project sponsor for approval. This may be a go/no go decision point. There may be funds for an expansion or updating of the IT infrastructure that was included as part of the project estimates. If not, or if these estimates will be exceeded, the project sponsor will be the point person for the final decision on continuing with the project. If the project will continue, the estimates will need to be formally adjusted with a description of the reasons for the adjustment.

Changes to any company's IT infrastructure must be timed with the construction, testing, and delivery of the business solution. It may be timed to be "just in time" for use, but it must be timed to allow sufficient testing and stabilization as the new hardware and communications capabilities are installed and made operational. The new equipment should be certified by the vendor before it is considered to be operational. This will help avoid costly delays.

A business analyst from the project team should be given responsibility for the completeness and accuracy of all testing of infrastructure changes from a business perspective. This includes actually participating in the installation testing of PCs, printers, communication capabilities, web site use, social media app use, and equipment use stability. This is NOT a certification that the hardware is functioning; this is the vendor/IT technical services role. This certification is a test that the PCs are properly loaded and ready for use and that the printers actually work. The business analyst is not responsible for doing the installs, but rather to ensure that the results work.

The project manager should work with IT closely and insist on formal weekly status reports against a formal IT infrastructure modernization/expansion plan. This reporting against a formal IT plan should be the basis for a section of the weekly status report to the project sponsor.

5.7 Customer interaction/contact optimization

Customer experience or a customer journey in any interaction with the company is recognized as being of critical importance. All customer interaction points and all communications should be carefully considered from the customers' perspectives. Nothing in the use of any social application or web site interaction should be based on assumption. All design considerations should be based on personal experience with competitors' and other industry application designs, uses, and capabilities. This should be augmented with mobility application research and possibly internal and external customer focus groups.

We cannot over-emphasize how important it will be to get this interaction right. As the buying public moves ever more toward the use of mobility applications, competence in this area is critical. The way that these mobile applications and the company's website support interaction between the customer and the company will be a significant competitive factor in attracting and keeping customers.

However, while many customers today are extremely computer savvy, many other possible customers will not be up on the latest technology. Any solution will need to address both groups through use design that is obvious to the less informed and simple for all to use. This complicates the design of any social mobility application and should be a key part of any design – what is intuitive to a technically savvy person is a mystery to someone who is not technically sophisticated.

This can be tested in customer focus groups and comments used to improve the interaction design and interaction flow. It is critical to "remove all barriers between the customer and the company" (by Edward Deming).

In today's world, there are no enterprises solutions that are designed to service only one type of customer. This is because no matter the geographic location, there are many types of customers and just as many types of customer segments. One starting point is to understand how customers are related to the company. For example, are these customers internal, who are grouped by the various functional areas that touch processes that are being improved, or are they external customers such as consumers, outside sales partners, suppliers, shippers, wholesales, etc., who are external to the processes that are being improved? Any solution must therefore address interactions with multiple customer segments. That having been said, the point at which the solution touches these segments will be primarily, if not exclusively, through the User Interface (UI) designed for that particular segment. A BPMS generally makes adjusting a UI easy and quick.

For consumers, as well as for partners, expectations regarding web and mobile solutions are becoming increasing sophisticated. These expectations need to be carefully considered in solution design and validated in test settings before the solution is made operational. It is quite possible to devise solutions that improve internal operations, but have unintended negative impacts on consumers and/or partners.

For most customer segments, except consumers, the role of the individual determines the relevant segment, internal functional area or external partnership type. For those roles that are external and, increasingly in some companies for select internal roles, the channel that carries the User Interface (UI) also must be considered such as web, smartphone or tablet. Role determines the content and channel determines how that content is best handled. UI development and refinement must address both role and channel.

Consumers subdivide into additional segments by characteristics such as country, language, age, etc. Since there can be a wide variety of additional factors to consider, how content is presented is extremely important. User Interface (UI) development and refinement must address those customer segments that are relevant as well as the channels that are selected. For retail, some approaches now make each consumer his/her own segment by applying browsing and buying history in determining what content to present, or by automatically presenting shipping status at log in. While these types of intelligent activities may affect the content and therefore the overall solution design, in the end it is the UI that has the most impact on customer interaction.

UI Design is one of the trickiest areas in customer experience because it is constantly changing as mobile technology changes, which can lead to an ever increasing set of expectations by the customer. For this reason, it is recommended that the business area managers and IT managers periodically use customer focus groups to test the acceptability of the way they need to interact with the company. This may generate change requirements or total reworking of the way the company supports the customer experience.

The first testers of customer experience should be the more advanced mobility computing app users in the company. These people represent the future of customer interaction. Once this group has evaluated the solution, we suggest that the solution be tested by people who are not technology savvy. This second internal test will help to make the User Interface more intuitive and easier to use.

If possible, we also suggest that a series of user focus groups be given the apps and try to use them to purchase company products or interact with customer service. This final user test will provide the final feedback and will guide the final adjustments of the solution.

6.0 Deploy/implement the solution in the business

In a typical implementation, there are two major components. The first is the technology component, where the IT solution is built and then moved into the physical locations where they will reside and operate. The second is the business component. This component's focus is to test the IT solution that was developed and train the managers and staff on the new "To Be" activities, which include updated policy and procedures, customer interaction, and evaluation, to name a few. It is important to note that while a typical implementation will have both technology and business components, there are some cases where only the business component may apply.

The IT side of this deployment will probably be fairly well thought out from past deployments, and IT should at least have a list of tasks that can be considered to be IT standards. These lists of tasks, (or considerations), should include BPMS-generated applications, legacy application updating, licensed application use, interfacing, database modification, web services, social mobility applications, and any other hardware or software upgrades or changes that are part of the solution. Any existing deployment plan from past efforts should be updated and customized to this solution's deployment. The same should be true for any manufacturing equipment deployment or upgrade, including any manufacturing automation upgrades. If these past plans and standards are not available, the project team will need to work with IT and/or manufacturing to create them. This is not a trivial exercise and sufficient time should be given to research actual deployment and implementation procedures and needs, as applicable in your company. This is critical because the best solution will fail if improperly deployed and implemented.

The other main cause of failure at this point in the project is related to people and human acceptance and human error. If people don't feel comfortable with training, the new ways their work will be measured or how that measurement will be used against them (or hopefully for them), they will make the project fail. It is critical that training and change management programs be put in place to build staff confidence in the way the new solution will work and in their ability to work in the new environment. This cannot be over-emphasized. It is also a good idea to extend training programs with mentors who are available and walking around during the actual solution cutover.

The people side is worth spending additional time on. If people do not feel that they were part of creating the solution, they may be pre-disposed to find fault instead of working with the team to get past any issues. This is a key success factor and is a major component of the BPM drive for collaboration in all phases of any transformation or improvement project.

6.1 Review implementation standards and prepare for cutover

Every organization will look at the deployment of IT and manufacturing equipment installation differently than they will look at software implementation. While the basic functions might be similar, organizations will customize their installations based on the corporate culture, type of IT environment, type of industry, and whether or not it has an international or domestic operation. What is acceptable for one company may be totally unacceptable for another company.

This is further complicated by the fact that many types of equipment rely on a variety of software to operate and that most application installations include some form of IT equipment acquisition or upgrade. Today, most things in business rely on intertwined technology which adds a new level of concern for any solution development or licensing since all components of the solution must be designed to work together, built to support interfaces between the components, and tested differently than in the past.

Security policies and capabilities can come into play here, as well as financial and legal requirements, to protect companies from new equipment problems or application "bugs" and potential business interruption due to either the new equipment and/or the new applications. These considerations need to be identified, and then built into the design, development and testing tasks in the business improvement or transformation project.

This may also include a need for new short-term business interruption and potential damage liability insurance. A formal approach and plan to control deployment risk and then implementation risk must be put in place. This plan must address all security, business interruption, and other risks. Accordingly, the team should check with legal and finance, along with IT and manufacturing, to make certain that all risks are known and controlled.

Note: While this will probably be a minimal concern for small improvements, it will be a major consideration for transformation level projects.

The planning requires that the project management and sponsor look carefully at potential post implementation problems and then take steps in the solution design and development to avoid or mitigate as many as possible. For those potential issues that remain, advice should be obtained from legal and finance regarding options in dealing with risk to the business.

In addition, the project manager and team should work with collaborative partners to identify any standards or policies that will need to be considered, and then align these considerations to the points in the project where they apply. This is especially important for legal compliance and reporting. Although this is important in every business, extra care should be taken in healthcare where service reimbursement for Medicare and Medicaid patients is related to performance metrics and complex service coding rules.

Actual solution cutover should be firmly based on IT application and hardware cutover procedures. Any cutover should also have back out points built in, places where quality measurements are taken. If there is a problem, the solution can be backed out and the original version restored. This will help avoid business interruption and allow the project team to correct problems and then try the install and cutover again.

Both IT and manufacturing hardware deployments will have likely happened in the past and there should be experience-based tasks and plans that can be found and reused as a foundation for identifying standard approaches and tasks. These should be found and reviewed for common considerations, tasks, and problems.

Any deployment of hardware for IT or manufacturing equipment (including engineering CAD systems, and document management systems) will need to adopt a policy of, "do no harm". Do not cause a business interruption or disaster of any magnitude. Do not cause a situation that is seen as a risk to the deployment of the implementation. The deployment must consider backup and solution back out. Business interruption, risk avoidance, and risk response activity must be built into the deployment plan, and later into the business solution and hardware cutover in actual implementation. This is extremely important. Also, understand what may void warranties and what may void insurance that may be in place, and take specific steps to ensure that no insurance or warranties are affected by the approach or planned activities.

Once company standards and past plans have been obtained, they should be reviewed within the context of the nature of changes they were designed to handle. If the scope was narrow, there may need to be modifications to address the current project. Also review the nature of the components of the implementation standards and past plans to see if each of the components of the current project is covered. If not, you may have to seek out or develop additional plans or develop new standards.

If company standards and/or past plans do not include readiness assessments and checklists, it is suggested that they be created for each component that is relevant. Components can include:

- Hardware
- Software
- Technology infrastructure – such as PCs and digital mobile devices
- Communications equipment
- Manufacturing equipment
- Processing equipment (scan, copy, OCR, etc.)

- Physical plant
- Staffing
- Work stations
- Access
- Security
- Training by role and location
- Proficiency testing/certification
- Etc.

Timing is an important issue for two reasons that may sometimes conflict. The rule of thumb is generally to identify a cutover date and time when both the business and the systems are the least stressed. Hence, holiday seasons may be avoided, year-end may be avoided due to financial closing of the books, and 10:00 am to 6:00 pm may be avoided based upon the nature of the business and its cycles. Potentially conflicting pressure may arise when the nature of changes is such that the company is counting on a big bang and resulting market bump when whatever is new goes live. Despite such pressure, it is usually better to make certain all your ducks are lined up, and then check them quietly before you create a big bang.

Cutovers of large implementations should be done on weekends. Ideally find a "long weekend" that includes a holiday so that the team has three or more full days to execute the cutover plan and ensure that all systems are performing per plan before operations are started up on a normal workday.

6.2 Plan for business solution implementation

The business operation should be considered to be somewhat fragile. It can absorb only so much change in any given time period. When that limit is exceeded, problems begin to occur. If care is not taken, new solution implementation can push the business operation over this invisible and hard to detect line.

The project team and project manager should build checks into the implementation plan that will initiate specific change management activities to deal with this situation. These change management activities may include hiring temporary staff to work with the business unit staff and handle the workload, while senior staff members work with the solution team to get past any issues. They may also include additional training and business staff mentoring as the solution is implemented. The change management activities will vary, but should be based on assurances that people will not be penalized for mistakes and that the staff should not hesitate to ask questions and ask for help. These steps will require additional time in the cutover to the new solution; however, the activities are important and they should not be ignored.

In addition, a formal implementation plan should be built with input from the business manager and staff, IT, and collaborative partners. This should address timing issues, staff training issues, equipment installation and certification issues, compliance reporting timing, and solution interface (with other applications) issues. This plan should be detailed and define each activity and show how any issues will ripple. It should also be approved by everyone who will be involved in the installation and cutover.

Planning for implementation is the most critical set of tasks in the project. Everything else that has been done and will be done can be simulated, role played, and tested without disrupting the business. Since planning for the implementation has such a great effect, it should really be treated as a project itself, and full participation of the team is required to ensure all aspects belong to someone, and that all aspects are then checked and verified.

Most solutions involve both people and systems. While the systems can be tested in simulations, the interactions between the systems and the people cannot be tested within the BPMS itself. We recommend that an instance of the solution be built to run and in a Model Office environment. This Model Office should use a fully functioning version of the solution and should utilize data that comes from the operational activities that are being carried out in the business. Ideally, several months of input data are copied and then processed in the Model Office. This approach has several benefits:
- Hands on learning of the solution with real data in an environment that duplicates how the work is going to be performed after cutover
- Quality, experience-based input about ease of use, problems, short cuts, etc., that can then be used to make the UI changes that the BPMS supports

- Test of the IT components under stress duplicating normal daily work demands
- Actual outcome of transactions that can be compared to expected outcome, and/or reference set outcomes. Depending on the data source, it may be possible to check the Model Office outcomes against the actual outcomes that resulted from "As Is" use of the data.

Planning should include deliberate overstaffing of experts and "go to" people at the time of cutover. While there may be technical issues that arise, the most likely problems will be the result of staff not being fully acclimated to the new activities and steps. Those who are there to assist should be specifically assigned to providing help and should not be expected to assume their regular work responsibilities, at least initially. As the level of needed support becomes less, the experts can gradually be transitioned back to their normal assignments.

If any part of the solution touches any customer segment, customer support for each segment should be beefed up for implementation. Keep in mind that there will normally be multiple customer segments defined by role (consumer, broker, wholesaler, shipper, etc.) and by channel (website, mobile app, tablet, snail mail, phone, etc.). If the business is multinational, there may also be customer segments that are defined by language.

Implementation planning should start with cataloguing everything that needs to be in place before implementation. Based on this list, a "ballpark" estimate can be made for when cutover to the new "To Be" business operating model might take place. The "ballpark" should include a generous margin that supports verification and validation that everything is in place and works as planned. It is a big mistake to start with a date and work backwards. Rushing, pressure, and skipping things can seriously increase risk.

There should be a fully developed plan ready to back out from the solution and completely restore the status quo to prior to the cutover. You may never have to use this, but you must know in advance how this will be done because the alternative may be a serious business interruption. This plan must be as detailed as the disaster recovery plan and must specify roles that can track to individuals.

Remember, no one ever reads help FAQs. People learn early in their use of apps that FAQs cover everything but what they are looking for, and no one wants to spend a lot of time reading through things they don't need. So the default for most of us is to experiment - and at times to get into deeper trouble. This is why all user technology interaction points should be intuitive.

6.3 Orchestration - control implementation participation

With the move to collaboration, more people are involved in each part of a project than ever before. These people represent a wide range of business groups, project approaches, disciplines, techniques, methods, and planning styles. In addition, as the number of participant groups grows, priority, project focus and actual commitment can become issues. Strong personalities may also become a problem as weaker personalities hold back opinions and ideas as others dominate discussions. All of these factors must now be considered and managed in any solution implementation and cutover to its use.

Orchestration is the ability to manage this participation and to focus on contribution, timing, and priority. Interaction control must be employed by managing the way participants interact and making certain that the less vocal members have an opportunity to contribute (even if this is one on one contribution with the project manager or team leaders). This human contribution is one of the more difficult parts of the project because it impacts not only the solution content, but also the expectations of the delivered solution and the way success will be defined and measured.

As with collaboration in any part of the improvement or transformation project, the solution implementation and cutover need to be a blending of concepts and activities that the collaborative partners bring to the project. The creation of the implementation and cutover approach and actions should, therefore, be a composite of actions that all can agree on. This includes timing, and both business and IT manager/staffing commitment.

Further, orchestration of the contributions from each collaborative partner determines how the work from different groups will fit together. This activity also controls the type of training each participating group will receive, when they will receive it, and how they will use the skills the group brings and acquires.

In summary, orchestration determines how everyone will work together, what they will do, and how disagreements will be resolved.

Solution Orchestration directs the right mixture of skills and disciplines at the right points in the project and at the right time to make the project succeed. It leverages the capabilities from a set of critical solution disciplines which, when combined in well-designed BPM projects, will deliver true business transformation.

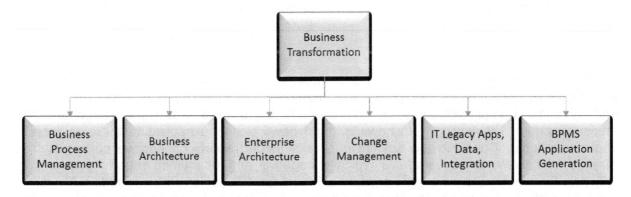

Each of these disciplines, as well as potentially others, need to be reviewed for their possible contribution to the project and, where beneficial, incorporated, and harnessed to deliver an effective BPM or BPMS-enabled BPM solution.

A BPM project should include participation from the project sponsor, the project manager and team, the business managers and staff in the business areas in scope, IT specialists, affected business area managers whose areas may be outside of the project's scope, vendor specialists, and possibly HR, Legal, Finance and manufacturing advisors. Contributions from all of these participants need to be coordinated and integrated as a key responsibility of the project manager. These efforts will consume a significant amount of time and should be deliberately planned for. It is a mistake to think that orchestration can be squeezed in when a schedule already consumes most of the available time with other responsibilities and tasks. Since orchestration pivots on people activities, you should actually allow for more of your time than you initially think is needed. Ask yourself how many "I only need ten minutes of your time" conversations actually only take 10 minutes?

Projects can only be done one of two ways: *with* someone OR *to* someone. With managers and staff, doing things *with* people is the preferred way. However, in many cases where business managers abdicate their responsibility in the creation of an outcome or the design of a solution, the change really has little to do with the way they actually may want the business to work and will instead deliver a business operation that works the way someone outside the actual business area thinks it should work. This is the root cause of a delivered solution that is a technical success (it works) but a business failure (it is not accepted by the business managers or staff). If the "do it to someone" approach is forced on the project team by a disengaged business manager, strongly consider stopping the project.

Many IT managers believe that they know best in determining what a solution should do, how it should do it, and how the business should work. They don't. IT professionals are experts in systems and technology. It is the role of a BPM professional, working together with the business experts, to determine what and how business processes should operate. Do not allow business transformation or improvement projects to be considered as IT projects. These projects involve much more than simply building an application.

The fear of implementing a new solution is common and often impedes a company's willingness to consider adopting change. As we all know, many projects exceed budget, suffer from delays, and can even be implemented incorrectly. However, there are also projects that go well, and are successful. The saying, "No news is good news," can be applied to these successful implementations. Consider how seldom our news media reports on positive outcomes. The majority of newsworthy coverage is typically negative and oftentimes reports problems or failures. So why should we expect anything different from business status reports? There are ways to protect your company from becoming one of those newsworthy and unsuccessful implementations.

1. **Prepare**. Be clear about what your company wants to achieve with the implementation of the new solution. Take the time to determine what functionality is necessary for your company, what functionality you would need to achieve the company's long-term goals, and what functionality would simply be nice to have, but is not essential.

2. **Have a plan**. Taking the time to plan and communicate an implementation process is a key element. This is where you want to work closely with your implementation team. Implementation teams have (hopefully) gone through many implementations and can assist in creating a realistic timeline and budget for the project. Often, especially in organizations which have a poor implementation success rate, the implementation can cost the company more to correct than if they had utilized professional implementation services.

3. **Allocate enough time**. Do not misjudge the amount of time that will be required of your managers, the implementation team, and various personnel. Implementation is a full time job. You are asking people within your organization to lend their expertise regarding the company's processes to an implementation project. These are employees that already have full time positions within your company. The project will require some moving of responsibilities for a period of time, and the understanding that in addition to their current roles, some employees will be providing vital knowledge and work throughout the implementation process.

4. **Identify**. Determine what reports, interfaces, forms, and enhancements will change in your production and operations process. The point of most projects is to provide a greater level of visibility into your business as well as streamlining and becoming more efficient. It is necessary to not be taken by surprise when certain interfaces and enhancements behave differently than what you are accustomed to.

5. **Test**. Testing is a vital part of the process. Testing will assist in working out any final questions and helps to ensure that the production and operations processes are running smoothly. This is your trial period. It is the period of time where you are able to test and make any changes prior to your "go-live" date in order to ensure that user adoption goes smoothly.

6. **Train and mentor**. Some of the biggest concerns with project implementations are "will my people learn fast enough, will they retain what they need to know after the team completes its work, and will we lose core knowledge if key people leave the company?" If you are a multi-site company and have implemented your solution at least in one of your sites, but still have others on the implementation to-do list, one way to mitigate all of these concerns is to use an internal Mentor Program. A Mentor Program utilizes your previous investments (in the form of trained and knowledgeable people who already went through an implementation) to assist in the implementation at other corporate sites. Connecting "mentors" with "protégés" (people who are challenged with a new project implementation) can be very successful.

Taking the time to create a training programs with job aids and support materials that place emphasis on the aspects of the new solution that are meaningful to the employee will save the company lost time and money in the long run. Properly designed training programs, especially ones that employ at least some hands on experiences, reduce implementation confusion and bring operations back up to full speed more quickly.

Management of collaboration in any project requires that debates and disagreements be controlled using consensus management techniques. Agreement is important because disagreements among collaborative partners will build up and eventually kill a project. Collaborative projects must therefore be based on the establishment of relationships and a foundation of mutual respect of one another's skills, disciplines, and points of view.

Without these supporting factors, collaborative projects can turn into ugly battlegrounds that fail to deliver anything of much use. It is important for any project manager to focus on building the right culture in the project to support open discussion and collaboration.

A mix of knowledge of the company's culture, internal politics, the real power brokers, and what each key project sponsor, business manager and supporting area manager (IT, Legal, Finance, Sales, Customer Service, etc.) expects, will help in understanding the complexity of a project implementation and how to avoid a project implementation (and career) disaster.

Studies reveal Electroshock is Preferred Over Boredom! Have you ever sat in a training class and been so bored you would rather go through electric shock treatment? Science Magazine confirms it (http://www.sciencemag.org/content/345/6192/75.abstract). Good training is a time and money saver. However, poorly designed and executed training can deal a death blow to your implementation. Training should be focused and relevant for those in attendance. It should have "Aha" moments, where the employees are introduced to functionality they didn't have or know about before.

Create a checklist of what each key business manager and collaborative partner in the project expects. This should be aligned with the project goals and requirements and any expectation disconnects noted. The project sponsor should then adjust expectations or possibly the project's goals and/or requirements. The result should be a description of what each of these people are looking for and a brief description of how the expectations will be met. These adjustments must be reviewed by the sponsor. If these changes can be accommodated, they should be added to the list of capabilities that must be delivered for the project to be a success.

It is important to continually confirm the project priority and timeline for availability of staff, dependencies on one another at given points in time, and other things the project may need with all collaborative partners. This helps control relationships and keeps the collaborative partners focused.

The biggest incentives for managers and staff to become collaborative partners are peer pressure and the visibility of their involvement/contribution/value to senior management.

No manager wants to be shown as the cause of a failure. This is a cultural issue that is even more important in a situation with multiple collaborative partners. The problem is that this fear can get out of control and cause some managers and staff to procrastinate or follow an approach that continuously finds fault with little things. This approach is believed by many to ensure that they can never be blamed for anything because they have found fault. This is extremely disruptive and if encountered, it should be brought to the attention of the project manager or the sponsor.

It is clear that all roadblocks to success must be eliminated or at least mitigated. This can be accomplished in frequent, formal project status/planning review meetings. Share praise and also meet with managers who are behind or causing problems before the meetings, and see what can be worked out to bring their work back into alignment with the schedule. This is a main role of the project manager, to work with team members to help them succeed by removing all obstacles in the way of their personal success as well as the project's success.

Do not simply trust any estimation of progress, especially in a collaborative group with parts of the solution spread among different groups. Too many managers tell others what they think is best for them or what they think the project manager wants to hear. It is necessary to rely on the actual deliverables to determine progress. If the deliverable is under development and there are any signs of possible inaccuracies when status is reported, the works in progress should be checked to see if they are on track. Also, beware of anyone who nuances their message or couches their message in a way that makes it difficult to understand.

Estimating any business or IT project is an educated guess, at best. This is especially true if a formal execution-based methodology that defines activity and provides guidance in a step-by-step manner is not used. Estimation in a collaborative environment is even more difficult, because it relies on the cooperation and ability of multiple groups to provide meaningful estimates that are built from a list of activities that must be performed.

6.4 Plan technical cutover

BPMS-enabled BPM construction is easier in many ways than traditional application development. However, BPMS solution construction is still challenging and requires staff experienced in all aspects of both traditional IT application development and BPMS application generation, including rules definition and use, and data modeling/flow/transformation/access. In an iBPM environment, these skills will need to be augmented by experience with simulation setup/execution/reporting and with a firm knowledge of advanced analytic reporting. If the project will include true collaboration, experience in setting up collaboration and controlling it in projects will also be required.

In addition to the technical side of any solution development or implementation/cutover, a successful implementation requires the active involvement of people with experience in business operational change implementation, BPMS solution implementation, and IT implementation, including interfaces and data routing.

Although it requires specialized knowledge to design, create, and test BPMS-generated applications, application solutions built in traditional computer languages (such as JAVA, .net, COBOL, etc.) require the programmer to manually consider many things that the BPMS generator takes care of. However, when it comes to data, both generated and custom-built applications require fairly complex data use definitions, as well as complex architecture of the databases that will be used at different points in the solution.

However, a word of warning is appropriate here. If not designed and built the right way, the data interfaces, data source quality, and use may be slow, and application use may be disappointing. This will become apparent after solution implementation and cutover to the new business workflows, their activities, their rules, and their applications and performance reporting.

Therefore, at a minimum, BPMS-generated applications, application interfaces, changes to legacy and licensed applications, and data delivery/removal must be carefully tested, both for the traditional IT application's function and the way the new business area will operate. For this final full operation test, we suggest that a model office environment be set up to simulate the actual operation and used to optimize the final solution before it is formally delivered and implemented.

The way in which these components of the technical side of the solution are moved into a live production operating environment must be carefully planned and tested after each step in the cutover to the new solution. It is also suggested that the IT team be prepared to back out the solution at any time that a problem surfaces and then reinstate the current application. This approach takes more time, but reduces risk and is part of the cutover process in most IT shops.

Planning and executing a cutover to a new multi-application solution is difficult and requires experience and expertise in all areas of IT, from application development, to interface development and data movement/storage, to application operations/technical services, to communications, and more. This must be done by specialists. The project team leader has responsibility for the overall solution and its implementation, and he or she will need to understand some of the things in the cutover to the new solution that can reduce risk. These include:
- The entire solution's application support environment and applications/data uses/user interfaces should have been fully tested and certified as being operational before the implementation begins.
- The solution should have been reviewed and approved by all collaborative partners prior to implementation.
- No significant problems should remain in the applications/data/technology support at the time of implementation.

- The implementation should have a formal plan with roles and tests, and back out/restore points.
- The implementation of the applications in the solution should follow the database loads and data quality certification from the responsible data architects.
- All required support hardware (PCs, specialized 3-D and other printers, communications capabilities, etc.) should be in place and tested prior to solution implementation.

Note: This list is not meant to be a full list of considerations of items that should be put in place prior to a solution deployment.

The real keys to solution implementation and cutover success are to take extra precautions in monitoring progress and be ready to back out the solution, even if it delays the project and even if it represents a temporary setback in management's eyes. We guarantee that it will be much better to move a solution's delivery date than to implement and cutover to a solution that does not work well.

Remember Wendan's three rules of business transformation. The first, "Do no harm to the business operation!" The second rule, "Take no risk unless it is planned, controlled, and approved by anyone who might be affected." Finally, Wendan's third rule, "Never do anything without first being able to back it out and reinstate the current business operation without any noticeable effect on the business."

Cutting over to a new solution for the operation is scary at best and is seldom stress-free. That is because it is something that can literally kill a business operation if not performed the right way. We have seen companies shut down for weeks with poor cutovers due to solutions that did not fit the business. We have also seen companies do this the right way, and we have helped companies plan for recovery and success when variables outside of direct control go well or if they don't. The key is that you must remember Murphy's Law, "If it can go wrong, it will." There are many who also say that Murphy was an optimist, just think about that one. No one can anticipate every possible thing that can go wrong. If a good job is done anticipating and planning for problems, the impact will be small and all major potential issues will be addressed. However, then comes Mr. Murphy. It is the unforeseen things that can kill a cutover. That is why you must always be ready to back out the cutover and restore the operation to the previous application support. Then re-plan, reschedule, and try again. This is a little longer process and maybe it will seem more expensive, but it is much less intrusive and disruptive than a failed cutover.

There should be an IT cutover specialist who will lead the cutover planning and execution. He or she will leverage the expertise of technologists within multiple technical disciplines to create a low risk cutover plan that includes testing at each step of the cutover and allows for back out and recovery at key points in the cutover.

A good IT Department will have a formal cutover approach with past cutover plans as the basis for the IT plan. They will have standards that apply to all tasks and lead the team's evaluation of things that need to be considered in the company's operating and IT environments. If they don't, the team will need to take the time to create this.

No cutover should take place without a detailed plan which includes activities, "go/no go" decision points, clearly assigned responsibilities, time estimates for activity completion, escalation paths, etc. The risk is too high.

The cutover should certify the operation of the application, the creation of any databases, and database loads. This certification must be based on tests during cutover.

The cutover can be a gradual application by application process or it can be performed in a single cutover involving all of the technology that will change with the solution. Both approaches have their own risks and both have ways to mitigate the risks. The key is that the risks must be listed and then the way each is mitigated should be defined.

The cutover team should have a script that helps them test each step in the cutover and identifies what they think could go wrong with each step. The plan should also provide step by step guidance as to the action that should be taken if a problem is encountered.

The training programs should be coordinated with the cutover plan for the new solution. Actual training should take place close to the cutover date. Following cutover, a group of highly trained mentors should be available to help people with problems.

6.5 Cutover to the new business operation with BPMS support

Once cutover is complete and certified, this represents "Day 1" of the operation under the new solution. With the new operation implemented, the new activities should be taking place. The business operation will now be responsible for modifying its process and procedures based on the new solution in the live environment.

Part of the cutover to the new business operation is formal change management and formal training. Both are critical to business activity initiation and the implementation of the new business operation and solution. Performance measurements will now be run in order to identify the true outcomes and benefits of the new business operations. Staff mentoring should augment the formal just-in-time training to ensure that the staff becomes comfortable and familiar in the new operation.

The deployment of the new applications and other parts of the technical side (PCs, specialized 3-D and other printers, communications capabilities) of the business transformation or improvement should have been tested before the deployment is scheduled. This testing should result in formally certified (approved/accepted) application functionality and hardware/communication installation. This should be confirmed and any slippages in the plan should be used to modify the implementation schedule. It is important that the implementation go smoothly to build confidence within the business managers and staff that will use the new solution. For this reason, the solution should not be rushed into implementation before it is complete and stable. If the solution is implemented before it is fully tested (under the reasoning that the bugs will be worked out as they are identified in production/operation), the solution will never be accepted by the business users, and the project will be declared a failure.

The implementation/cutover plan will need to be coordinated with the IT application solution migration, and with all collaborative partners to make certain everyone is in sync with what will happen, when, how, and each is familiar and comfortable with their roles.

Although an implementation/cutover business operation plan is critical, you cannot expect it to lead to actual implementation without adjustments to additional situations as they arise. It is not possible to foresee all possible events and issues. The plan is a guide, but it is not cast in stone. It must be used in a flexible manner that includes management adjustment. This adjustment will need to involve different collaborative partners, depending on the events and issues that arise.

As implementation and cutover are underway, any adjustments to applications, data sources, etc., must be handled quickly to avoid delays and possible implementation cancellation. If the adjustments cannot be made properly and the results verified as correct, the implementation will need to be cancelled, the applications backed out, and the old applications moved back into IT operating production.

The cutover should be scheduled for an evening or weekend to minimize potential impact on the business and allow back out and recovery, if needed. If your company has international operations, take time zones into account as well. If you truly have to be up and running 24/7, identify the time zones that represent the greatest and the lowest volumes and use those as a guide to planning timing.

As the technical members of the team are implementing the new solution, be sure to set expectations with the business sponsor, operations managers, and operations staff that this version of the solution will not last forever. As business conditions change, and products/customer experience expectations continue to mature, new problems will emerge and new solutions will need to be found. This mindset is critical to building an expectation that even optimal solutions will need to change as the business and its operational needs change. This is the foundation of expectation management and proactive business operations evolution.

Just-in-time training should be used to provide training that will not be mostly forgotten when it is time to use it. A detailed training program should take place close to the cutover date. Skills should be tested at the end of this program. Anyone who needs further help should receive it for any part of the new operation they are uncertain about.

It is important that business operation training be monitored and tested. This includes the understanding of new policy and procedures, as well as the new applications that will support the business. Those that need additional training should be given it discreetly to avoid feelings of inadequacy and to build confidence.

In addition to formal training, it is recommended that formal change management concepts be woven into preparations for cutover. This should include holding general discussions to help calm business staff fears and to help staff members function as a team. They should understand the processes, why they need to do what the work requires, how they will basically interact in the team (their role), how everyone will be evaluated, how the evaluations will be used, and what will be expected of them. It may be necessary to have an HR or union representative involved in these discussions.

New procedure training should be part of the overall training program. This includes new standards, any changes in union related work/performance limits, new security, new federal and state government compliance requirements, and new workflow and workflow bottleneck alerts.

Once the technical deployment and cutover have been certified by IT, it will be time to execute the business cutover plan. Specific timing should be closely tracked by the project leader and the project team. Collaborative partners should also be counting down the activities that lead to this point.

The execution of the cutover plan is a move to a live new business operation. All forms and data feeds to the business area in scope will be rerouted, and all activities will begin to use the new applications and reports. It is important that a highly trained set of mentors walk the business area floor helping people who get stuck in performing their duties in the new operating environment. As issues arise, the mentors will help correct the process as well as help to give the business staff members the confidence they need to perform at expected levels.

6.6 Move models to the process model library in the BPMS

The creation of business process models and the collection of supporting information represent an investment by the company and should be considered to be a company asset. However, in many companies today, this is not the case and models are virtually discarded at the end of projects. This practice totally eliminates the reuse advantage to BPMS-supported BPM because it eliminates the context of any solution and therefore the thinking behind the solution. This makes each project in any business area start from scratch. Remember, out-of-date models are worse than no models because the team has no idea of what is good and what is wrong. This issue has been the root cause of many bad decisions in the past.

Since business process models and supporting information are to be treated as an asset and kept up-to-date for reuse, the company will need to have a formal policy requiring that they be updated at the end of a project, and formally indexed and stored. Most likely this storage will be in a special log in the BPMS tool. If this approach is used, the BPMS administrator will need to create a formal directory for this storage with a unique indexing structure to keep it separate from "live" projects.

This business model library will need to be managed by the BPMS administrator and operated using formal sign out and sign in procedures that capture information on access authority, timing, a summary of what was changed, and who, what, when, where, why information.

All finalized business process models and supporting information should be reviewed with the business managers and IT to create a final version signed off by the project manager, business manager, and collaborative partners. Signoff includes signatures and date.

The new process model should be saved along with all supporting information, including notes from all interviews, and the reasons for each operating and design change decision.

The BPMS models will be stored in the BPMS or a database that is open to the BPMS. Other information should be stored in a repository that is accessible to the team for easy updating. This information should be kept secure and protected by formal security protocol and access management.

The solution models for any project should be considered to be of critical importance. They are the foundation for the next iteration of the solution as the business changes. The more accurate these models are, the less time the new iteration will take to design, build, test, and implement. These models should be managed by a BPMS administrator or security specialist with access being given on an as needed basis.

It is critical that models be kept up-to-date. Any change to the operation should be made through documentation that updates the model to reflect each change. Any changes that are not reflected in the master models and information will lessen the value of the models and the ability to reuse the information and to make changes in an efficient manner. We recommend that the BPMS administrator require each solution model to have a business owner who will need to review and recertify or update his or her area's models annually. If this is not done, the models will soon become useless and the model library will become irrelevant.

Many companies fail to update the project's business process models and supporting information at the close of a transformation project. As a result, many business process models are incomplete and many do not reflect the current business operation or how it has changed since it was initially designed. This may save time, but it increases the risk for future changes. Incomplete models are a problem, but they can be dealt with by obtaining missing information. The real problem is related to out-of-date business process models and information, especially those from recent projects where people are likely to assume that they are current. These are worse than no models or information. The reason is that no one will know what is still current and accurate and what is not to be trusted.

The result is that if the BPM/BPMS project team assumes that the models are OK, they will have a very inaccurate view and understanding of the business. To avoid this, we recommend that all business process models, supporting information, and rules be checked at the end of each project and have their accuracy certified by the project manager. Unless a set of models has been certified by the originating project manager as being updated, any other project manager who needs to use these models should assume that the models are out-of-date and redo them.

> Note: The current models (if any exist) should be evaluated for quality prior to planning the project. Time for any current state or "As Is" model creation/re-creation should be built into the project's schedule. If it was not, the project manager should work with the project sponsor to assess risk and adjust the schedule to reflect needed improvement time.

Following the implementation of any solution, the project team should update and certify the models and information and move them and their supporting data to a model library for easy access and use/modification control.

6.7 Check project success

Project success must be determined based on pre-agreed upon formal measurement criteria with agreed upon data sources and evaluation formulas. Without this formality, success is opinion. Determining success by using opinion is risky and benefit determinations cannot be considered to be accurate.

Immediately following the acceptance of a project, the sponsor and project manager should have determined what the requestor considers to be a success and how success will be measured in terms of performance and the delivery of a function. This is the foundation for measuring improvement and benefit and for determining success. If this is not done, success will be based on opinions and perspectives that can be influenced by history and corporate culture, as well as personal style. That should be avoided if at all possible.

For this reason, if success and how it will be measured was not defined at the beginning of a project, it should be defined as soon as possible, before the project solution is evaluated.

Additionally, if a formal business improvement methodology (different from the IT Agile method) is used, it is likely that project state phase gates and other check point approaches will be used to monitor status. This checking helps control the quality of the design from phase or task group to task group and greatly improves the chances for a successful solution. If the business improvement methodology supports collaboration orchestration and advanced iBPM concepts, it will align both IT methods such as Agile and specialty methods such as Business Architecture, Enterprise Architecture, and change management. The control that is available through this combination of disciplines in a formal methodology greatly improves the likelihood of success and the acceptance of the implemented solution's evaluation.

If you cannot measure improvement, it does not exist since anything that cannot be proven becomes opinion. This is to be avoided because no one can really "succeed" when success is not backed by a formal definition of what success entails for the project, namely, how it will be measured, where the information will come from, and who will be responsible for the measurement.

What constitutes success in the case of the project? Who will make the decision and what will it be based on? This must be defined as early in the project as possible and it must be agreed upon and a formal definition signed by all relevant managers to show their agreement.

Equally as important as agreeing on what constitutes success, is an agreement on how success will be measured and the sources of the data. If this is not done, the evaluation of success is still open to disagreement.

Project success measurement should be a key consideration in creating the new business design and supporting automation. This definition will point out the key things that the business managers want to have happen as an outcome. The ability to monitor and measure these success criteria in production will help show trends and help focus improvement over time.

Once a solution is deployed, mechanisms need to be put in place to ensure that it is adopted by the business area managers and staff and that the old ways of doing business do not creep back into the operation. This is done with post cutover mentoring and analyses of reported problems/complaints. This assessment includes measuring post cutover performance and the benefits that are being delivered to the business. By comparing these measurements against baseline/new design simulations, management can see if actual results are within an acceptable range of predicted results. This can be used to identify where problems are occurring, and the managers and staff in those areas can be first assessed by observation and then by interview to determine root causes.

Before success is measured, we suggest that the quality of the information from different defined sources be confirmed and that all reporting software be double-checked. This only needs to happen at implementation time.

If a project is measured and considered a success, the team is finished with the solution and it will move to a state of continuous refinement.

If a project is measured and does not hit the target numbers, it will be necessary to go through another iteration that is focused on the places where the performance needs further improvement. Performance measurement will be carried out on all changes until the changes deliver target outcomes.

6.8 Formal project closure

All projects will share some similarities with other projects, but each will also have unique aspects. Each project will have its own challenges and each will require creativity in dealing with challenges. For this reason, each project should be looked at as a learning opportunity. However, many project managers and staff members may see the need to learn and grow as possibly also creating a risk of being viewed negatively by management. This is a corporate culture issue. If it exists, there is little that can really be done and ongoing experience-based learning and skill improvement will be limited.

If the teams and managers can be open, an evaluation of lessons learned should be shared and is an important part of any project closure.

Overall, project closure should be directed by formal policy supported by standards. These policies and their supporting standards should address both business and IT project closing activity with formal acceptance and comments that roll up from the team (business and IT members) to the project manager and the sponsor. We believe that there is additional value in project approach, tactic and team evaluation notes from the business area manager and staff who were involved in the project. These evaluations should be used to improve future projects.

At formal project close, all models and supporting information should be turned over to the BPMS administrator for entry into the company's business model library.

It is important to learn from each project. A post mortem should be conducted once a project is completed. This information should be formalized and added to an improvement or "lessons learned" library and indexed by topic so others can benefit from these project close reviews.

It is valuable to make time in each project Sprint or at key deliverables to discuss what is working well and what is not working as well as desired. At these checkpoints, the team should discuss what to change (and how to do things differently), what to keep the same and what to eliminate. This "live" learning environment will engage the energy of the team and bring the team closer together as a true collaborative group. These adjustments and observations will become part of the project close meeting and part of the notes and recommendations that will be formalized and placed in the "lessons learned" library.

The project closing meeting should be considered mandatory. It consumes some time, but it is well worth it. The commitment to have a formal project close meeting should be obtained at the beginning of the project, and the importance of the close should be stressed by the sponsor and upper management. There can be a tendency to want to avoid extending project activities once cutover has taken place and participants may very well be weary of the project. It may help to combine the close with a bit of celebration for a job well done.

Identify project closing and evaluation standards and data collection. Pull the project team together in a workshop or two and discuss each major activity and how it could be improved.

Recommend changes to the BPM methodology and techniques, building your case as to the benefits of each recommendation. Have all team members sign the recommendations. It will mean more if the whole team is behind a change.

Create a small committee that looks at all project closing recommendations on how to improve the business transformation process and also has the authority to make beneficial changes. This committee will need to include a few business project managers, IT project managers, and BPMS developers.

7.0 Improve – sustained operation

As soon as any solution is implemented it will begin to morph in order to accommodate changing business operation needs, legislative requirements, market trends, and opportunities. We call the process of addressing this continuous change "Evolutive Management."

Evolution happens in every company to varying degrees. You cannot stop it, but you can leverage it to guide how the company will operate and how it will be able to respond. Many call this ability to respond being nimble. However, few companies have reached a state of operation where they can respond quickly, for low cost, and with confidence in the outcome of the changes. Creating this ability began with the adoption of BPM and the move to BPM product suites. If you have moved to iBPM, even better.

The successful deployment or implementation of a business transformation solution is the proof case of all the work done by the project team. You are installing the changes and are counting on the business, its leadership and the employees to accept and adopt the change. More to the point, it is vital that the solution address the original business needs, satisfy key business objectives, and provide a solution which is not only adopted but becomes the new way business is conducted. We call this "project stickiness." The intent of stickiness is to limit the degree to which the solution degrades to allow the business area to slip back into old ways.

We have found that the adoption and continued use of a solution can be improved by:
- Involving the business and users of the solution throughout the development, building and testing of the solution – promoting a sense of ownership by the business users
- Communicating with all impacted stakeholders frequently – and listening to responses
- Providing training designed specifically for each stakeholder group – limiting anxiety
- Removing the old, e.g., shutting down old applications, eliminating access to old templates – promoting one way of doing each job
- Creating champions within the business who will carry the flame and be both responsible and accountable for adoption – mentors build confidence and lower the risk of rejection
- Measuring success after the solution is deployed - revisiting the solution 3, 6 and 12 months after implementation to ensure that the solution has been completely adopted and is working as designed. Adjustments may be made at each of these reviews.

In addition, periodic reviews of the solution with the sponsor and the business manager will help expose them to emerging technology and the way it can be leveraged and lead to innovations. These reviews should be hosted by the BPM Center of Excellence and are introduced below in Chapter 7, section 1.

7.1 Create ongoing business transformation BPM Center of Excellence support

Although optional in the past, companies are now finding it advantageous to have a single place where they can focus BPM and BPMS business transformation skills, capabilities, knowledge, and standards. This also often includes Business Architecture. The CoE being recommended will need to have strong business and IT representation and if the company manufactures a product, it will need manufacturing representation. The purpose of the BPM CoE group is to make certain that changes to all cross functional process solutions and solutions that impact multiple areas in the business remain well coordinated, and that the collaborative groups are managed by a central governance body that will have the best interest of the process or collaborative group of business areas in mind.

This provides a broader and more complete picture of operational change and improves the potential for benefit and operational streamlining.

To equip and enable change, many companies today have some form of Business Process Center of Excellence. In some cases, this is a BPM CoE, while in others it may be a Six Sigma group or a Continuous Improvement Group. Regardless of the name given to the group, it is clearly there to help business operations improve.

However, even as organizations continue to invest significant resources and money into BPM programs, the results often fall short of leadership expectations. Leadership has been sold BPM as a way to align and deliver the improvement objectives of an organization by integrating and more effectively leveraging its technical and management potential. BPMS tools that support the overall BPM concept are often improperly promoted, set up, and turned over to company BPM and IT organizations. This has caused problems for many in realizing the potential of this powerful discipline and its supporting technology. However, when set up properly, BPMS-enabled BPM can deliver significant results and provide a competitive advantage across the entire organization. It can also drive high value business operation streamlining and sustained operational optimization – thus reducing cost and increasing the ability of the company to change quickly, with low risk.

Some of the most serious challenges that a typical BPM CoE must address and resolve:
- How to be positioned in the business structure
- What services should be provided and when
- Elevate the project type from department level process improvement to enterprise-wide value stream transformation
- Offer solutions outside of the existing BPMS
- Identification of the most serious projects along with correct prioritization
- Develop deep business unit/BPM CoE partnership

To address these challenges, the CoE needs to have a solid plan to:
- Solidify Foundation: Ensuring the BPM/BPMS CoE has a solid foundation of methodologies, internal processes, level of certified training, as well as the exposure to and support of the business partners. Investing in this phase will result in improvement of the overall success of the project.
- Institutionalize Core BPM Capabilities: Building on the foundation to expand the capabilities to support 'rescue' projects and formalizing benefit realization.
- Investing in iBPM: Expanding the BPM capability to be comparable to that of a contemporary CoE by leveraging analytics and simulation tools, as well as the establishment of key standards, and ensuring the selection/leveraging of the 'best fit' BPMS tools/business partner.

Demand for BPM support fluctuates based on the submission of project requests from business area managers. As demand for BPM support increases, BPM CoE managers need to recognize that the traditional approach to project request, definition, and scheduling will need to become more formal and decisions will have to become rule-based.

Establishing and properly staffing a Center of Excellence (CoE) is core to enabling business objectives. The challenge is often establishing the credibility with leadership that the CoE should, and can, deliver strategic/enterprise wide level projects. This is done by establishing relationships with key business leaders, demonstrating your understanding of their business and the issues they face, and providing them solutions which directly address their pain points. Too often BPM COEs confine their projects to efforts requested by the business, which may not actually be their most pressing issues. Engaging with the business and focusing on all of their issues, not just the issues they believe you can solve, allows you to move up the ladder and focus on more strategically aligned efforts.

The following are vital areas for an effective BPM CoE:

Capability Areas	Success Area
BPM Organization	BPM Strategy
	Align BPM Objectives to Business Objectives
	Creation of a BPM Organization
Services	Business Improvement Organization
	Project Size and Criticality
	Project Requesting
	Formal Governance
	Formally Defined Services
	Performance Management
	Business Redesign Skills
	BPMS Application Generation and IT Solution Creation
	Implementation
Benefit Realization	Formal Benefit Estimation
	Formal Benefit Measurement in the Solution Design
	Formal Benefit Realization
	Solution Benefit Measurement - After Deployment
Methodology and Tools	Formal BPMS-Enabled BPM Methodology in Use
Competencies	Business Operation Performance Analysis
	Business Operation Modeling, Analysis and Improvement Design
	Lean Analysis and Design Modeling
	Six Sigma
	Requirements Definition
	BPMS Use - Business Designers
	BPMS Use - Application Developers

A BPM CoE should strive to become a high value internal consulting group that not only offers guidance but also provided input into line of business strategies.

Getting funding for the BPM Center of Excellence can be greatly enhanced by demonstrating how the team directly contributes to the business objectives. Establishing targets, such as delivering a 5 to 10 X return on the COE's annual budget in realized benefit (real money eliminated from business operations budgets, not just identified), will get leadership's attention. After all, you are giving them 10 times in real return for their investment. A good BPM team can easily achieve this target and much more.

A BPM CoE needs to have a core set of standard practices including:
- Clear and consistent methods to define the business problems and scope of a project,
- A compelling process to prioritize projects based on the contribution they will make to the business objectives. This process needs to be aligned with, and fully supported by, leadership. Ideally, you will incorporate this process into the leadership strategy and budgeting process at an enterprise level,
- A framework to ensure sponsor alignment and participation,
- A clear methodology to manage, run, and deliver projects on time and within budget

This greatly increases project success and improves the reputation of the BPM team.

A BPM team should aspire towards a vision built around the following key points:
- Expand support to the entire organization
- Increase the level of impact, scope, and complexity that projects address and thus increase the level of impact/benefit to the business
- Provide seamless solution development for complex projects
- Become a group of highly skilled operations improvement professionals
- Work with business area managers and provide input into their annual planning process
- Work with senior managers to help identify the potential impact of strategy on the business operation and what will need to be changed to support strategy and goals

The BPM CoE is the governing body in BPM projects. As a result, a business-oriented business transformation methodology is needed to provide project execution guidance – who, what, when, why, where, how. IT Agile and other methods are needed for the IT development efforts, but they are not business change methods.

If your BPM team has hit a project size/scope plateau within your organization, but nonetheless has developed a solid reputation for delivering on a certain type of project, your days as a team may still be limited. A BPM team should never be pigeon-holed into a limited set of project types. BPM professionals are trained to address and provide optimized solutions to a wide range of business problems while directly contributing to achieving business objectives. If your team is narrowly focused and limited to small process improvement processes within a functional area, or relegated to facilitating meetings for the business, then the team is not living up to its potential. We call these "fingers & toes" projects, projects that have a limited scope and impact on the business. A shift in focus is needed to move up the organizational impact scale to more significant projects which have an enterprise impact. This is done by engaging with the business leaders and having them participate in defining the role which the BPM should be playing in enabling their business. This process will help to educate the business in the true potential of the CoE and serve to align the team's objectives with those of the business.

To implement BPM-based planning and management a CoE should:
- Design the internal BPM/BPMS processes to improve solution delivery with creation of standards, formalized alignment to other internal 'resource' groups, e.g., Information Technology, Strategy Planning, Human Resources, Legal, Compliance and Audit in solution delivery
- Create role definitions and tie skills to roles to ensure effective BPMS development and execution
- Work to establish clear RACI model amongst the various internal teams, so that each of their unique capabilities can be leveraged in concert, therefore dramatically improving the impact on overall business operations effectiveness, and ensuring that each of the teams are working on the highest leverage projects

Building internal awareness and business sponsorship while undertaking enterprise level projects is vital to the long-term success of a BPM team. This is done by:
- Providing formalized business awareness/education on how BPM/BPMS can affect operational efficiency/effectiveness,
- Working with the CoE to identify high value projects that either cut costs in expensive operations areas and/or projects that directly impact revenue generation/experience engineering
- Creating collaborative relations with other needed groups (Information Technology application development and interface/data architecture, Compliance, Legal, etc.)
- Partnering with the CoE to deliver on these enterprise level projects by leveraging the new CoE methodology to ensure that the projects are aligned to the enterprise business objectives, are well sponsored and executed, and the planned benefit/value on an enterprise/customer level are realized

BPM CoE should play a role in reshaping how the Information Technology component of business transformation or improvement projects will be approached – focus first on process and the business operation.

The maturity of a BPM team can be assessed on the following ten (10) dimensions. These, in turn, can provide a roadmap on how to continue to invest in and create a multi-year roadmap to mature your team's overall BPM capabilities.

10 Categories Essential Areas for BPM COEs	COE Areas of Investment
1. Clear vision of the future 2. Commitment to the vision 3. Leadership 4. Stakeholder buy-in 5. Reality-based planning 6. Balancing people, process and technology 7. Nimble execution 8. Clearly defined success metrics 9. Run the business 10. Organizational transition	1. Leadership 2. Sponsorship / stakeholders / communication 3. Methodology 4. Tools – BPMS, simulator, BPMS 5. Project management 6. Change management 7. Implementation / adoption 8. Metrics 9. Training 10. Coaching / mentoring

As BPMS technology continues to evolve and IT organizations continue to grow, there has been a trend towards viewing the BPM group as part of IT and for BPM projects to be IT projects. Careful consideration needs to be given where the BPM CoE reports within your organizational structure. Remaining part of IT will mean that BPM will be perceived as a technology solution and forever will suffer the typical complaints that business leaders have of IT. An alternative is for the BPM CoE to report directly to the leader of operations. In this reporting structure, the BPM CoE can more effectively impact the enterprise level business processes and become recognized as a "strategic asset," rather than a complex cost drain that is too often associated with IT.

For many projects, especially those with long timelines, benefits are often unproven and do not seem to meet business expectations. This can be a result of a loss of focus or leadership interest in the project, or simply a function that the project has been underway for so long that the business needs have changed and the project team never recognized that they were at risk of developing irrelevant solutions.

The real question for BPM COEs is: "How can you increase the benefit delivered from your current business transformation program to a level that is makes the group indispensable to the company?"

The goal is to move from tactical projects that deliver small incremental and often unappreciated value, to projects that enable the transformation of the organization. To do this, a BPM team must demonstrate that they are business change experts who understand the business strategy, the key variables that drive the delivery of business objectives, and are capable of providing solutions that deliver clear and tangible business value. This can only be done if you are seen as a partner to the business. You need to attend their staff meetings, understanding their scorecards/dashboards, anticipating how technology can enable the business, and providing immediate and longer term solutions to ensure the core business capabilities continue to mature.

A formal effort should be conducted to reach out to groups that drive serious change in business operations and partner with them to identify new areas for the BPM CoE to expand into. These groups include highly manual business operations, groups that deal with mandated change (like compliance), high cost areas, areas with quality problems, and so on. To deliver a maximum impact from each service, the BPM CoE should consider how it will interact with and support key business areas. Based on good work, it will be possible to leverage success to expand into new areas, and by partnering closely with managers, to develop close business advisory relationships. This increasing reliance on the BPM CoE for recommendations will alert the BPM CoE managers to more serious business problems and opportunities to solve increasingly difficult, complex problems and other issues.

Becoming more relevant is vital for a BPM CoE. The challenge is to take BPM to the next level of maturity. This is really all about building a business transformation capability which is so beneficial to the company so that the group becomes indispensable! There are four simple steps to seeing a compelling BPM CoE future and achieving it:

- Understand where the CoE is and the constraints preventing the team from becoming engaged in more significant projects
- Conduct a formal status analysis to understand the team's true capabilities and assess the gap between your current state and where the team should be
- Identify where you need to focus BPM operational enhancement to improve the team's capabilities
- Determine the gap between where your team is vs. where management envisions BPM to be

Engaging in this as a serious assessment of the COE's BPM capabilities will help create a roadmap to improve your relevance and position the team into making a more significant impact on the organization.

When attempting to move from small process improvements to larger initiatives that have a significant impact and are transformational in nature, you will need to demonstrate that your team not only can consistently deliver project requirements, but that it can deliver significant measurable benefit. You will also need to show the ability to manage large and complex initiatives, while mitigating risk to the ongoing operation. Leaders often become anxious when large-scale change is to be done within their operations; they need reassurances that you have their back and can deliver on expectations. We found that a formal business-oriented methodology provides the framework and credibility needed to take on larger and more significant projects. This will help reposition the BPM team from being focused on incremental improvements to being a strategic asset for leadership to rely on to drive and deliver transformation.

Streamlining of the process/methodology of the solution development process must always be in complete alignment with business needs. When organizations establish separate and organizationally disconnected BPM and BPMS design teams, risk may arise from the way information is collected and ultimately the way solutions are designed and deployed. Examples are business rules, data use, data flow, data transform, application use, etc. Both of the design teams may talk to the same business managers and staff about these information needs. Each team will approach this from a somewhat different perspective, but the result is that the same business people need to answer the same questions twice.

Create and execute an internal marketing program for the BPM COE "selling" to the different business units outside IT. This will include establishing close relationships with the compliance monitoring function, the customer relations function, the new product initiative managers, and those managers whose group's operations are mostly manual – under-automated.

7.2 Create an evolution plan for the solution

The new business solution that is put in place will, like the rest of the business, begin to evolve. This evolution will really begin as soon as it is installed. If the design is frozen at some point, the evolution will begin before the solution is completed. This is why many new solutions and virtually all changes to legacy applications go into production with a list of change orders. While this situation is not as bad with a combination of BPMS-supported BPM (due to iteration) and applications built following Agile techniques (due to the ability to adjust small Sprints quickly – if the ripple is not too much), it is still something that must be considered.

Recognizing this reality, the project team should plan for the solution's evolution as the solution is being implemented. This may be part of a continuous refinement program or a Six Sigma program – but it must be considered. In addition, volatile technology and digital mobility will change during many projects, and creative ways to adjust and keep improving need to be defined within the context of the capabilities of the IT group and the BPM Center of Excellence and the standards of the company.

In addition to changes during the project, this review should continue after solution implementation, focusing on the ways customers are reached and served. This review really needs to be performed and the solution updated at least semi-annually. This review should be used to create an evolution plan that will guide an ongoing modernization of the solution and the way it leverages new technology and business concepts.

> Note: Regardless of the industry any company is part of, the company will clearly also be in the technology business. Falling behind your competition in the creative use of

modern technology is no longer really acceptable. The world of technology has changed in the last 20 years, and the expectations of customers, suppliers, partners, and the competition are not remotely what they were five years ago. This is among the greatest challenges facing management today and will be a deciding factor in determining winners in the near future. This is exacerbated by the cost reduction in IT over the past fifteen years. Many companies are simply not well positioned for the digital enterprise revolution that is arriving today.

Once a solution is deployed, mechanisms need to be put in place to ensure that it is adopted and that the old ways do not creep back into the business. For example, old forms, templates, processes, etc., must all be removed from the operating environment so that people are not tempted to revert to the old way of doing things.

When establishing the evolution plan, the people whose input is solicited should go beyond the key managers in business and IT and should include some line staff that were identified during the project itself as being especially aware of details and especially creative in their thinking. This balances higher level considerations with information about the current reality of the process. The folks actually executing tasks and activities are in a position to notice subtle things that will not be as apparent to those who are managing things.

A key focus of the evolution plan is to plan for (when possible) and address changes that may impact the solution. Those changes that can be planned for include external events such as pending legislation, draft regulatory requirements, supply and pricing trends, software releases and upgrades, transaction trends such as chip cards and mobile payments, dynamic market changes, and many more.

Internal events that may impact the solution should also be planned for and monitored. These might include things such as system changes, physical space, staff reductions, new vendors, outsourcing/re-in sourcing, new technology, acquisitions/mergers, new methodologies, etc. Internal factors arising from IT and/or technology will normally be included because the team managing continuous refinement should always include IT and/or technology. It does not hurt, however, to specifically check whether those items on the radar screen include everything. Other factors might be a bit more elusive and, as a result, there should be periodic inquiries made to the key responsible parties to capture anything that may be changing.

Do not just assume that someone in the company must be monitoring for future changes and trends. Find the people who are monitoring various factors and include them in the plan. If it turns out that no one is responsible for monitoring an area, the gap should be brought to the attention of executive management or alternatively, the CoE might have to take on responsibility and report their information upwards, so it can be considered at the strategy level as well as for continuous refinement purposes.

Solicit input regarding potential changes at regular intervals. Depending on the nature of the business, this might be monthly in some cases, quarterly in others. The staff monitoring key factors should be requested and reminded to provide input as soon as they become aware of something. The regular intervals should catch anything not reported immediately and if particular areas of concern seem to be moving fast or notifications are not timely, the CoE may have to reach out to these individuals to follow up at least weekly.

Even with well-developed planning and monitoring, there will be unplanned changes that arise from time to time. Identification of unplanned changes generally occurs in three ways:
- Changes in performance indicators
- Information provided by employees actually executing activities and tasks
- The occurrence of an event that either was not foreseen or could not be foreseen.

Routine monitoring of performance measures should have been assigned to appropriate managers during the solution design. It is good practice for the CoE to also periodically check these indicators to confirm current results. If there are aberrations, they will appear either as emerging patterns or as isolated events. Normally, identification of patterns is the most important since patterns not only indicate a trend, but they are the way to identify changes that may be impacting other activities in an overall process. For example, a work-around that evolves in one unit may not impact their metrics or may even improve their metrics and the problem, only discovered by a pattern of deterioration in another unit. Isolated events may be less of a concern unless, when examined, it is determined that a negative effect will occur and the trigger may likely repeat at some point. Many isolated events will already have been planned for if there is a well-developed disaster recovery plan, but there may be some that do not fit into the disaster recovery plan at present. Isolated events should be reviewed to determine if there needs to be additional planning.

As the solution was being developed and refined, there will have been relationships established with some selected people in operations who actually do the work. It is a good idea to periodically sit down with these people again and ask questions about anything that may have changed in the interim: work-arounds, changes in the sequences of manual steps, differences seen in input information, problems and/or "clunkiness" that was not identified before, and similar questions. There may even be significant changes that have not been caught because the change is external to the BPMS flow, for instance, use of a different tool to calculate something or to capture some information that only becomes part of the BPMS flow when it is entered later on.

There may be subtle undocumented changes that do not have any negative impacts on any performance metric. It is even possible to have such undocumented changes produce improvements in some metrics. Why then bother to try to identify these? The BPMS assumes a model that is now incorrect and continuous refinement changes may have unforeseen consequences because the model is no longer accurate.

A critical perspective that should play a central role in defining all BPM project approaches is that of the various customers. Tracing how activities support customers and how the customer might interact with the company is more than important. Almost every process will involve consumers, suppliers, broker/sales, vendors, etc. and how easy, non-threatening, and pleasant the interaction is will make a big difference in retaining customers. As a result, the BPM project team should consider gathering information on past and current customer reactions, problems, suggestions, complaints, support requests, and also feedback posted to social media. This means gathering information not only from the points where each customer type interacts with the company (sales support for brokers, purchasing for vendors, customer service for consumers, etc.), but also across all the channels available to each customer – such as web, chat, call center, text, mobile app. There should also be social media monitoring by either an internal resource or outside vendor and the trends, as well as the nature of topics fed into the overall process of continuous refinement.

7.3 Create a collaborative (business/IT committee) for innovation ideation

Beyond the focus of the evolution plan for the solution, the team will need to both recognize that any evolution plan will start to be outdated as soon as it is accepted and that the solution is part of a broader set of processes and capabilities that define the company. As such, the solution evolution plan represents a vision starting from the current technology capabilities and constraints and the current market environment. But we know both will change and we need to adjust to these changes.

Every company faces a challenge in keeping up with emerging technology and competitors in their use of this technology. It is a leap frog game that requires the ability to predict when a given technology is stable enough to use and then spending the money to obtain it and learn to use it. This is a game that is growing in importance as competition finds new ways to leverage these digital tools to reach out to customers in new ways and provide new conveniences.

All managers claim to want to find innovative solutions to their operational problems. But to do that, companies will need to create an environment for innovation. This needs to be a formal goal, with formal funding, mandatory manager participation, and viewed as being a critical tool in the continuing transformation of the company.

More progressive companies are monitoring these changes in emerging technology and ways to both improve the business operation and interact with the customers. While cost management is important, it is a distant secondary concern (or at least should be) to customer interaction and retention. This is the critical factor in company growth, including profitability. It will be necessary to focus on the customers and creatively look at how the market and societal changes are being driven by new technology, such as digital mobility. The BPM Center of Excellence should be monitoring this changing technology and help the company plan to stay even with the buying trends and expectations of the company's customers.

We believe that this is best approached by a collaborative committee with representatives from the major areas in the business. We have found that the findings of this committee must be viewed from a business capability and impact perspective, not a technology perspective. This is important and we urge executive management to promote this concept.

A structure that is worth considering is to have some committee members who are consistently part of the committee over long periods of time, while there are other members who are part of the committee for 3-6 months, and then rotate out. Of course, if a person scheduled to rotate out is actively working on a committee issue or project, extending the period should be considered. This helps to bring in fresh ideas and thinking, while ensuring some consistency and familiarity with best practices and approaches that work for solving problems. It also helps reduce burnout and gradually increases buy-in as more people contribute over time.

The committee should create channels that feed issues and problems from customer service segments as well as operational areas. These feeds should be reviewed to identify patterns of issues that may help locate where things are not working as smoothly as they should. The feeds can also help identify trends that show building problems that can then be addressed before too much damage occurs.

An ongoing challenge is to find ways to encourage employees at all levels to identify issues as well as to express ideas. There are, of course, the physical and online "suggestion boxes" and they work in some companies and are not effective in others. Reward programs should be considered as well as simple things such as naming a project for the person who identified it, or adding that person to the committee at least for the life of the project. One thing that should not be overlooked is simply walking around and talking with people.

Most companies only leverage a small portion of the knowledge and experience that exists just because information never gets communicated to a level where someone could take action. Co-workers may share thoughts and ideas, but unless there is a clear culture that encourages and rewards people for pushing forth an idea, it may often just die without ever being noticed. One of the worst thing that happen, and happens frequently, is for a supervisor or manager to be dismissive and not listen. The idea is lost and the employee just won't bother again. An important role the committee must adopt and play is fostering and maintaining a culture where ideas are sought after and communicating ideas are rewarded.

The collaborative committee needs a blend of creative idea people and those with a thorough understanding of the details of business operations and IT. There are some individuals who are adept at both and they should be at the top of the list of potential participants. The committee should also span positions in the company from the executive level through to those involved in the direct performance of activities. Such a variety of individuals helps to balance different perspectives as well as to promote innovation within the context of the company's strategy and operating environment.

The tone taken must be one of problem solving; being innovative and figuring out how to get there within the limits of any constraints. Objections and concerns should be welcomed as problems to be solved, but "wet blanket" behavior should result in the change of a team member if that is at all possible. If a required participant is being the "wet blanket," the overall project sponsor should be consulted for assistance.

Just as for the initial project itself, committee participation requires commitment from each individual, support at the executive level, and cooperation from managers and supervisors. The enterprise must embrace continuous refinement as a key characteristic.

7.4 Implement continuous refinement and Evolutive Management

Taken as a whole, all delivered solutions and all legacy operations will change how the company can respond to multiple factors. Some of these factors cannot be predicted and some will change the playing field. As a result, change is continuous and results in operational evolution. We have found that there are only two possible ways to deal with this evolution. One is to let it take its course and try to react to it. The other is to understand what is coming (to the extent that it can be predicted) and leverage it to your advantage. This latter approach requires the ability to change quickly with little disruption, low risk, and low cost. It also requires creativity and an environment that promotes innovation. To achieve this, company management must be ready and must be able to make accurate decisions on how to leverage every tool at their disposal and define how the business as a whole will change.

The key is to predict needed changes and then use them to evolve the ability of the company to produce services or product, the ability of IT to deliver solutions quickly, and the ability of the company to interact with customers and serve their needs.

To do this, the company will need to leverage the predictive work of the collaborative BPM Center of Excellence and its collaborative committees. Senior management will need the ability to use the COE's findings as a guide in determining the way the company can evolve and the timing and cost of that evolution. This ability will help support a series of steps in this evolution that tie to funding reality and control risk, turmoil, and development.

This allows the management team to tie continuous refinement to operational evolution and allows changes to align with strategy, evolution, and opportunity.

Determine how to build BPM into the overall business strategy process as a key enabler in achieving business objectives. By moving beyond small tactical projects that deliver small levels of benefits to larger enterprise transformation projects, the BPM CoE will be considered a vital asset to leadership and become part of the larger strategic dialogue vs. being "assigned" projects.

Continuous refinement is approached with repeated cycles of information gathering, creative problem solving and innovation, simulations to refine, live testing, and implementation. These cycles should be planned as regular activities. Provision should also be made for ad hoc cycles to address urgent problems and opportunities.

Continue to create and execute an internal marketing program for the BPM CoE "selling" to the different business units. This will include establishing close relationships with the compliance monitoring function, the customer relations function, the new product initiative managers, and those managers whose group's operations are mostly manual/under-automated.

To move beyond an "order taker" becomes a valued capability for an advancing organization's strategy. The BPM team should work with business partners to identify opportunity by:
- Establishing internal training programs for business operation improvement with business managers – train them and their key staff members in what to look for
- Establishing improvement identification rewards programs.

Formalize benefit targeting, estimation, and evaluation to formally determine how a benefit is identified or tested following solution delivery. This moves the determination of project success from the realm of opinion to objective understanding. We believe that if you cannot measure a benefit, it really doesn't exist.

BPM approaches, techniques, concepts, and needed skills are constantly changing as BPM matures. BPMS tools and concepts are also in a constant state of change as vendors try to beat one another with new features that will make people select their products. This creates a need for frequent training and skill updates. However, care should be taken in selecting training providers, as many really do not have the needed expertise in BPM or business transformation.

Project requesting tends to evolve in BPM teams from ad hoc into a formal process, with formal data requirements and formal benefits estimation. For small to moderate size projects, ad hoc can work. However, as larger mission-critical projects are requested, the BPM CoE will need to formalize the requesting process and create rules that will control what projects are accepted and provide the foundation for making these decisions. Such requests should include a formal description of the problem, the harm being caused, the potential impact to the scope, the performance issue it is creating, the constraining factors, an assessment of damage to the operation, and a description of what must change.

Formalize the BPM CoE project request review process with rules that govern how requests are evaluated and prioritized. This evaluation and prioritization will require agreement between business requestors and IT, with all participants agreeing to priority, start time, resource commitment, key objectives, targets, and measurable results.

Building internal awareness and business sponsorship, while undertaking enterprise level projects is vital to the long-term success of a BPM team. This is done by:
- Providing formalized business awareness/education on how BPM/BPMS can improve operational efficiency/effectiveness
- Working with the CoE to identify high value projects that either cut costs in expensive operations areas and/or projects that directly impact revenue generation/experience engineering
- Creating collaborative relations with other needed groups (IT application development and interface/data architecture, Compliance, Legal, etc.)

BPM supports rapid change, so cycles can and should overlap with various steps in various cycles ongoing simultaneously. Avoid completing one cycle before starting to gather information for the next.

Since some improvements can be designed and implemented in a very short period of time while others may take longer, the CoE should look for opportunities to combine improvements even if they started in different cycles, so long as this approach does not create significant delays.

Continuous refinement must be proactive and not wait until some change, problem, or opportunity forces it into action. Some activities will be pursued to accommodate for changes in the overall business environment. However, the CoE should also leverage the capability to innovate and redefine the business environment.

Organizations talk a lot about continuous refinement and how it should be built into everything people do, and even into the underlying culture. For this mindset to exist, the BPM team should lead the discussion and define for leadership and the employees what continuous refinement means in your organization. Make the definition specific and relevant to the business, provide training mechanisms for the employees to identify improvement opportunities, and finally, provide the tools to enable people make improvement real.

BPM COEs not only need the skills to execute the projects on their roadmap, but they also need a CoE Capability Investment Plan that outlines which BPM key competencies will be evolved over time and how this will be accomplished. This plan should be synced up with the vision of the BPM COE and how, over time, it will become even more aligned with the overall business strategy and move up the value chain in terms of the scope, size, and overall impact that BPM-enabled projects will deliver to business leaders.

About the authors

Any book, conference presentation, column, or article is only as good as the experience of the authors. It is this experience that makes this book worthwhile as a collection of things that will help you succeed and things you really may want to avoid.

The authors are widely published and recognized "Thought Leaders" in the business transformation industry. They have also taught a great many people who they have worked with, who worked in client companies, and who attended training courses about how to be successful in business transformation.

Together they bring over 100 years of professional experience - as Dan likes to say, "We have stumbled onto a lot of business land mines and we have learned to watch where we put our feet."

This experience is shared in this handbook.

Dan Morris, CBPP, CBA

Dan is the coauthor of four books on business process transformation, a columnist for PEX, and the author of over 50 white papers and articles on a variety of business transformation topics. He has spoken internationally at over 30 conferences and serves on the International Board of Directors for the Association of Business Process Management Professionals (ABPMP™). Dan has also served on the Business Architect Association Board and the Forrester International BPM Council.

Dan's previous books:
- *ABPMP™ Common Body of Knowledge* v3, ABPMP 2013
- *Just Don't Do It*, McGraw-Hill 1998
- *Re-engineering Your Business*, McGraw-Hill 1994
- *Relational Systems Development,* McGraw-Hill 1989

Dan is a frequent Webinar host for ABPMP™ and other groups and has held several formal training sessions for different organizations. He is also the co-author of the ABPMP™ International BPM Practitioner's certification test, the Business Architect Association certification test, and the ABPMP™ Common Body of Knowledge® (v3). He has led training courses for ABPMP™ and PEX as well as internal training for major consulting firms.

He is the designer and the co-author of the Architect, Design, Deploy, and Improve (ADDI) BPM/BPMS Execution methodology. He is a leader in melding Business Architecture, Process Architecture, Enterprise Architecture, and current/legacy technology into a single integrated approach to transformation. Working with a small group of senior colleagues, Dan is involved in defining new approaches to leveraging tools and concept, and inventing new ones (where needed) to address the leading problems in business transformation. These approaches, concepts and techniques are all integrated into the ADDI methodology.

Dan is currently a Managing Principal with Wendan Consulting **www.wendan-consulting.com**. He has also served as North American Practice Director for Business Transformation at Infosys, Capco, and TCS - three leading international consulting firms and as an Executive Consultant with IBM Global Services. In his career, he has led business transformations and smaller operational improvement projects in insurance, healthcare, manufacturing, banking, automotive, pharmaceuticals, retail, food processing, energy, and government.

Note: CBPP – Certified Business Process Professional
       CBA – Certified Business Architect
Contact: daniel.morris@wendan-consulting.com

Keith Leust, Six Sigma Black Belt, CBA

Keith Leust has extensive experience in Business Architecture and strategy, change management, leadership development, large-scale business reengineering & BPM, technology implementation, and is an expert in driving transformation to enable modern business design.

With over 30 years of work focused on ensuring "... *organizations are designed to achieve their desired business results*," Keith has helped drive significant transformation efforts.

Keith is a Managing Principal with Wendan Consulting. Prior to joining Wendan, Keith served as a Client Advisor and Business Architect with Oracle leading Business Transformation and Strategy Execution projects. Keith works directly with leaders to create and execute holistic solutions to align the leadership, build business roadmaps, and implement organizational change. Keith has led engagements with Mayo Clinic, BCBS IL (HCSC), AvMed Health Care, The Home Depot, Cordis Medical Devices, Optum Pharmacy, Parsons Construction, and Donaldson Manufacturing, working with leadership to define and execute business transformation.

As an executive with Motorola, Keith was instrumental in the re-architecting of the cell phone business as well as the transformation of the global IT organization. At Prudential, Keith was the VP of Business Transformation and led the reengineering of front and back office operations. As an executive with American Express, Keith reengineered processes, organized business segments around the customer, and installed technology to simplify operations.

Keith began his consulting career with Arthur Andersen where he co-managed the Northeast Change Management practice. He holds a Bachelor of Science degree in Engineering from Lehigh University, MBA's in Finance and International Business from Fairleigh Dickenson University, and an HR/OD Certification from Columbia University. In addition, Keith is a Certified Business Architect, a Motorola Six Sigma Black Belt, and is certified in Myers Briggs.
Contact: keith.leust@wendan-consulting.com

Rod Moyer

Rod has over 25 years of experience as a consultant improving businesses from a strategy perspective straight through to step by step implementations and improvements. As a co-author of the ADDI BPM methodology and a Managing Principal with Wendan Consulting, he has devoted the past several years to improving the way businesses approach BPM so that addressing business needs becomes the primary focus and actual result.

As an executive consultant, Rod has served in leadership positions in both international firms and boutique companies. His clients also extend from international companies to local ventures. He has assisted start-ups as well as turnarounds and process improvement projects in established companies. In his engagements, he has frequently served as the "bridge" between business and technology to ensure solutions leverage technology, while at the same time meeting business needs in a way that works for the business managers.

Rod has authored and co-authored numerous columns, papers, and presentations. He has also co-authored reference manuals and designed and presented training programs.
Contact: rod.moyer@wendan-consulting.com

Jim Sinur - Foreword Contributor

Graduated from Cardinal Stritch College with a Bachelor's of Science in Management after graduating from Milwaukee Area Technical College with an Associate in Arts in Business Data Processing achieving a Summa Cum Laude in both cases. Jim then spent over 24 years developing advanced business processes and systems for several blue ribbon companies (American Express, Northwestern Mutual and Wehr Steel). After many successful large scale implementations, Jim joined Gartner Group where he guided many premiere Software Providers and Fortune 500 organizations to success in their journey with process and application technologies for nearly 20 years. For the last three years, Jim became an independent consultant helping organizations plan and implement their incremental transformations to advanced digital organizations. Jim is also an author of several books and white papers and is known best for his visionary, yet practical, blog and social presence.

https://www.linkedin.com/in/jimsinur
Current Blog: http://jimsinur.blogspot.com/
Current books on Digital Transformations and the Future of Process
Digital Transformation: Innovate or Die Slowly
Business Process Management: The Next Wave http://www.mkpress.com/aoBPM/

Neelesh Harmalker **Lead Content Editor**

Neelesh has over 10 years of experience within the Financial Services industry, including experience in Asset Management and Capital Markets. He has successfully led several groups within the financial services industry, including broker dealer services, global business development, back/middle office transformation projects, and Business Process Management (BPM). Neelesh has experience working in 7 institutions, covering approximately 13 separate engagements, covering process management improvement projects, business process mapping initiatives, and project management roles.

Companion Books from Meghan-Kiffer Press

CPSIA information can be obtained
at www.ICGtesting.com
Printed in the USA
LVOW03s0024240117

521943LV00032B/772/P